CAMBRIDGE LIBRARY COLLECTION

Books of enduring scholarly value

History

The books reissued in this series include accounts of historical events and movements by eye-witnesses and contemporaries, as well as landmark studies that assembled significant source materials or developed new historiographical methods. The series includes work in social, political and military history on a wide range of periods and regions, giving modern scholars ready access to influential publications of the past.

A Brief Description of the Holy Sepulchre Jerusalem and Other Christian Churches in the Holy City

As the purported site of the resurrection of Jesus, the Church of the Holy Sepulchre has been a centre of pilgrimage since at least the fourth century CE. The church has survived through fire, invasion, neglect and near-destruction. The result of such a turbulent history is an extraordinarily intricate and intriguing building. George Jeffery's 1919 book, compiled from his own meticulous scrutiny of the site, is an in-depth chronicle of the church's amazing history and serves as an informative guide to many of its most interesting details. The book features plans and illustrations of the church's numerous phases of construction, and historical accounts of the building from its earliest origins, as well as descriptions of the nearby Augustinian convent and other holy sites of interest within the walls of Jerusalem. Also included is a comprehensive discussion of the many European copies of the church constructed during the middle ages.

Cambridge University Press has long been a pioneer in the reissuing of out-of-print titles from its own backlist, producing digital reprints of books that are still sought after by scholars and students but could not be reprinted economically using traditional technology. The Cambridge Library Collection extends this activity to a wider range of books which are still of importance to researchers and professionals, either for the source material they contain, or as landmarks in the history of their academic discipline.

Drawing from the world-renowned collections in the Cambridge University Library, and guided by the advice of experts in each subject area, Cambridge University Press is using state-of-the-art scanning machines in its own Printing House to capture the content of each book selected for inclusion. The files are processed to give a consistently clear, crisp image, and the books finished to the high quality standard for which the Press is recognised around the world. The latest print-on-demand technology ensures that the books will remain available indefinitely, and that orders for single or multiple copies can quickly be supplied.

The Cambridge Library Collection will bring back to life books of enduring scholarly value (including out-of-copyright works originally issued by other publishers) across a wide range of disciplines in the humanities and social sciences and in science and technology.

A Brief Description of the Holy Sepulchre Jerusalem and Other Christian Churches in the Holy City

With Some Account of the Mediaeval Copies of the Holy Sepulchre Surviving in Europe

GEORGE JEFFERY

CAMBRIDGE
UNIVERSITY PRESS

CAMBRIDGE UNIVERSITY PRESS

Cambridge, New York, Melbourne, Madrid, Cape Town, Singapore,
São Paolo, Delhi, Dubai, Tokyo, Mexico City

Published in the United States of America by Cambridge University Press, New York

www.cambridge.org
Information on this title: www.cambridge.org/9781108016049

This edition first published 1919
This digitally printed version 2010

ISBN 978-1-108-01604-9 Paperback

THE CHURCH OF THE
HOLY SEPULCHRE

CAMBRIDGE UNIVERSITY PRESS
C. F. CLAY, Manager
LONDON : FETTER LANE, E.C. 4

NEW YORK : G. P. PUTNAM'S SONS
BOMBAY ⎫
CALCUTTA ⎬ MACMILLAN AND CO., Ltd
MADRAS ⎭
TORONTO : J. M. DENT AND SONS, Ltd.
TOKYO : MARUZEN-KABUSHIKI-KAISHA

The Holy Sepulchre Church. Exterior.

A BRIEF DESCRIPTION

OF THE

HOLY SEPULCHRE

JERUSALEM

AND OTHER CHRISTIAN CHURCHES
IN THE HOLY CITY

WITH SOME ACCOUNT OF THE MEDIÆVAL COPIES
OF THE HOLY SEPULCHRE SURVIVING
IN EUROPE

BY

GEORGE JEFFERY, F.S.A.
Architect

CAMBRIDGE
AT THE UNIVERSITY PRESS
1919

PREFACE

TO add yet another to the innumerable volumes which have appeared on the Holy Sepulchre seems a somewhat thankless venture. The only excuse for so doing is that notwithstanding the multitude of students whose names are linked with that of the Holy City in modern times or in passed away centuries, and the voluminous results of their studies, there are certain aspects of the greatest of Christian Monuments which still remain comparatively unknown. My ambition has been to cast into book form the notes which I made some few years back to satisfy my own curiosity—I trust I have presented these studies in such a way as will interest others in the most famous of Christian relics.

This account of the Holy Sepulchre first appeared in a published form in the pages of the *Journal* of the Royal Institute of British Architects in 1910. I have to thank the editor of that journal for permission to make use of the original illustrations for the present purpose.

I am also under a special obligation to a leading authority on Christian Archæology—Dr M. R. James, Provost of Eton—for very kindly reading the proofs, and affording me the advantage of his valuable advice and criticism.

To my wife I am indebted for the laborious compilation of an index.

G. J.

Cyprus, 1918.

CONTENTS

LIST OF ILLUSTRATIONS

PART I
HISTORY

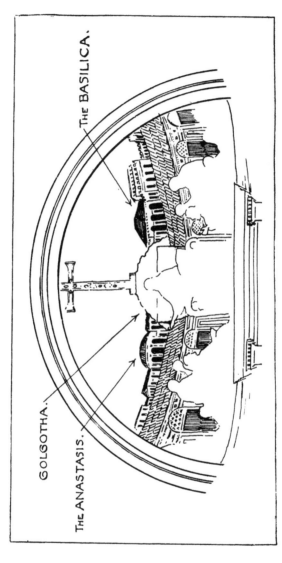

Fig. 1. Apse Mosaic in St Pudenziana, Rome. From a photograph by Alinari 1875.

CHAPTER I

PRIMITIVE CHRISTIANITY

EUSEBIUS, Bishop of Cæsarea, who flourished in the early part of the fourth century, is the first writer who gives a clear and intelligible account of the Holy Sepulchre after the events recorded in the Gospel. It is to be hoped that in the new discoveries constantly being made in Egypt, some references in Christian documents may be found throwing additional light upon this most interesting subject; nothing, however, of an earlier date than the middle of the fourth century seems to have been found up to the present.

The finding of the Holy Sepulchre is described by the Bishop of Cæsarea as a simple operation. We are given to understand that the site was well known, and the presence of the pagan temple built to desecrate it was sufficient to indicate its exact position. Eusebius seems to have been present at its discovery when a boy; he speaks as an eye-witness.

The temple, already venerable after, as it is supposed, 200 years of heathen use, was first pulled down; then the podium or platform was completely cleared away, and the materials and earth carried to a considerable distance, adding possibly to the enormous accumulations in the Tyropœon valley. Roman temples in Syria were frequently erected on more or less artificial mounds, as, for instance, Baalbek, the greatest of them all. The Holy Sepulchre when laid bare by the removal of the temple podium seems to have astonished the explorers by its intact condition.

The tendency of the historians of the early Christian Church is to magnify the position of Christianity at its first recognition by the Roman Government. It is not perhaps sufficiently recognised that, although Constantine seems to have personally and privately favoured Christianity, and the famous Edict of Milan removed all restrictions as to its development, the Roman Imperial Government remained officially heathen until the time of

Theodosius at the close of the fourth century, when the Olympian Games were abolished and the central shrine of the State religion, the Temple of Vesta in the Roman Forum, was officially closed (394). Christianity was viewed by Constantine's Government much in the way that it is viewed by the Turkish Government of the present day, and tolerated for similar reasons. Christ occupied a place in the Roman Pantheon long before the middle of the fourth century, and even Antoninus Pius, one of the builders of Baalbek, severely repressed anti-Christian riots. But Constantine went a step farther than any of his predecessors in that he permitted the destruction of a temple of the Imperial State religion for the purpose of substituting the central shrine of Christendom—the Monument of the Resurrection. It is the first instance of the kind on record.

The exact dates of the destruction of the temple and the building of the Christian church are unknown. Eusebius is supposed to have witnessed the first when a boy, and to have been present at the consecration of the latter in his capacity as bishop of the region. Some little time must therefore have elapsed between the two events, and the legendary account generally gives the period of transformation as 326–335. In the year 333 the new buildings seem, however, to have been seen in an unfinished condition by the Bordeaux Pilgrim.

Descriptio fabricæ Sancti Sepulchri

The Holy Sepulchre—this, as the chief part of the whole monument, the Emperor caused to be decorated with the greatest care, and with magnificent columns. Outside was a vast court, open to the sky, paved with polished stone, and with long porticoes on three of its sides. Towards the east, opposite the Tomb, was joined a Basilica, an admirable work of immense proportions. Its walls were encrusted with vari-coloured marbles, whilst its exterior was built of polished stonework little inferior to the marble in beauty. The roof was constructed with a lead covering impervious to winter weather, and on the inside it presented a vast surface of gilded coffers. At both sides of the Basilica were two-storied aisles, with gilded ceilings divided from the nave by colonnades.

Outside the Basilica, on its front, were enormous columns, and three doors opening towards the east as public entrances. Opposite these doors was the apse[1] or principal part of the church. This apse was enclosed or decorated with twelve columns to symbolise the Apostles, and on each column was a silver vase, the special gift of the Emperor.

In front of the church was an open space with porticoes on either hand, and also gates into the Atrium. This grand entrance to the Basilica stood in the midst of the.market-place; and its gates of beautiful workmanship afforded a view of the interior to the passer-by, who could not but be filled with astonishment. Eusebius Pamphili, *De Vita Constantini*. Migne, *Pat. Gr.* t. xx.—supposed date of writing, A.D. 335.

The meagre account of Jerusalem by the first Christian pilgrim known to have recorded his travels (the Bordeaux Pilgrim) confirms the statements of the Bishop of Cæsarea. He seems to have been attracted on his arrival in Jerusalem by the sight of the Acropolis (modern Haram), with its Roman temple and other buildings, and its statues still standing of Hadrian. He then mentions the Domus Caiaphæ on Sion, which would appear to have been the great Christian hospice of the period as well as *Mater omnium ecclesiarum*, a title afterwards transferred to the church of the Cœnaculum. Lastly, he describes the New Buildings on the Holy Sites, and makes the first recorded mention of the *Monticulus Golgotha*. He speaks of passing through the wall of Sion by the gate of the New City, which may mean either a new district rising round the Holy Sites, or from its facing Neapolis (Nablus). On the right hand he observed the ruins of the Pretorium, on the left were Golgotha and the Sepulchre.

After an interval of fifty years another native of France followed in the footsteps of the Bordeaux Pilgrim. This was Silvia of Aquitaine, whose account of her travels, discovered accidentally at Arezzo in 1887, is as tediously voluminous as the Bordeaux Pilgrim's tale is short and meagre. Silvia seems to have visited the Holy City during A.D. 380–385, when Cyril, the author of the "Catechetical Discourses," was Bishop of Jerusalem.[2] She

---

[1] *Hemisphærium:* this possibly means the Anastasis, and not the western apse of the Basilica.

[2] The Bishops of Ælia Capitolina were dependent on the Bishopric of Cæsarea until A.D. 451, when the Council of Chalcedon made Jerusalem the Fifth Patriarchate.

does not mention him by name, but he doubtless was the bishop whose ritual and ministrations she watched with so much care. The *Peregrinatio* takes the form of a letter addressed to certain ladies, possibly the sisters of some convent in Aquitaine. The first few pages, a fragment in the centre, and the conclusion are missing, but the greater part of the description of the Holy Sites is fortunately intact.

At the date of Silvia's visit the buildings were in their pristine condition as planned by their first builders. The Anastasis (Tomb-enclosure) is unfortunately not described in detail, but its doors (or the doors of the Tomb itself) are mentioned, outside which the catechumens stood, whilst the faithful entered within. On several occasions the Anastasis is spoken of as a "Church," and the sound of the voices of those offering praises within it, heard outside, is noted.

Silvia's descriptions of her religious life in Jerusalem are vivid and full of interesting particulars, which may be epitomised as follows. After a service of prayer in the Anastasis, the pilgrims were conducted by the Bishop (who seems to have played a very active part in the ceremonies) to the "Cross," whilst interminable kyries were sung and benedictions performed. This Cross, covered with jewels and gilding, stood on the " Monticulus Golgotha." The seat of the Bishop was placed in different positions around the hillock during these ceremonies,[1] and the open space of Golgotha is described as decorated with innumerable lamps and lighted candles, hanging presumably within the surrounding colonnades, as we see them, for instance, represented in the mosaics of Thessalonica. This illumination of Golgotha was specially important at the *Licinicon* (λυχνικόν) or *Lucernarum* festival, but whether before cockcrow in the morning or at evensong these illuminations of the colonnades seem to have been very noticeable.

Silvia is probably the first person to mention the veneration of the relics of the "True Cross," which she describes as taking place on a table covered with a linen cloth arranged at the side of Golgotha. During all the ceremonies connected with Golgotha, the Bishop is always mentioned as assisting "in

---

[1] "Though I should deny the Crucifixion, this Golgotha confutes me near which we are now assembled" (St Cyril, Lect. XIII. 4 (*c.* A.D. 350), Newman's translation).

cathedra." She then gives picturesque details of the pilgrims' visit to *Imbomon*, or the scene of the Ascension on the Mount of Olives: the return to Jerusalem after a night spent on Olivet; *candelæ ecclesiasticæ* or candle lamps throwing a weird light on the crowd of men, women, and children carrying palms and olive branches and singing hymns, the little ones overcome with fatigue being carried on men's shoulders, and the noise of the returning multitude ever increasing to those who lay awake in Jerusalem. Then arriving at the city gate "at that hour when one man can distinguish another," the Bishop leading the way into the Basilica, the great eastern doors were thrown wide open for the entering crowd.

On other occasions Silvia mentions the Bishop examining the candidates for baptism. The Bishop's *Cathedra* was placed behind the great altar in the apse of the Basilica, and the neophytes were conducted to him one by one. No mention, however, is made of the Baptistery which fifty years before had attracted the notice of the Bordeaux Pilgrim.

Cyril, Bishop of Jerusalem in the concluding years of the fourth century, has left sermons (we can almost fancy Silvia may have heard them) which contain interesting details about the Holy Sepulchre. He mentions the great modifications the Tomb had undergone more than fifty years previously when the Anastasis was erected. The monument had been reduced to a mere rock-covering of the sepulchral chamber, and the outer or entrance part of the cave (such as is usually found in tombs near Jerusalem) was hewn away for the general adornment. He mentions this fact in several parts of his lectures. Here it is interesting to remark that in the very wonderful reproduction of the Holy Sepulchre at Bologna (possibly fifth century in origin) it is represented without any outer chamber. Another curious detail mentioned by Cyril would imply the roofless state of the Anastasis. He speaks of the evidences then remaining of a garden surrounding the Tomb, as if it had been treated as a rock-hewn monument like those of Petra, or the well-known "Absalom's Pillar" in the Valley of Jehoshaphat with somewhat natural surroundings.

A great deal of interest attaches to the few contemporary representations of the Holy Sites in the fourth century which have been identified up to the present. The most important is the apse mosaic in the Church of St Pudenziana, Rome, which the present writer was the first to bring into public notice for this purpose [fig. 1]. Very careful drawings of this most interesting work of art were made by the late Cav. De Rossi. He has given an elaborate sectional diagram in his great folio work on the Roman Mosaics showing all the portions which have been restored at different periods, and he has been able to define the portions which undoubtedly belong to the fourth century. The general design and the architectural background are original: the inscription on the book held by Christ may have been altered, and the sky portion with evangelistic symbols seems to have been a good deal restored. But as a whole this most valuable monument of ancient art gives us a wonderful idea of the buildings, and coincides remarkably, considering the inherent conventionality of the representation, with the remains in Jerusalem and the ancient descriptions.

The picture has evidently been executed under the careful supervision of some returned pilgrim of the period, who with true Italian poetic imagination wished to represent not only the Holy Sites of the terrestrial Jerusalem, but also the courts of the celestial Sion with Christ and His Apostles sitting in conclave. It answers both these purposes, and as a decorative work of art magnificently fills the apse of the church. Behind the figure of Christ rises the *monticulus* of Golgotha surmounted by an immense jewelled cross. This is evidently the "Cross" so often mentioned by the pilgrim Silvia—an addition to the Holy Sites of fifty years after the time of Constantine. On each side of the cross may be seen the arcades of the Atrium, and behind these rise the Anastasis and Basilica in their correct relative positions, but without any idea of proportionate size.

It will be noticed that the view is supposed to be taken in a very natural manner from the high ground, overlooking the Holy Sites, of the upper part of Sion, where the Christian quarter of the Roman city was situated. The pilgrims would be most familiar with this view of the buildings as they would usually approach them from this side.

It is curious that there should be no history, traditional or otherwise, about this very important representation of the Holy

Sites in the Church of St Pudenziana, which is believed to have been built on the site of the house of Pudens, friend of St Paul, by Pope Pius I in A.D. 142. The restoration of the building and consequently of the mosaic is supposed to have taken place in the eighth century, and the mosaic may have again been touched when the church was modernised by the Gaetani family in 1598. De Rossi and Garrucci believe the original work to have been executed at the command of Pope Siricius in A.D. 390.

Fig. 2. The Trivulzio Ivory, Milan. From the *Bulletin* of
the Russian Palestine Society, 1894.

Representations or models of the Anastasis on ivory diptychs, caskets, or other small objects of the fourth and fifth centuries frequently occur in museums. Amongst the best known are the Trivulzio ivory (evidently of the same period and design as the mosaic in St Pudenziana) now preserved in the museum of Count Trivulzio of Milan [fig. 2], the example in the British Museum (Maskell Collection) [fig. 3], the Quedlinburg ivory (cast in the South Kensington Museum) [fig. 5], and that in the Bibliothèque Nationale, Paris [fig. 4].

From such evidence as we possess at the present—descriptions by contemporaries, pictorial representations, and a few traces on the rock-cut site—we conclude that about the year 333 A.D., after the laying bare of the Holy Sepulchre, the Christians were permitted to level the whole area around the Tomb for the purpose of the "adornment" spoken of by Cyril. This levelling of the rock surface was carried

Fig. 3. British Museum. One of four plaques of stained red ivory, 4 inches by 3 inches. Italian, fifth to eighth centuries. On the door of the Holy Sepulchre is a representation of the raising of Lazarus. On the lower panel a seated figure of Mary weeping. Above the soldiers are the two Maries in attitudes of grief.

out in such a way as to admit of the spot identified with the Crucifixion being left as a hillock or "monticulus" standing in the midst, whilst on the west side of the levelled space the Tomb was treated as a kind of chamber with walls and covering of rock in the style of the numerous tombs of the Valley of Jehoshaphat, which are precisely similar in character. Incidentally it may be remarked that this type of rock-hewn architecture is worthy of a special study; the tombs of Palestine and Idumea, Egypt and India, are amongst the most interesting monuments of archæology, and it is curious to consider that the great Christian Memorial is perhaps

Fig. 4. The Anastasis and Basilica within the Walls of Jerusalem. Early Ivory (Bibliothèque Nationale, Paris). One of the few representations extant of the Martyrion Basilica, and possibly of the same period as the Madeba Mosaic, which it resembles.

ous to consider that the great Christian Memorial is perhaps one of the last examples of the kind ever hewn out of the living rock.

In detaching the cubicle of rock, containing the Tomb, from the surrounding cliff, a much larger space was given to the encircling pathway on the west side than seems to have been common in the cases of more ancient tombs, such as those in the Valley of Jehoshaphat. This was doubtless in consequence of the important character of the monument, and in anticipation of large numbers of people assembling within the area. It is not sufficiently clear whether Eusebius means by the word "hemisphærium" the semicircular space surrounding the Tomb, or the apse of the adjoining Basilica. The probability seems that he means the latter, and that round this semicircle there were twelve magnificent columns, each bearing a silver vase, the special gifts of the Emperor Constantine. These columns would, of course, form a colonnade supporting a cornice.

Fig. 5. Cast at South Kensington Museum. On top of richly decorated casket. German, tenth to eleventh centuries. Treasury of Abbey Quedlinburg. Presented by Emp. Henry I.

In endeavouring to realize the appearance and arrangement of the Holy Sepulchre monument as designed by the unknown Architect of the Constantinian government, it must be borne in mind that the Roman colonization of the Levant had introduced the current styles of Roman Art. The circular form given to the excavation, unusual in the East, where a square outline is almost universal in tomb structures, seems reminiscent of the characteristic tomb at Rome, which is itself the descendant of the Etruscan rock-cut circular monument such as still survives at Castel d'Asso (Bieda).

The colossal monument to Hadrian or the smaller examples on the Roman "Via Appia" would be spoken of as models for the new tomb monument to be set up by the still despised Christian section of the community. Amongst the early Christian pilgrims to Palestine in the first days of the "recognition of the Church" would undoubtedly be many Roman patricians, familiar with all the still unfaded glories of the Imperial City—

its splendid basilicas, its sumptuous tombs, its temples and palaces—and these probably wealthy and enthusiastic promoters of the scheme would very much influence the character of its design.

The general plan and idea of the monument were thus Western in origin, but the details of carving and mason craft were undoubtedly similar to the local style of mighty Baalbek, or the theatrical types at Petra. This was but natural under the circumstances, seeing that the artists and workmen employed must have been natives of the country who in their youth would have laboured in erecting the last temples of the decaying heathenism of the Roman Empire.

In making so large an excavation as the plateau surrounding the Tomb presented when finished, it would appear that an idea of congregational use was contemplated—probably much of the same kind as prevails at the present day on the Easter festival. A similar circular enclosure on the Mount of Olives, around the traditional place of the Ascension, was made use of in a like congregational manner.

The Christian sentiment about pilgrimage to Jerusalem quickly developed into a veneration for relics, and instead of the older religious customs of visiting a temple as the abode of the deity, the new faith seemed identified from its beginnings with a special regard for tombs.

The artist rock-cutters of Petra may have been engaged in carrying out this entirely original monument, and in so doing doubtless lavished all the ornamental profusion upon it which we associate with the rather bizarre style of the Petra tombs. The city of Petra was in the height of its Roman splendour fifty or a hundred years before the commencement of the Holy Sepulchre monument.

The so-called "Tomb of Absalom" in the Valley of Jehoshaphat, which so closely seems to resemble the Holy Sepulchre as described in ancient notices, is finished with a remarkable pyramidal covering constructed in masonry and resting on the cubical base of the monument. This type of tomb, partly excavated from the mountain side, partly constructed, was doubtless common in the Levant, but unfortunately the ease with which it could be broken up by quarrymen has led to the destruction of the larger examples. At Akhiropietos, in Cyprus, a singularly large tomb of the class, still covered with its rock ceiling, survives. Elsewhere in the Levant small rock-cut tombs, formed by cutting away the rock, leaving the tombs standing like works of sculpture, are common enough of all periods in earlier history. They seem to be particularly numerous in Asia Minor.

For nearly 300 years the monuments of the Holy Sepulchre remained as originally built in the days of Constantine, doubtless influencing by their presence the course of early Latin ecclesiastical history, although they do not seem to attract so much attention perhaps as at a later period.

During the Dark Ages succeeding the fall of the Roman Empire, and the era of barbarian invasions from the East, the monuments on the Holy Sites at Jerusalem suffered the same fate as befell the still magnificent remains of the decaying Roman civilisation elsewhere. Père Lagrange, in *La Science Catholique*, 1890 (p. 14), seems to have discovered that the Persian invaders of the Syrian provinces in 613 spared at first the buildings on the Holy Sites, but owing apparently to a revolt of the conquered district whilst the Persian army was encamped on the other side of Jordan busy about the building of the remarkable palace at Meschitta, they returned and decided upon the destruction of the Tomb of Christ. In this destruction the famous basilica is said to have been completely destroyed by fire, and the relics contained within it were carried away to Persia in the month of May 614.

Fifteen years after the first destruction of the basilica an attempt was made to restore it. The names of two celebrated ecclesiastics are associated with this work: Modestus, Abbot of St Theodosius, and St John the Almoner, Patriarch of Alexandria. The work seems to have been achieved by the year 629, in time for the triumphal return of the Emperor Heraclius with the relic of the Cross, and for the solemn dedication of the new buildings on the 14th September of that year.[1]

---

[1] Modestus proceeded to build again from their foundations the churches of the Resurrection and of Calvary. (*Antiochi Epist.* in *Bib. Patr. Græc.* Tome 1, p. 1023, quoted by Robinson, vol. i. p. 388.) The Abbey of St Theodosius in Jerusalem is referred to at different periods, and perhaps for the last time in a bull of Pope Honorius III in 1216, "cum hospitali et apothecis."

The records which survive of this period of destruction and restoration are more scanty and less intelligible than those we have of the erection of the basilica and its colonnades in the fourth century. An equal obscurity reigns over the remainder of the Byzantine period. In 637 Jerusalem was occupied by the Arab Mohammedans for the first time, and the last vestige of the Roman Imperial protection of the Holy Sites disappeared. The Arabs do not appear to have injured the restored basilica or the Tomb, but on the contrary they became to a certain extent friendly partners in the property with the Christians. The entrance to the basilica on the east side, which seems to have been provided with a portico by Modestus, was converted into a small mosque for their convenience, whilst the area of the eastern hill on which the city stands (Mount Moriah) with its ruins of the Temple of Jupiter, was assigned to their exclusive use.[1]

The description of the Holy Sites by the pilgrim Arculf, with his remarkably preserved plan (as reproduced in numerous recensions), affords us the best idea of their condition at this period. It is evident that after the rebuilding by Modestus the basilica was reduced to a very insignificant condition compared with its pristine importance; this part of the question is however of considerable obscurity. The Tomb was becoming the more important monument on the sacred area, and the time was approaching when the circular enclosure surrounding it would be converted into a regular circular church.

The plan and description by Arculf stand in need of some little interpretation. The three walls which he mentions surrounding the Tomb must in all probability be understood to mean an outer wall of enclosure, an inner line of wall or colon-

[1] The earliest writers who describe this event are Theophanes (c. 830) and Eutychius (c. 870). The Arab authors are of the thirteenth century. Arculf (697) does not seem to refer to the presence of a mosque within the portico. Under the friendly monarchs Charlemagne and Haroun-er-Raschid the possession of the Holy Sites appears to have been in the hands of the Jerusalem Patriarch, although the Moslems presumably continued to occupy the small mosque within the portico. The early Abbaside Khalifs employed Christians as officers of trust and attendants on the person of the Moslem sovereign. (Robinson, vol. i. p. 393.)

nade, such as is often introduced in any kind of cloistered court, and the third or innermost wall is the outside casing of the rock-cut Holy Sepulchre. No covering over of the enclosed space around the Tomb is mentioned either by Arculf (c. 700), Willibald (c. 722), or Bernard the Wise (c. 867). Arculf speaks of the "Basilica of Constantine," but already it had become especially identified with the Cross-finding legend of St Helena—a legend which assumed such vast proportions in the later Middle Ages. Two entirely new buildings are mentioned as having been added to the general group—presumably by Abbot Modestus—the large new church covering over Golgotha, and a square church of the Virgin Mary.

The friendly terms on which Moslem and Christian at first lived together in the Holy City seem to have been continued during the ninth century, if we may credit the legendary history of Charlemagne and his friend Haroun-er-Raschid. To this period also belongs the first notice which we have of the covering over of the round or semicircular enclosure of the Tomb with a wood roof such as protected it until 1870. The *Annals* of Eutychius provide a picturesque legend in this connection. The Patriarch Thomas (813–821) is credited with the design of the very remarkable piece of timber construction which was eventually set up, and the ideas for which are supposed to have been revealed to him in a dream. In his vision he appeared to see forty phantoms, whom he recognised as martyrs, issue from one side of the Holy Sepulchre enclosure. These strange figures mounted the encircling wall, and stretching their arms and bodies over the space beneath, they seemed like caryatides supporting a central circular cornice and forming to some extent the outline of a domical roof. On awaking, the ingenious Patriarch seems to have been convinced of the important suggestions in his dream, and forthwith ordered forty great tree trunks from Cyprus—reminded no doubt of the wood of Shittim used by Solomon. He seems to have been advised by experts of the period to use a larger number of tree-trunk supports in this novel construction, but he adhered to the number forty of the vision, not forgetting to institute a memorial altar of the forty martyrs which happens to survive even at the present day within the precincts of the Holy Sepulchre. The mention of Cyprus as the place whence the timber was procured suggests the idea that possibly the method of construction adopted may be traced in the roofing of the curious little Byzantine churches of that island. (*Vide* "Byzantine Timber Building," *Journal R.I.B.A.*, 1907, p. 575.) As far as can be gathered from the legend the circular wood roof at Jerusalem must have been constructed in the same way with tree-trunks resting on a wall plate *against* the wall, the upper ends supported by a circular curb of wood leaving a large opening in the middle. Eutychius describes the outer covering of the roof as being supported by the inner or lower circle of tree trunks, and between the two was a space sufficient for a man to walk upright along the top of the wall under the outer roof which rested on the *outside* of the wall. Even this brief description serves to show that the mode of construction consisted in the tent-like covering which is represented in the early copperplate views of the interior of the Anastasis at a much later period.[1]

The Holy Fire ceremony seems to have been instituted about the same time as the covering over of the Anastasis, and some little difference in the general arrangement of the group of buildings is referred to by the pilgrim Bernard Sapiens.

A change in the conditions between Moslems and Christians took place when Jerusalem passed into the hands of the Fatimite Caliphs of Egypt in the year 969. A period of persecution on the part of the new government against the Christians culminated in the furious acts of the mad Caliph El Hakim-bir-Amr, the founder of the Druse sect, who ordered the complete destruction of the monuments on the Holy Sites. This devastation was apparently carried out about the year 1008 according to most authorities, and to judge from many of the accounts it was executed in a manner which could have left but few traces of the buildings identified with the sacred area.[2]

---

[1] Willis (p. 74) states that the wood roof over the Holy Sepulchre was constructed of 131 squared cedars, in the form of a single cone, truncated at the top, where the light was admitted through a circular aperture, 12 feet, or perhaps more, in diameter.

[2] According to Will. of Tyre the ruin of the monuments was complete, and even the rock-cut Sepulchre itself was defaced and destroyed with much labour. "Prædicta ecclesia usque ad solum diruta" (Will. of Tyre). For about thirty years the Holy Sites appear to have

Between 1046 and 1048 the buildings of the Holy Sepulchre were rebuilt at the command of the Caliph Abu Tummim El Mostanzir Billah, eighth Fatimite Sultan of Egypt. For thirty years the area had lain waste and unoccupied. Pilgrims still made their way to Jerusalem, and a great number of brief notices of their adventures are preserved by the numerous writers of the age; but they brought back with them little more than complaints of the profanations to which the holy places were exposed, and of the wretched conditions to which their brothers in faith had been reduced. The celebrated Gerbert, afterwards Pope Sylvester II, was one of the first of these pilgrims in the time of El Hakim. Descriptions of the Holy Sites immediately before or after their restoration by El Mostanzir are hard to discover, and this may perhaps arise from the usual insignificance of Byzantine buildings of that period. Nâsir-i-Khusrau, an Arab traveller of the period, gives an account which conveys the impression that the restored church was decorated internally with considerable magnificence.

lain desolate, and not until 1048 was any attempt made to restore them by the building of a small chapel on Golgotha.

"Anno D. 1033, ex universo orbe tam innumerabilis multitudo cœpit confluere ad Sepulchrum Salvatoris Hierosolymis, quantam nullus hominum prius sperare poterat" (Glaber, 4, 6). Now commences the great era of mediæval pilgrimage; of princes like Robert of Normandy and William of Angoulême, the German archbishops and bishops, the innumerable nobles and knights with their men-at-arms, ending in the decisive occupation of Jerusalem by the Crusaders of 1099.

CHAPTER II

THE MIDDLE AGES

AT the time of the first, or great Crusade, Jerusalem was under the rule of the Fatimite Caliph of Egypt; but the different races composing the Caliphate of the period were at constant war with each other, and their dissensions allowed of an easy conquest of the Levant by the enterprising colonists from Western Europe. A short time before the Crusaders arrived on the scene the Holy City had been occupied by the famous Sokman son of Ortek the Seljuk Turk, who a few years later founded a powerful Seljuk dynasty in the region of Mesopotamia. The Egyptian Caliph had however succeeded in driving the Turks out of Jerusalem in August 1098—only in turn to be driven out himself by the Crusaders on the 15th July of the following year.

The settlement of the Franks within the walls of Jerusalem was evidently accompanied by an immense revolution in the condition and ownership of properties within the city; from the Temple area the Moslems were ejected, and it is not clear how far the Christians who were not Crusaders were allowed to occupy the Christian Holy Places.

Possibly the Orthodox monks may have been allowed an equal share in the use of the Holy Sepulchre as a shrine, although we do not hear of such being the case, and it was only at a later period, when the feudal law had been firmly established, that the rights and privileges of the native Christian communities were clearly defined in the usual documents and decrees. Customs connected with the Church of an earlier or Byzantine period were continued by the Latin hierarchy established at this time—such for instance as the ceremony of the Holy Fire, a custom which has been repudiated by the Roman Church since the Moslem occupation of Jerusalem in 1244.

The Latin Kingdom of Jerusalem came into existence on the

22nd July 1099, at a meeting of the chiefs of the Crusade, when it was determined that the conquered territory should be administered under the European feudal law by the Frank seigneurs, instead of becoming the patrimony of a theocratic form of government such as was advocated by certain of the Crusaders. The crusading aspirations were perhaps as much secular or commerical as they were religious, and immediately the ostensibly religious goal of the crusade had been won, all ideas of founding a simulacrum of the mediæval Papacy in the Levant were abandoned.

The feudal kingdom, with its Prince bearing the title of the "Advocate of the Holy Sepulchre," having been established, the next important step was to settle the ecclesiastical questions involved by a Latin occupation of the Holy City. For the moment a vicar of the Patriarch, who was to be eventually anointed, was chosen in the person of Arnulf, the chaplain of Robert Duke of Normandy. Daimbert, Archbishop of Pisa, was soon after created the first Latin Patriarch, and as such became the representative of the party in favour of a theocracy; but his reign was of short duration, and with his downfall in 1102 the regular feudal system of law and order was established without further opposition.

The paucity of information upon the condition and the appearance of the Holy Sites during the eleventh century is compensated for by the numerous accounts of pilgrimages containing interesting details on the subject which were compiled by the first visitors to Jerusalem after the occupation of the city by the Crusaders in 1099. The narratives of the Anglo-Saxon Sæwulf (a monk of Malmesbury?), 1102, and the Russian Abbot Daniel, 1125, give an excellent idea of the arrangements of the buildings at the time of the Crusaders' occupation, and before they had been touched with the object of erecting a vast Gothic cathedral in place of the group of Byzantine churches.

The group of churches seen by the first Crusaders on their entrance into the Holy City may not have been as originally rebuilt by the Caliph El Mostanzir, for it would appear that towards the close of this disastrous period Jerusalem was subjected to all the horrors of pillage and massacre by the Seljuk Turks, who spared neither mosques nor churches. The date of this barbarian inroad is supposed to have been 1071.

The date of Sæwulf's pilgrimage to the Holy Sites is important. His editor, M. d'Avezac, seems to have established it as the year 1102 (*vide* Bohn's translation, Introduction, p. xxi), and consequently his very graphic descriptions of the round church and adjacent chapels represent them as they stood *before* the Crusades. He states that "the Holy Sepulchre was surrounded by a very strong wall and roof, lest the rain should fall upon it, for the church above is open to the sky." He then mentions that "in the sides of the church itself are attached, on one side and the other, two most beautiful Chapels of St Mary and St John. On the other side of the Chapel of St John is a very fair monastery of the Holy Trinity, in which is the baptistery, to which adjoins the Chapel of St James the Apostle, who first filled the pontifical see at Jerusalem. These are all so composed and arranged that anyone standing in the farthest chapel may clearly perceive the five churches from door to door. Without the gates of the Holy Sepulchre to the south is the Church of St Mary called the Latin, because the monks there perform divine service in the Latin tongue. Adjoining to this church is another Church of St Mary called the Little, near which is the hospital and monastery founded in honour of St John the Baptist." The large church built in honour of Queen Helena, "which has since been utterly destroyed by the pagans," is, of course, the still famous basilica of the fourth century.[1]

The travels of the Russian Abbot Daniel are usually dated

[1] Sæwulf (*c.* 1100) describes the Rotunda of the Holy Sepulchre as we see it now. He also mentions the different "stations" of the open courtyard and the basilica ruins, and the place "Calvary" with Golgotha. The Chapels of St Mary the Latin, St Mary the Less, and St John the Baptist appear to have been then in use. Two most important Chapels of St Mary and St John were attached to the Rotunda, and the existing Chapels of the Monastery of the Trinity formed, as at present, the west side of the "parvis." The "place of the baptistery" and the Chapel of St James are mentioned as on the other side of the Chapel of St John, which was afterwards enclosed within the base of the thirteenth-century bell tower built by Frederick II, and now forms the Chapel of the 40 Martyrs.

The ceremony of the "Holy Light" on Easter Eve would appear to have been remarkably popular amongst both Latins and Greeks at the time of the capture of the city by the Crusaders. See Abbot Daniel, Foulcher of Chartres (1100), in *Gesta Dei per Francos*, and Sæwulf.

1125, during the reign of Baldwin II. The orthodox abbot seems to have been a special envoy to the newly instituted Latin court, and during the ceremonies of the "Holy Fire," which he describes in detail, he was accommodated with a seat of honour near that of the King. He describes the arrangements of the church as a circular building with a large apse towards the east containing the high altar, and with apparently the thrones of the King and the Patriarch respectively on the north and south sides. The Tomb, overlaid with marble decorations, was surmounted by a colossal figure of Christ in silver, "made by the Franks," and perhaps somewhat distasteful to the iconoclastic orthodox. In spite, however, of this great image introduced by the twelfth-century artists into what was doubtless otherwise a Byzantine interior, the two great branches of Christianity seem to have shared the building in a more amicable manner than in subsequent times. It is interesting to learn from this description that the great circular church was covered with the same kind of roof as was originally put up by the Patriarch Thomas of 300 years before. It is evident that it could not have been the same roof because of the two destructions of the church in 1008 and 1071. From an architectural or engineering point of view this remarkable roof was the great curiosity of the building, although from that point of view it does not seem to have attracted particular notice on the part of the mediæval pilgrims or those of a later date.[1]

[1] Daniel (c. 1107) describes the ruins of the place where Helena found the Holy Cross. "It was a very large church with a wooden roof; now, however, there is nothing but a small chapel. Towards the east is the large doorway to which Mary the Egyptian came, desiring to enter the church......" "She passed out of this door on her way to the desert of Jordan. Near this door is the place where St Helena recognised the true Cross, &c."

"Calvary and the place of crucifixion are enclosed by a (retaining) wall, and they are covered by a building ornamented with marvellous mosaics. On the eastern wall a life-like representation of the crucified Christ, and larger and higher than nature; on the south side a Descent from the Cross. There are two doors; one mounts seven steps to the doors and as many after. The floor is paved with beautiful marble. Beneath the place of crucifixion, where the skull lies, is a small chapel, beautifully decorated with mosaic, and paved with fine marble, which is called 'Calvary'; the upper part is called 'Golgotha.'"

Daniel describes the Holy Sepulchre: "Approached by a little door

The mosaic decorations within the Rotunda are described by the twelfth-century pilgrims as if they were works of art of unusual magnificence.[1] Traces of these mosaics are referred to in the comparatively modern times of Quaresmius and Sandys as of an imposing character.

It would seem probable that the transference of the old Byzantine buildings from their former orthodox occupants to a body of Latin ecclesiastics, constituting a patriarchal court and eventually an Augustinian convent, was effected by degrees. During the earlier years of the Crusading Kingdom the Church of St Mary the Latin continued in use, and was probably not demolished until the commencement of the works of the new through which a man can scarcely get by going on bended knees. The sacred rock was visible through a covering of marble slabs by three small round openings on one side. The Sepulchre was surmounted by a beautiful turret resting on pillars, terminating in a cupola covered with silver-gilt plates, and on its summit a figure of Christ in silver above the ordinary height; this was made by the Franks."

The Patriarch resided in spacious apartments attached to the upper part of the church.

"The Church of the Resurrection is of circular form, containing twelve white monolithic columns and six pillars. There are six entrances, and galleries with sixteen columns. Under the ceiling, above the galleries, the holy prophets are represented in mosaic as if they were alive; the altar is surmounted by a figure of Christ in mosaic. Over the high altar is an 'Exaltation of Adam' in mosaic, and the mosaic of the arch above represents the 'Ascension.' There is an 'Annunciation' in mosaic on either side of the altar. The dome of the church is not closed by a stone vault, but is formed of a framework of wooden beams, so that the church is open at the top." The number of columns mentioned in this description varies in different MSS.

From a translation into French by Mme de Khitrovo, published by the Soc. de l'Orient Latine.

[1] Nâsir-i-Khusrau, 1047. (Guy Le Strange: 1888.) "Inside, the church is everywhere adorned with Byzantine brocade (mosaic?), worked in gold with pictures. These pictures they have overlaid with a varnish of oil of Sandaracha (red juniper); and for the face of each portrait they have made a plate of thin glass, which is set thereon, and is perfectly transparent. This dispenses with the need of a curtain, for the glass is cleaned daily by the servants of the church."

Idrîsî, 1154 (G. Le Strange), mentions a bell-tower in the same position as at present over the south door (Gate of the Crucifixion). He does not appear to have actually visited the Holy Land, but he seems to have heard of the rebuilding of the Crusaders, and he describes the choir as finished.

cathedral. The Augustinian convent was founded in 1120, and the famous consecration of the new choir of the canons—the Chorus Dominorum—by the Patriarch Foulcher took place on the 15th July 1149. The new building seems to have been about twenty years in course of construction.

The magnificent new church in the early transitional style of the South of France was erected during the reign of Fulk of Anjou and completed during the minority of his son Baldwin III, or, more properly speaking, under the guardianship of the queen-mother Milicent. The Second Crusade, in which the French interest was chiefly concerned, and in which the French King Louis VII and his queen Eleanor of Guienne, the "Rose of Aquitaine," took part, was in 1148, and the consecration ceremony of a distinctly French piece of architecture was therefore appropriately witnessed by no fewer than four reigning sovereigns of French nationality. Under these circumstances it is not surprising to find the style adopted for the new buildings most distinctly French in character, representing doubtless a vast French influence not only in politics and social life, but especially in the arts and crafts of the settlers in the new Kingdom of Jerusalem during its palmiest days. In other monuments of the Holy Land of an earlier or a later period the traces of Italian and even German culture may be noticed, but in this great central memorial of the Crusades the French must be allowed to claim a complete ownership.

On approaching the Middle Ages—that period when the foundations of our modern life and thought and manners and customs were being laid—Jerusalem, instead of being a half-forgotten name, an inaccessible place but rarely visited by Frankish pilgrims at the peril of their lives, becomes the most interesting place on the world's surface to all Christendom, and to a great part of the Asiatic peoples as well. Chronicles, histories, travels, and government records, charters, monumental documents of all kinds, crowd upon the view, and the difficulty of digesting so much historical detail is probably greater than in almost any similar branch of study.

History from the eleventh to the thirteenth centuries—the epoch of the great Crusades—is of course the most important, in its relationships with modern Europe and civilisation, of any the world has ever seen. The very word *Crusade* conveys so much that it is needless to insist upon the absolute supremacy of the period in historical interest. And perhaps the most important monument—certainly the most remarkable for its history—which survives from those stirring days is the Gothic church of the Holy Sepulchre.

The church built by the Crusaders is an especially interesting example of artistic development. It exhibits most distinctly the dawn of a new era in architectural design, methods of construction, and perhaps, to some extent, in ritual arrangements. The Dark Ages preceding the twelfth century had passed away with their characteristic Romanesque art, and the civilised method of life, both religious and secular, which we identify with the Middle Ages, was about to create those stupendous architectural monuments all over Europe, the particular characteristic of mediæval Christianity. The splendid cathedrals which formed the centres of Christian life in mediæval times owe all their beauty to the development of that particular style of art and architecture of which we see the first beginning in the church at Jerusalem.

In this church we have evidences of a scientific and organic principle of design and structure which belongs to the famous mason-craft of the great French cathedrals. The presence of the *ribbed vault* in part of the construction is sufficient to differentiate it from mere Romanesque building, although the style of decorative carving employed may have a somewhat earlier feeling in it than we usually associate with the pointed style.

One very remarkable feature about the twelfth-century design is the way in which the general arrangement of the Holy Sites has been worked into the new plan, and the strictly conservative scheme by which the circular church of the Anastasis is preserved intact from its original conception in the early part of the ninth century (*vide supra*). The remarkable conical roof of timber covered with lead as at first designed by the Byzantine Patriarch Thomas seems to have been repeatedly restored and repaired, as we shall see later on. This roof would doubtless be renewed by the Crusaders during their occupation of the Holy City for nearly one hundred and fifty years, and in all probability at the time of the new building of 1130 such a restoration would take place, although no records remain of the fact. The only monument connected historically with the Holy Sepulchre which the Crusaders destroyed for the purpose of their new work was the church of Sta Maria Latina, and even that building, which of course became meaningless when the whole sacred area was in the possession of the Latin Church, is still marked by the apse which survives as an Armenian shrine on the east side of the Parvis (*vide* Sta Maria Latina in Part II, c. 1). The ruins of the "Basilica of Helena," as it is sometimes called, were probably of a scanty description in the twelfth century; we hear nothing about them after the time of Sæwulf (1102), and by the middle of the century they had completely disappeared beneath the buildings of the Priory.

The Patriarchate and the Augustinian Convent

The founding of the Priory is ascribed to King Godfrey by the chronicler Albertus Aquensis (*Gesta Dei*) writing, as is supposed, in 1184, who says: "In Templo Dominici Sepulcri viginti fratres in Christo divini cultores officii constituerentur." Other authorities place the date in 1120.

The Canons Regular of St Augustine, who are said to have been first established in 1061 at Avignon, represented a popular religious development of that period. The rule they observed differed but little from the older Benedictine, but they professed certain tenets peculiar to the teaching of the great Augustine. Like the Benedictines they lived in common, eating together in a refectory, and sleeping in a general dormitory. The Augustinian Order at a later period gave birth to the Premonstratensians and other branches. Although designated "Canons," and holding prebends (Theodoric, 1175) they were virtually monks and lived a cloistered life. Their habit was black with a white rochet, and over all a black hood. At the present day the Augustinian Order is represented in Jerusalem by a small convent on Mount Sion.

The Augustinian Order may be said to have originated in the course of the eleventh century in consequence of a very large number of the clergy attached to cathedral and collegiate churches in different parts of Europe being imbued with the desire for a community life on the pattern of the monasteries of the period. There was no particular founder of the Order, but it was natural, under the circumstances, that the classical references in his sermons made by St Augustine to the mode of life led by himself and his clerics at Hippo should be taken for this rule. Based upon fundamental principles more than on a precise ideal, this rule was of easier adaptation to the requirements of cathedral chapters than the Benedictine Rule; hence such mediæval foundations in England as Carlisle; in Scotland, St Andrews; and in Ireland, Dublin; came into existence. The Cathedral of Bristol was formed by Henry VIII out of an Augustinian foundation, at a later period.

The Augustinian Order of Canons Regular, recognized by a Lateran Council of 1059, was not fully organized until Benedict XII published a Rule for their use in 1339.

The importance of the Augustinian Order in the twelfth century is sufficiently demonstrated by such important monuments as the Holy Sepulchre and the Temple in Jerusalem being committed to its care.

As an additional evidence of the intensely "French" character of the first Crusades this institution of the then recently founded Augustinians—who may be considered perhaps as one of the numerous religious developments of mediæval France—as the guardians of the recovered Holy Sepulchre, is of importance. As representatives of the religious interests of Western Christendom in the Holy Sites, they took the place of the Benedictines who had hitherto occupied the Church of St Mary the Latin.

De Vogüé in his account of the Holy Sepulchre Church, gives the following list of the Priors of the Augustinian Convent:

Gerard	1120	Nicholas I	1140	Arnauld	1157
Guillaume	1128	Pierre II	1141	Nicholas II	1160
Pierre I	1132	Amaury	1155	Pierre III	1167

The ownership of the Holy Sepulchre was divided between the Latin Patriarch and the Prior of the Augustinian Convent. The Patriarchate (which to a great extent still survives in the modern Christian Street—Rue du Patriarche of the Middle Ages) was situated on the west side of the church, and appears to have had a separate door of entrance into the gallery of the Rotunda. The Augustinians had their convent on the eastern side of the site, with, of course, a separate entrance to the church. A catalogue of the officials connected with the buildings is preserved in a MS. of uncertain date called "Commemoratorium de Casis Dei," which has been several times published in collections of documents relating to the period.

PRIORY OF THE HOLY SEPULCHRE

Canons	23	Notaries	2
Priests (Vicars) . .	9	Seneschal . . .	1
Deacons	14	Custodians of the Sepulchre	2
Sub-Deacons . .	6	Custodian of Calvary .	1
Custodians (fragelites) .	13	Custodians of the Relics .	5
Monks (!) . . .	41	Cellarers	2
Candlebearers to the Patri-		Treasurer . . .	1
arch	12	Water Guardian . .	1
Ministers . . .	17	Porters	9
Prepositors . . .	2	Hospitallers . . .	3
Accountants . .	2		

This large number of 166 officials would probably be attended by a considerable number of servants and hangers-on, who would perhaps have made up an even larger resident population on the Holy Sites than the multitude of sects constitute in modern days.

The Latin Patriarchs and Priors of the Holy Sepulchre resided within the precincts—the Patriarchs in an imposing palace, the outside of which is but little altered by its subsequent use for Mohammedan purposes; the Priors in some part of the buildings on the eastern side long since pulled down or altered beyond recognition.

Latin Patriarchs.—The following list taken from De Mas Latrie's *Trésor de Chronologie* is of a certain architectural interest. These important personages, coming from various European districts which are characterised by schools of art, may be supposed to have influenced the design of the new buildings to some extent, by patronising artists of their own nationalities during the progress of the work.

Daimbert (Dagobert), Archbishop of Pisa	.	.	1099
Ebremar	. . . .	.	1103
Gibelin, Archbishop of Arles .	.	. .	1107
Arnoul de Rohes	.	. .	—
Germond, Bishop of Amiens .	.	. .	1118
Estienne, Archbishop of Chartres .	.	.	1128
Guillaume, Bishop of Mechlin	.	. .	1130
Foulcher, Archbishop of Tyre	.	. .	1146
Amalric, Bishop of Noyon .	.	. .	1157
Heraclius d'Auvergne, Archbishop of Cæsarea	.	1180

From 1180 to 1227 doubtful occupants of the Patriarchal Throne are mentioned.

Girold, or Geraud, Abbot of Clugny	. .	.	1227
Guy, Bishop of Nantes .	. .	.	1240
Robert	. .	.	1244
Jacques, Bishop of Liège	. .	.	—
Pierre, Bishop of Agen .	. , .	.	1263
Guillaume, Bishop of Agen .	. .		1265
Tommaso d'Agni, Bishop of Cosenza	.	.	1272
Giovanni, Bishop of Vercelli .	. .	.	1278
Eli	. .	.	1279
Nicholas de Hanapes	. . .	.	1280
Raoul de Grandville	. . .	.	1294
Landulf	. .	.	1295
Anthony Beak, Bishop of Durham	.	.	1305
Pierre de Plaine Chassagne, Bishop of Rodez .	.	1311
Raymond	. .	.	1324
Pierre de la Palu, Bishop of Limassol	.	.	1329
Eli de Nabinaux, Archbishop of Nicosia	.	.	1342
Guillaume Amici, Bishop of Chartres	.	.	1351
Philip de Cabassole, Bishop of Cavaillon	.	.	1366

The last nine names are those of mere titulars who had no residence within the territory of Jerusalem, Nicholas de Hanapes being the Patriarch who lost his life in escaping from the siege of Acre in 1291.

Pierre de Plaine Chassagne was apparently at one time Bishop of Limassol, Cyprus. He was also Papal Legate, and in that capacity was charged with the suppression of the Temple Order in the island. On the 7th November 1313, he read the Papal Bull in the cathedral of Nicosia dissolving the Order, and conferring their estates upon the Hospitallers.

Pierre de la Palu, Dominican, left Cyprus in 1337, and died in Paris in 1342.

Eli de Nabinaux, of Perigord, Franciscan, Cardinal de St Vitalis, Archbishop in comm., died at Avignon in 1367. (Hackett, *Hist. Ch. of Cyprus.*)

For above fifty years the splendid memorial of mediæval religion and romance continued to be used in the manner its builders intended. During this period (1130–1187) the Holy Sepulchre Church would appear as it is described for us by the pilgrim John of Wurzburg in 1150 and Theodoric in 1175.

In 1187 the siege and capture of Jerusalem by Saladin marks the beginning of the decay which for more than a hundred years sapped the vitality and stifled the growth of those once brilliant little principalities founded by the adventurers of 1099. Saladin seems to have treated conquered Jerusalem with leniency in spite of his threats to butcher the inhabitants and destroy their churches. The Holy Sepulchre is even said by some authorities to have remained untouched.

For more than forty years Jerusalem remained in the hands of the Mohammedans whilst the princes of Europe continued to threaten with fresh Crusades, most of which enterprises ended in disaster to their originators. Lastly the astute Emperor Frederick II and Melek Kamel, Sultan of Egypt, came upon the scene in 1228, and by their friendly and politic arrangements the Holy City was divided between Christians and Moslems as in the days of Charlemagne and Haroun-er-Raschid.

We unfortunately have but little information about the condition of the Holy Sepulchre Church during the Moslem interregnum, 1187–1228.

In 1239 Richard Earl of Cornwall, brother of Henry III of England, with William Longsword, Earl of Salisbury, and many other nobles of England, ventured on what was practically the last of the Crusades which had any successful issue. Richard obtained a settlement by which the great object of the Crusades seemed to be accomplished; Palestine belonged to the Christians. Richard then returned to England, and was received everywhere on his journey as the deliverer of the Holy Sepulchre.

There was one thing, however, which marred the prospect, the government of the country was left virtually in the hands of the great military Orders, instead of under a responsible king, with the natural results of divided counsels, opposing interests, and want of cohesion in face of a common danger which very soon appeared on the frontiers.

In 1245 the terrible Carismian Tartar invasion from Central Asia took place, and in spite of the union of Christians and Moslems in a common cause against these savages, Jerusalem was sacked and most of its inhabitants were massacred. To this overwhelming event is perhaps due the very complete destruction of certain parts of the precincts—the cloister of the Priory for instance. The wooden roof over the Rotunda would be destroyed at the same time in all probability.

Since 1245 the Holy Sepulchre Church has been considered the property of a Mohammedan State, whether under the Sultans of Egypt or their successors, the Sultans of Turkey, and the Latin Christians who then lost their sovereignty over Jerusalem have ever since been tenants of the Holy Sites by virtue of *capitulations* or treaties with the Mohammedan landlord; by simply renting the property as Turkish subjects under the patronage of the Russian Government and the Negus of Abyssinia, the Eastern Christians occupy the greater part.

During the fourteenth century innumerable stories of pilgrimages to the Holy Sites were written, many of which have been published in different collections. One of the most interesting is that of Ludolphus de Sudheim, a Westphalian priest, who describes the condition of the Holy Sepulchre in 1348. According to his account the use of the church seems to have been regulated by this time very much in the way in which we see it at the present day. Latins, Greeks, Armenians, Nubians (Copts and Abyssinians), Syrians, and Georgians occupied different parts, but it is singular to find that "Canons Regular" are said to have still officiated for presumably the Latin section. The pilgrims were admitted at stated times within the church, which must have been enclosed in much the same way as at present to allow of such arrangements. The pilgrims were obliged to pay four florins for the privilege of passing a day and a night adoring the Sepulchre, and this tax was exacted by a

Saracen official called *Amil*, a sort of prefect appointed by the Sultan. Twice in the course of the year admittance to the church was granted gratis—at Easter, and on the festival of the Invention of the Holy Cross—at which times the different nationalities of Christendom celebrated their particular rites in different languages, and made processions with their bishops and clergy, carrying censers and candles according to their different customs.

Earlier in this century the Italian Dominican of Sta Maria Novella Florence, Fra Ricoldo, describes in his *Itinerarium* a somewhat similar condition of affairs. He made two pilgrimages to Jerusalem; on the first occasion he was refused admittance to the Holy Sepulchre, but was more successful on his second attempt. At the end of the century Simone Sigoli wrote one of the earlier guide books for pilgrims, a mere list of the stations where "perdono di colpa e di pena" might be obtained by the devout pilgrim, showing that the visit to the Holy Land had become a matter of system and custom. Simone gives the cost of the pilgrimage at the end of the fourteenth century as 300 gold ducats, inclusive of visits to Mount Sinai and Damascus. Each pilgrim travelling in such a style took a personal attendant with him.

During the fifteenth century we approach more clearly the conditions of modern days. The absolute abandonment of the idea of crusading colonisation in the Levant synchronises with the discovery of America. The European colonial enterprise is attracted to a new world, and we hear no more of Frank adventurers attempting to carve out for themselves feudal principalities in the nearer East. On the eve of the great changes, political, social, and religious, which divide the Middle Ages from modern days, the history of the Holy Sepulchre also suffers a change. Instead of a religious relic to be fought for, and the possession of which by Christians was perhaps regarded as a symbol of a united Faith and a talisman for the good of the Christian Commonwealth, the Monument of the Resurrection becomes one of a series of places to be visited for a purely religious sentiment. The *Evagatorium* of Felix Faber, a monk of Ulm (1484), is a voluminous and amusing account of pilgrim adventures at this period. The young German nobles,

whom Felix accompanied as a sort of bear-leader, seem to have
conducted themselves in the Church of the Holy Sepulchre very
much as such young men would do in the present day, inscribing
their names and coats-of-arms upon its walls in a truly modern
way [fig. 6].

Fig. 6. Examples of Pilgrims' Graffiti on the
Entrance to the Holy Sepulchre Church.

CHAPTER III

MODERN TIMES

WITH the advent of printing begins the long and incalculable series of more modern descriptions of the Holy Land.

During the sixteenth century one or two events took place of a certain importance in the history of the Holy Sepulchre. In 1516 the whole of Syria and Palestine passed from the possession of the Egyptian Caliphs into the hands of the Turkish Sultans, who from henceforth became the owners of the Holy Sepulchre. Selim I is credited with being the most bigoted of the Turkish Sultans, but fortunately for Christendom his religious animosities were directed more against dissenters from his own faith than against the Christians. Passing on his devastating campaign of 1520 close to Jerusalem, he contemplated the total destruction of the city, but changed his mind in consequence of a lucky dream, and is even said to have presented gifts to the Christians in the Holy City.

The Turkish occupation of the Holy Land seems to have been inaugurated by friendly relations between the new governors and the Latins. The policy of Selim I was to subdue the Moslem world beneath the new Caliphate of Constantinople, for which purpose he employed the firearms and artillery, and even the bombardiers, lent him by the Grand Master of Rhodes and the Venetian Republic. He did not live long enough to turn upon his Christian allies, as he doubtless intended to do when once he had consolidated his empire; he left this for his son Solyman the Magnificent to attempt after his death.

With the advent of the new sovereign a change for the worse took place in the position of Latin Christians in Jerusalem. The Minorites, or Order of St Francis, who had owned the church known as the "Cœnaculum" or Home of St Mary (a holy site of great antiquity) for nearly three hundred years, were at this period the guardians of the Holy Sepulchre. In 1535 their troubles began by the imprisonment in the Tower of David[1] of Fra Tommaso di Norcia, Custode, and his brethren. Fra Tommaso eventually died a prisoner in Damascus. In 1549, according to the *Gesta Dei per Fratres*, the Minorites were expelled from the Cœnaculum, which thenceforth became the Moslem shrine of "David's Tomb," as it remains at the present day. A curious letter upon this subject of their expulsion written by Solyman the Magnificent to Francis I of France still survives. But although the Latins seem to have enjoyed but little favour with the new Sultan, it was during his reign that Fra Bonifazio di Ragusa was permitted to carry out a restoration of the Holy Sepulchre in 1555.

This remarkable fact is attested by the drawings of the restored monument in the early copperplates published by Bernardo Amico, *Trattato delle piante e immagine de' sacri edifizi di Terra Santa*, and by the descriptions published by Fra Bonifazio Corsetto himself in *Liber de perenni cultu Terræ Sanctæ*, in 1553. Within the outer chamber, which appears to have been added to the monument at this period, was placed a tablet with the following inscription:—

D. IESV SEPVLC A FVNDAM INSTA FVIT ANO S INCAR MDLV
PER F BONIFACIV DE RAGVSIO G S M SION SVPTIBS

The appearance of the restored monument, which has been preserved in the contemporary copperplate, is very suggestive of the usual Turkish *kiosk* style of architecture of the period. It seems to have undergone as great a change as was possible from the earlier designs which had occupied its place from time to time [fig. 24].

At the same time that the Franciscans (Minorites) were engaged in restoring the Holy Sepulchre, they were building their new convent (the "Casa Nova") within the walls of the city, and also about this time the Sanjak of Jerusalem presented them with the old wooden gates of the Golden Gateway of the "Haram" mosque, as a relic of the time of Christ and of His entrance into Jerusalem from Bethany. These gates were placed among the relics preserved within the Church of the Holy

[1] *Castellum Pisanum.*

Sepulchre, and this act on the part of the Moslems serves as another proof of the fluctuating state of mutual relations between the two great religions.

During the seventeenth century the Holy Sepulchre figures in history in a new and remarkable light. Completely dissociated from the crusading idea, it becomes an object for the cupidity of an Italian prince, Ferdinand I, Grand Duke of Tuscany. No page of history is perhaps more romantic and extraordinary than the story of the visit of Faccardino, Emir of the Druses, to the Tuscan Court in 1603, and of his return to the Levant with the captain-general Inghirami and the Tuscan fleet for the purpose of carrying off the Tomb to Florence. Faccardino and his confederates actually found means to enter the church and begin their operations for detaching the sepulchre, when, being discovered by the "malice" of the Greeks, they were compelled to take to flight. The ill success of the intending larceny was viewed as a great misfortune, and whilst the Emir retired to his possessions at Beyrout to carry out his schemes for introducing Italian luxury and art into the Lebanon, the Grand Duke of Florence had to be content with his magnificent Medicean Chapel, deprived of its central ornament, which was to have been the famous Tomb of Christ. How the Italians of that comparatively enlightened age could have been induced to consider such a project feasible is indeed astonishing. A rock-hewn tomb —even in the form of a kind of cabin, with thin rock walls and roof—would be impossible to remove except in fragments, which would be of little value when pieced together. But at an earlier age such a removal of the House of Loretto was attributed to angelic agency.

During the centuries immediately succeeding the loss of Jerusalem in 1245, the relics once contained in the Church of the Holy Sepulchre, and within its precincts, were considered to have been removed for greater security to Europe. Rome obtained the "True Cross" (St Peter's), the "column of flagellation" (St Prassede, presented by Cardinal Colonna in 1223); and the famous "Sudarium," or winding sheet of Christ, which is mentioned at an early period, after being removed to Cyprus, was presented by Marguerite de Charni to Louis II, Duke of

Savoy, at Chambéry, in 1452, and afterwards brought to Turin
in 1575 by Emmanuel Philibert, for the purpose of enabling
St Carlo Borromeo to venerate it without the fatigue of crossing
the Alps[1].

In 1621 appeared the highly important contribution to our
knowledge of the Holy Sites, written by George Sandys, of
London. His vivid descriptions and interesting "graven figures"
are most valuable. At this time the fabric of the church must
have been but little altered since mediæval days, the restoration
by Bonifazio di Ragusa having been confined to the "Monument." He mentions:—

The Temple of the Resurrection. A stately Round cloystered below
and above, supported with great square pillars, flagged heretofore
with white marble, but now in many places deprived thereof by the
sacrilegious Infidels.

Now between the top of the upper gallery and extream of the
upright wall, in several concaves, are the pictures of divers of the
Saints in Mosaique work, full faced, and unheightened with shadows
according to the Grecian painting; but much defaced by malice or
continuance. In the midst on the South side is the Emperour Constantine's opposite to his Mother's, the memorable Foundresse. This
Round is covered with a Cupola sustained with rafters of Cedar,
each of one piece, being open in the midst like the Pantheon at Rome.

The Ascent to Calvary. Prostrating themselves and tumbling up
and down (the stairs within the church)...Opposite to the dore of
the Temple, adjoyning to the side of the Chancell are certain Marble
Sepulchres without titles or Epitaphs....The chappell of Isaac,
without, and spoken of before; and where they keep the Altar of
Melchisedeck.—Sandys, p. 128.

At about the period of Sandys' *Travailes*, the guardian of the
Holy Sepulchre was Fra Francesco Quaresmius, the author of
a monumental book on the Holy Land—the famous *Elucidatio*.
In it he mentions many particulars about the buildings of the
Holy Sepulchre, and refers among other things to the ruined
mosaics in the Calvary Chapels, with their inscriptions.

Philip IV of Spain, perhaps the most powerful European

[1] A portion of the "Linteis sepulchralibus Christi" is supposed
to have been deposited at Besançon.

monarch of his period and at the same time a most religious zealot, naturally took an interest in the fate of the Christian monuments of the Holy Land. In 1628 he sent 30,000 ducats for their repair, and with this sum the timber roofs of the churches of Jerusalem and Bethlehem seem to have been reconstructed.

Towards the close of this century another Englishman, Henry Maundrell, wrote an account of his pilgrimage to Jerusalem from Aleppo, where he was stationed at the time (1697) as chaplain of the Levant Company. He does not enter into particulars as to the architecture of the Holy Sepulchre Church, but he describes how:—

In galleries round about the church, and also in little buildings annexed to it on the outside, are certain apartments for the reception of friars and pilgrims; and in these places almost every Christian nation anciently maintained a small society of monks, each society having its proper quarter assigned to it by the appointment of the · Turks, such as the Latins, Greeks, Syrians, Armenians, Abyssinians, Georgians, Nestorians, Cophtites, Maronites, &c., all of which had anciently their several apartments in the church; but these have all, except four, forsaken their quarters, not being able to sustain the severe rents and extortions which their Turkish landlords impose upon them. The Latins, Greeks, Armenians, and Cophtites keep their footing still; but of these four the Cophtites have now only one poor representative of their nation left; and the Armenians are run so much in debt that it is supposed they are hastening apace to follow the example of their brethren who have deserted before them.

Besides their several apartments, each fraternity have their altars and sanctuary, properly and distinctly allotted to their own use, at which places they have a peculiar right to perform their own Divine service, and to exclude other nations from them.

But that which has always been the great prize contended for by the several sects is the command and appropriation of the Holy Sepulchre, a privilege contested with so much unchristian fury and animosity, especially between the Greeks and Latins, that, in disputing which party should go into it to celebrate their mass, they have sometimes proceeded to blows and wounds even at the very door of the Sepulchre, mingling their own blood with their sacrifices, an evidence of which fury the father guardian showed us in a great scar upon his arm, which he told us was the mark of a wound given him by a sturdy Greek priest in one of these unholy wars. Who can expect ever to see these holy places rescued from the hands of the infidels? Or if they should be recovered, what deplorable contests might be expected to follow about them, seeing, even in their present state of captivity, they are made the occasion of such unchristian rage and animosity.

For putting an end to these infamous quarrels, the French King (Louis XIV) interposed, by a letter to the Grand Vizier, about twelve years since, requesting him to order the Holy Sepulchre to be put into the hands of the Latins, according to the tenor of the capitulation made in the year 1673, the consequence of which letter, and of other instances made by the French King, was that the Holy Sepulchre was appropriated by the Latins. This was not accomplished until the year 1690, they alone having the privilege to say mass in it: and though it be permitted to Christians of all nations to go into it for their private devotions, yet none may solemnize any public office of religion there but the Latins.

The daily employment of these recluses is to trim the lamps, and to make devotional visits and processions to the several sanctuaries in the church. Thus they spend their time, many of them for four or six years together; nay, so far are some transported with the pleasing contemplations in which they here entertain themselves, that they will never come out till their dying day, burying themselves (as it were) alive in our Lord's grave.

The Latins, of whom there are always about ten or twelve residing in the church, with a president over them, make every day a solemn procession, with tapers and crucifixes and other processionary solemnities, to the several sanctuaries, singing at every one of them a Latin hymn relating to the subject of each place.

Good Friday night, which is called by them *nox tenebrosa*, is observed with such an extraordinary solemnity that I cannot omit to give a particular description of it.

As soon as it grew dusk, all the friars and pilgrims were convened in the Chapel of the Apparition (which is a small oratory on the N. side of the holy grave, adjoining to the apartments of the Latins), in order to go in a procession round the church; but before they set out, one of the friars preached a sermon in Italian in that chapel. He began his discourse thus: "In questa notte tenebrosa," &c., at which words all the candles were immediately put out, to yield a livelier image of the occasion; and so we were held of the preacher for near half an hour, very much in the dark. Sermon being ended, every person present had a large lighted taper put into his hand, as it were to make amends for the former darkness, and the crucifixes and other utensils were disposed in order for beginning the procession. Amongst the other crucifixes was one of a very large size, which bore upon it an image of our Lord, as big as the life. This figure was carried all along in the procession, after which the company followed to all the sanctuaries in the church, singing their appointed hymn at every one.

The first place they visited was the Column of Flagellation, a large piece of which is kept in a little cell just at the door of the Chapel of the Apparition. There they sang the appointed hymn, and another friar entertained the company with a sermon in Spanish touching the scourging of our Lord.

From hence they proceeded in solemn order to the Prison of Christ. Here likewise they sang their hymn and a third friar preached in French. From the prison they went to the Altar of the Division of Christ's Garments, where they only sang their hymn without adding any sermon. Having done here they advanced to the Chapel of the Derision, at which after their hymn they had a fourth sermon, in French.

From this place they went up to Calvary, leaving their shoes at the bottom of the stairs. Here are two altars to be visited—one where our Lord is supposed to have been nailed to the cross, the other where His cross was erected. At the former of these they laid down the great crucifix upon the floor, and acted a kind of resemblance of Christ's being nailed to the cross: and after the hymn one of the friars preached another sermon, in Spanish, upon the crucifixion. From hence they removed to the adjoining altar, where the cross is supposed to have been erected. At this altar is a hole in the natural rock. Here they set up their cross, with the bloody crucified image upon it; and leaving it in that posture they first sang their hymn, and then the father guardian, sitting in a chair before it, preached a passion sermon in Italian.

At about a yard and a half from the hole in which the cross was fixed, is seen that memorable cleft in the rock, said to have been made by the earthquake which happened at the suffering of the God of Nature "when the rocks rent and the very graves were opened" (S. Matt. xxvii. 51). That this rent was made by the earthquake that

happened at our Lord's Passion, there is only tradition to prove; but
that it is a natural and genuine breach, and not counterfeited by any
art, the sense and reason of everyone that sees it may convince him:
for the sides of it fit like two tallies to each other, and yet it runs in
such intricate windings as could not well be counterfeited by art,
nor arrived at by any instruments.

The ceremony of the Passion being over, and the guardian's
sermon ended, two friars personating Joseph and Nicodemus
approached the cross, and, with a most solemn and concerned air
both of aspect and behaviour, drew out the great nails, and took
down the feigned body from the cross. It was an effigy so contrived
that its limbs were soft and flexible, as if they had been real flesh;
and nothing could be more surprising than to see the two pretended
mourners bend down the arms, which were before extended, and
dispose them upon the trunk in such a manner as is usual in corpses.

The body, being taken down from the cross, was received in a fair
large winding sheet, and carried down from Calvary, the whole
company attending as before, to the Stone of Unction. Here they
laid down their imaginary corpse, and, casting over it several sweet
powders and spices, wrapped it up in the winding sheet. Whilst this
was doing they sang their proper hymn; and afterwards one of the
friars preached, in Arabic, a funeral sermon.

These obsequies being finished, they carried off their fancied corpse
and laid it in the Sepulchre, shutting up the door till Easter morning;
and now, after so many sermons and so long, not to say tedious a
ceremony, it may well be imagined that the weariness of the congregation, as well as the hour of night, made it needful to go to rest.

March 27.—The next morning nothing extraordinary happened,
which gave many of the pilgrims leisure to have their arms marked
with the usual ensigns of Jerusalem.

In the afternoon of this day the congregation was assembled in the
area before the holy grave, where the friars spent some hours in
singing the Lamentations of Jeremiah.

March 28.—On Easter morning the Sepulchre was again set open
very early. The Mass was celebrated just before the Holy Sepulchre,
being the most eminent place in the church, where the father guardian
had a throne erected, and being arrayed in episcopal robes, with a
mitre on his head, in the sight of the Turks, he gave the Host to all
who were disposed to receive it, not refusing children of seven or

eight years of age. This office being ended we made our exit out of the Sepulchre, and, returning to the convent, dined with the friars.

This account of one of the principal ceremonies of the Churches in Jerusalem, still practised annually by both Greeks and Latins on their respective Eastertides, is of interest as showing how unchanged the use of the building has been for more than two centuries. The ceremony of the Latins, at which the present writer has assisted, is absolutely the same at the present day as it was in 1697, but for the introduction of a German sermon after the hymn on Calvary.

The Rev. Henry Maundrell does not mention the curious cups containing the spices, and decorated with the arms of the Emperor and the King of Spain, which are carried in the procession and must be as old as his time.

During the eighteenth century all interest in the Holy Sepulchre waned to its lowest ebb. The world was filled with wars and revolutions amongst Christian States, whilst the Turkish Empire had sunk into a state of lethargy after its last struggles with the decaying Venetian Republic. A good many books were written by travellers in the Levant during this period, but in place of the pilgrims' guide-books we have scientific treatises by students of natural history. Amongst such visitors very few display much interest in the architectural remains of the Holy City. Such books are illustrated with the deplorable copperplates of the period, mere sketches from memory and utterly useless, as a rule, for any purpose of study. One of the most interesting of these ponderous folios is Pococke's *Description of the East*, 1745. In it there is a reference to the Rotunda of the Holy Sepulchre which is of interest: "The roof was of cypress, and the King of Spain giving a new one, what remained of the old roof was preserved as reliques, and they make beads of it to this day." "To the north of it (the Stone of Unction) are the tombs of four Kings of Jerusalem, not well known, whose bodies, it is thought, were carried to Christendom when the Saracens took the city" (the view of Calvary shows two tombs at the entrance). The roof referred to as given by the King of Spain must be the new one erected in 1628 by Philip IV.

In the latter part of this century the church had fallen into deplorable neglect and almost oblivion—an oblivion from which it was dragged for the purpose of affording material for German speculation and investigation. But the bookseller, Jonas Korte, who started a theory to discredit the traditional character of the Holy Sites, unintentionally revived an interest in the monument by polemical discussions which have endured for the past hundred years.

At the beginning of the nineteenth century the Church of the Holy Sepulchre once more underwent a destruction by fire, which completely obliterated the mediæval character of the Rotunda, and caused much damage in other parts of the church, especially to the Calvary chapels. This unfortunate conflagration originated in the portion of the gallery round the Rotunda which was occupied by the Armenians, and according to the official report of Callinicus, Patriarch of Constantinople, the fire began at 8 a.m. on 30th September 1808. It consumed the cupola of wood covered with lead of the Rotunda, destroying the small kiosk built on the top of the Holy Sepulchre. The whole of the fittings of the Rotunda, with its surrounding galleries and chapels, and the " treasuries " and convent apartments were burnt. The interior of the great choir with its iconostasis, stalls, &c., was reduced to a mass of ruins, and the semi-dome of the apse above the " Cathedra " was severely injured. The only portion of the Holy Sites unaffected by the fire was the sub-terranean Chapel of Helena. The chapels on Calvary were gutted by the fire, and according to the Latin version of the catastrophe (*Breve notizia dell' incendio*, 12. *Ottobre*, 1808, published by the Franciscans) a wooden building over these chapels fed the flames and caused much damage to this quarter of the church. The roof of the Rotunda fell in upon the Sepulchre, but the latter, though crushed without, was uninjured within. The marble columns supporting the great roof were calcined and the walls injured. The buildings of the Latins on the north were all saved, and, of course, the external tower was untouched.

After much difficulty and many negotiations permission was obtained from the Porte to rebuild the church. In spite of the endless disputes amongst the Christian sects themselves concerning their respective shares in the ruined property, all the high dignitaries of the Empire at Constantinople and all the petty officials at Jerusalem had to be bribed. But, notwithstanding all the delay involved, the restored buildings are said to have been completed for reconsecration in 1810. The architect employed by the Greeks for their share of the work was a certain Comnenus of Mitylene.

In 1840 the Roman Catholics made some repairs to their property around the Chapel of the Apparition. Here it may be mentioned that this chapel and the convent attached are said to have been secured to the Franciscan Order through the mediation of King Robert of Sicily in 1342. At the back of the chapel stands a disused font of a quatrefoil plan, somewhat similar to the famous one in the basilica at Bethlehem. *Vide* note on p. 91.

The revived interest in the Holy Sites on the part of both orthodox and Roman Catholic Christians during the nineteenth century culminated in the Crimean War of 1854–55, which is usually attributed to the quarrels between the rival Churches. The Russian influence in Jerusalem did not, however, receive any very great check to its development, nor did the Roman Catholics succeed in obtaining any additional privileges within the Holy Sepulchre in consequence of this war; and about fifteen years afterwards we find the Russians putting up at their own expense the great iron girder dome covered with lead which now surmounts the Holy Sepulchre.

Since 1870 absolutely nothing has been touched in the fabric of the Church of the Holy Sepulchre, either in the way of repairs or structural additions. In these days of "restoration," how long will such a state of things continue—*ultima ora latet*?

PART II

DESCRIPTION OF THE MONUMENT

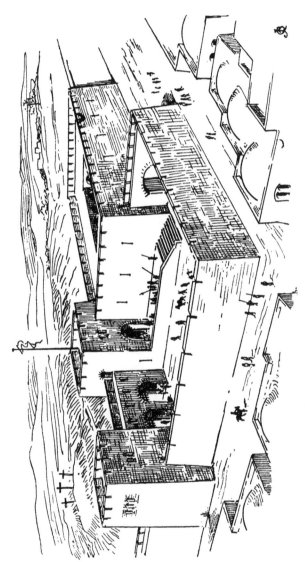

Fig. 7. Imaginary Bird's-eye Sketch of the Holy Sites in A.D. 33.

CHAPTER I

VESTIGES OF ANTIQUITY

THE traditional site of the crucifixion and entombment of our Lord occupies a plot of land which is apparently bounded on the south and east by remains of the city defences, which are certainly much older than the fourth century.

In describing these remains of walls of a remote age, it must be remembered that they cannot be precisely identified either in age or use, because they are without any architectural features. The methods of masonry construction adopted in the Levant have remained remarkably unchanged throughout the ages. The huge stones with a simple drafted edge, leaving the face in the rough, are common to the primitive builders of the "Haram area" (site of the Jewish Temple) as much as to the Crusading masons of thousands of years later. Also the method of building the city walls at different periods has remained practically the same, the masonry tending to become a little smaller in cases where rebuilding has taken place and the stones have been re-shaped to fit their new positions.

On the south side of the site a considerable length of the city wall lies buried beneath the accumulations of débris and the later buildings covering the area known during the past few centuries as the "Muristan." It was traced by Schick and others during the various alterations which have been carried out by the Germans and Greeks during the past quarter of a century on this site, and, although it was never very accurately noted at the time, the lower courses of the structure still remain below the level of the new German church and the Greek bazaar. This wall runs in a direction east and west, parallel with the south side of the Holy Sepulchre Church on a line passing through the foundations of the new German church (built on the site of Sta Maria Maggiore).[1]

[1] Apparently the only attempts to record the appearance of this

The traces of a fortified enceinte on the east side of the Holy
Sepulchre are very much more complicated with later alterations
than the southern wall, and they have afforded a deeply interesting problem from many points of view. Herr Baurath Schick, of
Jerusalem, who devoted so much of his time to the elucidation of
archæological difficulties in the Holy City, was perhaps most
successful in what he did for the Christian antiquities. Herr
Schick was employed during his long residence in Jerusalem of
some fifty years as sanitary engineer to the "medjlis" or town
council. He also prepared very complete and careful plans of the
Holy Sites for the Russian and German Palestine Societies, and
being constantly on the
spot whenever anything
was discovered during the
progress of alterations in
the centre of the city he
was able to amass a vast
amount of information.
The area on the east side
of the Holy Sepulchre
Church was laid bare to
a considerable extent during the eighties of the last
century by the Russian
Palestine Society, which
had obtained possession
of a convenient corner of
the premises for the erection of a large new hos-

Fig. 8. Model of the Holy Sepulchre by
the late Dr Schick (c. 1875). Preserved in
the Library of the Anglican College,
Jerusalem.

pice or hotel for pilgrims. This area on being freed from the
squalid tenements and hovels which always cover any ancient
site in the East revealed the presence of most interesting fragments of buildings which had been completely lost sight of.
Herr Schick was induced by these remarkable discoveries to
wall are certain references to it by Herr Schick at different times in the
P.E.F.Q.S., and a view of it taken from a drawing made when the
Greeks were rebuilding their bazaar in 1905. Selah Merrill (U.S.
Consul) reproduces this drawing at p. 297 of his book, *Ancient
Jerusalem*, published in 1908; he does not, however, mention how the
drawing was made or by whom.

make elaborate plans of the property, and to construct (or
perhaps finish the construction of) a large-scale model of the
Holy Sepulchre Church, with its surroundings, in wood [fig. 8]
—the different proprietorships of the premises being shown by
painting the model in various colours. This very valuable record
of a period now passing away is preserved in the Anglican
College, Jerusalem.

According to Herr Schick's investigations the site of the new
Russian church was a rock platform which, with its fortifications,
had formerly constituted the guardhouse of the Roman garrison
at this point of the city—a defence as much against the turbulent
citizens within the wall as against the enemy without. The
position of such a mural fortification is reminiscent of the great
Pretorian Camp on the Aurelian wall of Rome, or of the usual
position of a mediæval citadel in relation to the city for which it
served as a defence. Jerusalem appears to have been provided
with more than one of these Pretorian camps for the use of the
Roman army of occupation.

The traces on the site—*i.e.* the scarps and rock levels as far as
they could be traced by Herr Schick at various times in the course
of many years, whenever his professional employment connected
with the cisterns and drains within this area led to such investigation—induced him to form the following opinion.

The wall, traces of which have been distinctly identified at
different points within the foundations of the new German
church and the new Greek bazaar, appears to be a primitive
enceinte wall of ancient Jerusalem running east and west. In a
line, corresponding with the present " Suk-el-Amud," Herr
Schick thinks that the enceinte of the city at the period of A.D. 33
continued from this primitive wall in a direction due north, thus
forming a right-angled recess in the city defences at this point.
A city gate, of special plan and importance, was situated within
this re-entering angle of the wall, and forming an additional
defence to the gate on its north side stood the large square enclosure or tower of the Pretorian Camp. As already remarked,
this camp was intended to withstand any attack from the city
side as well as from the open country, and for this purpose the
gateway seems, according to Herr Schick's theory, to have been
planned in the shape of an elbow or of an L form, enclosing one

corner of the camp and having two doorways, one fronting the
country and the other facing the city, both of which could be
closed in the event of any fear of the population within the city
uniting with the enemy on the outside against the "army of
occupation" [fig. 9].

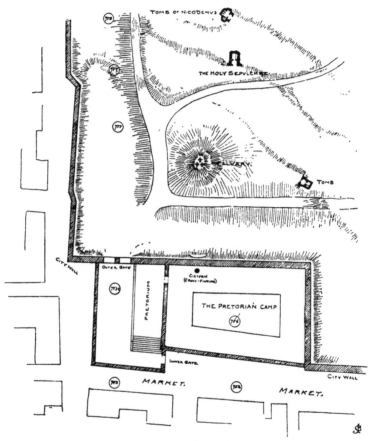

Fig. 9.   Plan of the Holy Sites deduced from the remains *in situ*.
Scale. $\frac{1}{1000}$.   Rock levels in metres above the sea.

The evidences for Herr Schick's theory—the theory which
seems also to have been endorsed and adopted by the Russian
branch of the orthodox Church—are based on a consideration
of the rock contours and levels, as they remain in a much

mutilated condition at the present day. Unfortunately, the site has been much changed in subsequent ages: first, by the monumental buildings of the fourth century; secondly, by the immense cisterns which have been formed all over it in later times.

An inclined plane, rock-cut, leading up to this rock platform of the supposed Pretorium on its south side from the street level on the west, seems to have been formed to receive a flight of stone steps, and one of the ancient steps still stands *in situ* on the top of this ramp[1].

The rock platform above described is a little below the level of the rock platform forming the floor of the Mount Calvary Chapel within the Church of the Holy Sepulchre, and also of the general rock level of Christian Street. The ground slopes in a direction from west to east, in the same way as it does at the Damascus Gate, but its exact limits on the north side are at present unknown.

There has always been a tendency to attach importance and value to any kind of ancient object which is found during the progress of alterations in Jerusalem. These remains, found by the Russians towards the end of the last century, attracted intense interest, and as is usual in such cases conclusions were drawn which have since become articles of belief with many persons, although there is little, if any, proof to be adduced in the matter. The Russian ecclesiastical authorities seem to have decided that the rock platform, with its inclined plane for steps, is the actual stage on which Christ was tried before Pilate, and the scene of "Christ before Pilate in the Pretorium" is represented in a large and quaint painting with life-size figures on a wall of the church which now covers the Holy Site.

Tombs of Jewish Character and Pagan Remains

These tombs may be classified as follows:—

(*a*) The Holy Sepulchre.

(*b*) The traditional tomb of Adam, forming Mount Calvary.

(*c*) The tomb of Nicodemus, a much mutilated tomb of the "kokim" variety, investigated with great elaboration by various

---

[1] The mysterious "Scala Santa" in Rome might be accounted for by these missing steps at Jerusalem perhaps?

writers in the *Palestine Exploration Fund Quarterly Statement* for 1877 (several Papers).

(*d*) The "Prison of Christ," possibly a tomb which had been almost entirely destroyed as far as its character is concerned. This chamber could hardly have been a cistern as has been suggested, as it stands at too high a level for such a purpose. Certain traces of graves are said to have been detected in the rock area not far from the north-east corner of the "Prison."

The area covered by the buildings of the Holy Sepulchre is broken into all manner of irregularities by innumerable cisterns which have been cut from time to time, partly for collecting water and partly for quarrying purposes. Many ancient vestiges have naturally disappeared under the circumstances. The most ancient of these cisterns is the famous "Cross-finding" Chapel, which is referred to in the first historical accounts of the mediæval period—*e.g.* Arculf. The holes in the rocky roof of this cistern are mentioned by Quaresmius (*Elucidatio*) as evidently used for buckets, and this idea has been advocated by the supporters of a theory as to the rock platform above being the ancient Pretorium.[1]

Every possible trace of the use of the Holy Sites for Pagan purposes has, of course, utterly disappeared. This would be but necessary under the circumstances.

During the excavation of the south-east corner of the site by the Russians, a curious fragment of inscription, evidently from the frieze of some public building, was turned up. It is the usual commencement of an Imperial dedication—

IMP......
PART.....

in two lines of finely cut letters of the second or third century.

The Russians have carefully inserted this fragment in the wall of their church, and there are not wanting enthusiasts who can imagine this to be one of the usual dedications beginning—

IMP . CAES . DIVO . TRAIANO
PARTHICI . &c., &c.,

[1] "Cistern of the Cross-finding." *Ord. Survey Notes*, p. 54. "Of irregular shape, hewn out of the *Malaki* bed, with the overlying *Missæ* left as a roof, one of the most ancient types of cisterns."

set up by the Emperor on the temple erected here according to the Christian legend about the period of Hadrian or Trajan.

Fig. 10. Fragment of an Imperial Inscription found on the site of the new Russian Church adjoining the Holy Sepulchre.

THE BUILDINGS OF THE FOURTH CENTURY

Fragmentary and much mutilated traces of the great monument erected by the early Christians on the Holy Sites can alone be discovered at the present day. These fragmentary evidences are chiefly in the form of rock-cut outlines and foundation walls, which serve, to some extent, to elucidate the accounts written by early pilgrims. In as far as they agree with each other, such traces and early descriptions taken together give a fairly exact and conclusive idea of the plan and arrangement of the monument at the period in question [figs. 9, 11].

The method of building in vogue during the later Roman Empire, and especially in its provincial style, may be studied at Baalbek. The later portions of the stupendous temple may be considered almost contemporary with the buildings of Jerusalem, and the mason craft would probably be identical. This mason craft is characterised by the effort to employ the largest masonry possible, and, as a consequence of such a large scale, the stones are, as a rule, placed in position without being completely dressed to the face of the wall; a finished surface was obtained when the building was completed and there was no further danger of injuring the stones during transport and handling. In some cases, as in the entrance façade at Baalbek, the stones (which have never been treated as finished work) are drafted on three sides but the edges are protected by a projection of 2 or 3 inches, which was to have been cut off when the façade should be finished; this façade, however, never was finished.

In recognising Christianity as one of the religions of the Empire, the Roman Government appears to have permitted the erection of sumptuous buildings in the New Jerusalem. No record remains of how or by whom they were planned; few names indeed of any architects of the Roman Imperial period have reached us with certainty, and, although we have many descriptions of these buildings, and even a mosaic picture evidently representing them, still the information upon the subject is far from complete. In other words, we have none of that official information which is always desirable.

The surviving evidences of the Roman buildings of the Holy Sepulchre on the site are as follows:—

(a) The plan of the Rotunda or Anastasis (Church of the Resurrection) as defined by the circular rock-cutting on the west side.

(b) The "monticulus" of Calvary (Golgotha), which was also formed into a rock-hewn monument by the Romans.

(c) The east front of the "Martyrion" basilica, of which the lower courses of stone and its three doorways are fortunately preserved.

(d) The Madeba mosaic.

(e) The evidences derived from contemporary monuments, such as the apse mosaic of the Church of St Pudenziana, Rome (the present writer was the first to suggest this identification, see *Quarterly Review*, 1899), the Trivulzio diptych, and other ivories of about the same period [figs. 1–5, Part I], which all possess a precisely similar character in design and detail in the effort to represent the Holy Sites.

(a) The remains of the Anastasis are indeed scanty. The outline of the enclosing wall—which outline appears in the earliest known copy of a plan—is only to be traced with difficulty in the rock-cut floor of the south-west quadrant of the Rotunda. All that we can assume is that, as the rock-cutting suggests a circle in accordance with the earliest descriptions of the place, the traces which remain at the present day are the actual foundations of the encircling wall of the fourth century

The rock-cut Holy Sepulchre is, according to many past and present authorities, now reduced to a mere mutilated fragment of rock, the upper portion of the little cubicle which the fourth - century stone-cutters left standing in the midst of the levelled plateau having subsequently been demolished.

No architectural detail or fragment survives of the fourth-century Anastasis.

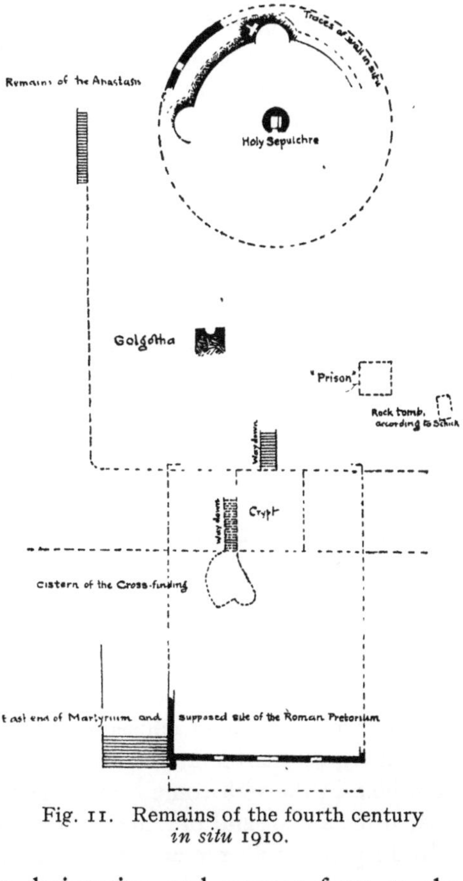

(b) "Mount Calvary," which owes its designation and present form to the Romans of c. 333, has perhaps suffered less from subsequent damage than any other portion of the remains of primitive times. If this little rock-cut chapel was originally a tomb, it has undergone a great change by being excavated and enlarged within to its present dimensions, but it is, of course, impossible

Fig. 11. Remains of the fourth century
in situ 1910.

to say how far the rock extends as a covering to the chapel; the apse of the chapel is perhaps a mere niche in the rock face, and was never anything more.

(c) The east front of the Martyrion or Memorial Church is the most interesting relic of the period now extant. Until the Russian Palestine Society commenced its explorations on the site during the eighties of the past century, this venerable relic was completely lost to sight, and a record of its existence seems to have survived only in the primitive descriptions, and in an assumption that the granite columns which have been found on the same side of the bazaar formed part of its decorations. These granite columns were first brought to public notice as the "Propylæa," by Schultz, in 1845, and made to do duty as the remains of the ancient "second" wall of the city[1] (see Robinson, vol. iii. p. 168).

The ancient east front of the fourth century has, however, no very clear connection with the columns, and it seems more than probable that this colonnade has been added to the façade at a subsequent period.

The three or four courses of large stones which are exposed to view in the Russian church and in the adjacent wood-store stand on the rock platform in a somewhat clumsily built manner, the inequalities of the rock made up with smaller stones, and evidently the whole is constructed with a view to being covered over by a veneer of marble, or in some other way. A sunk face on the stones and other indications show that the stones were to be dressed after they were in position. The southern door-way, which also shows in the Russian church, has this peculi-arity, that either it is of subsequent formation, or it has been covered with a marble architrave—in other words, it is now a mere hole in the wall some 8 or 10 feet wide; it is, however, rebated for a door and provided with a cill.

In the plans of the remains prepared by the present writer for

[1] The "Khan ez Zeit," "oil market," or Suk-el-Amud, takes its latter name either from the rows of columns with which the market-place was lined, or from a great column said to have stood in the open space within the "Gate of the Column," Bab-el-Amud. Both Willis and Schultz speak of the "Suk," east of the church, as "deserted" in their time (nineteenth century).

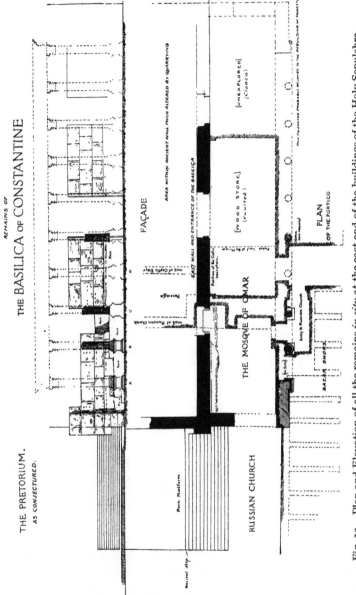

Fig. 12.   Plan and Elevation of all the remains *in situ* at the east end of the buildings of the Holy Sepulchre. Fourth to seventh centuries.   Scale, $\frac{1}{500}$.

publication by the Russian P. E. Society, in 1897, the central doorway of the façade was shown (as inferred) in the position where it has since been discovered (1907) during the process of rebuilding the Coptic convent on the site. Its dimensions and position are shown on the detail drawings of the front [*vide* illustration fig. 12], and a detail of its moulded architrave [fig.

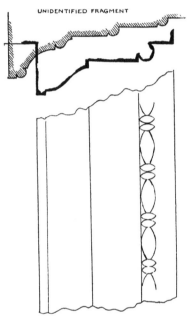

UNIDENTIFIED FRAGMENT

13]. It is somewhat puzzling to find this doorway existing with a moulded and carved architrave executed in the stones of the wall, whilst the side door, as above described, if contemporary, must have possessed a marble door lining.

The base of the wall, which has been brought into clearer evidence within the last few years, is certainly occupying the position of the east front of the fourth-century basilica, as shown on the mosaic of St Pudenziana and as described by St Sylvia of Aquitaine; the only question which arises is whether the stones we now see are the base of the original fourth-century monument, or of some later rebuilding [fig. 14].

ARCHITRAVE, EAST DOOR, BASILICA.

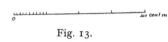
0   40 cent m

Fig. 13.

The problem presents itself under so many different aspects that perhaps we may consider it one of the most perplexing puzzles in archæology.

1. In the first place, the rock platform on which the wall stands has the appearance of having undergone great alterations subsequently to the erection of the wall—alterations which are so unaccountable and confusing as almost to baffle speculation. For instance, the great central doorway, on being discovered in

1907, proved to be without a rock cill as far as was observed, and the area within this doorway (westwards) appeared to be of a much lower level than the rock platform within the Russian church. Here there had been cellars under the Coptic convent, and within them were disused cisterns or mills for some primitive manufacture. This area was, unfortunately, not explored with any intelligent supervision—in fact, it was merely turned over by the ignorant occupants of the Coptic convent, whose object was to rebuild their premises in the cheapest and easiest manner possible, making use of all they found on the site for the immediate purpose of second-hand building materials. In this way a most valuable piece of archæological investigation has perhaps been completely lost, and many indications of the arrangement of the most interesting of Christian churches probably disappeared on this occasion.

Fig. 14. Foundation Stones of Constantine's Basilica in the Russian church.

It would seem sufficiently evident that the rock levels around the east front of the basilica have been cut away subsequently to the building of the church, because the wall and rock have been cleaned down (after building) to the depth of about three inches at some height above the present floor in the Russian church [see fig. 14]. The wall has been prepared to receive marble slabs supported by dowels, the holes for which occur all over the face of the stones, and this marble decoration evidently finished at a platform level, marked by the horizontal line of the sinking, beneath which the rock has subsequently been cut away in a rough unfinished manner.

2. A still greater puzzle presents itself when we come to consider the traces of a colonnade which at some period occupied

the usual position of such a feature in front of the east wall of the basilica.

The colonnade in question is represented by (*a*) the base

Fig. 15. The southern base remaining within the Russian church.

of a terminal pilaster towards the south, which is now to be discovered in a miserable little eating-shop only 6 feet wide on one side of the "Suk-el-Amud"; (*b*) the base of an engaged column of grey granite (a much-decayed fragment) standing within the new Russian church, of which the actual base of the column may be white marble; and (*c*) the mysteriously uncouth attempt (apparently) at a copy of (*b*) in a base to

Fig. 16. The northern base remaining within the Russian church.

another mutilated and decayed granite shaft, also standing within the Russian church.

These bases rest on a rock platform partly covered over with stone paving which prevents any investigation of their actual site.

In the building of the new Russian church these interesting fragments have been carefully incorporated *in situ*. At the same time it is a little difficult to realise their original appearance or to discover if they occupied the position of detached or attached columns. At present they are treated as if they belonged to the latter category, and they appear partly embedded in the external wall of the modern church.

The base mouldings of the column and its pedestal within the Russian church are precisely the same as those on the base in the little shop outside, and the pilaster base in the shop has a plan of an extra set-back to the adjacent

Fig. 17. Capitals found in the recent demolition of the Muristan.

wall, which seems to suggest its terminating a series of attached columns.

The bases of the two columns [figs. 15 and 16] preserved within the Russian church are very remarkable. Like the pilaster in the shop outside, these columns rest on low pedestals — that on the south being moulded in an ordinary style of Byzantine work, and apparently partly concealed by later masonry and cement. It is much mutilated. The northern of the two appears to be a mere block of stone, of which the moulding has only

Fig. 18. Capitals found in the recent demolition of the Muristan.

been commenced. In this latter the base of the column and the pedestal form one block, in the other example the base of the column is distinct from the pedestal.

The question arises as to whether these two pedestals are cut in separate blocks of stone or are part of the rock platform on which they stand. As the platform was covered over with paving at the time of the building of the new Russian church, it is of course impossible now to see if the apparent blocks of stone are part of the living rock or not.

In the *P.E.Q.S.* for 1888 (p. 17) Herr Schick appears to give the first regular report or statement on the discovery of the remains on the Russian property. According to this the Russian Society bought the site between the years 1859 and 1862 (in two portions). A visit of the Grand Duke Serge was commemorated by a general clearance of the ground under the supervision of Herr Schick, and an official report published in Russian and in the German Palestine *Zeitschrift* 1885 (p. 245). A more complete clearance of the site was made in 1887, of which a plan was made by Herr Schick and communicated to the Palestine Exploration Fund. A continuation of this report appears on p. 57 of *P.E.Q.S.* for 1888. Herr Schick begins by referring to the granite columns in " Suk-el-Amud," which at the time were three in number, a fourth having been removed twenty years before, also the remains of a pier or stone jamb (the pilaster base within a shop). The space between the columns appears to have been closed with masonry, "apparently built by the Crusaders" (and covered with a vault).[1]

Sir C. W. Wilson, commenting on the above statement in the same paper, states that "It is so important that researches should be carried on at this spot, that the Committee have taken steps, which they hope will be successful, to work in co-operation with the Russian Society." This hope seems not to have been fulfilled.

Herr Schick states that as far as he knew no plan except his own was made of the site before the building of the Russian and Greek property in 1887. (See *P.E.Q.S.*, 1888, p. 20.)

---

[1] The columns of the eastern façade referred to by Schultz in 1845 are perhaps clearly described for the first time by Willis in 1849. See Williams' *Holy City*, vol. ii. p. 250.

RESTORATION OF BUILDINGS BY THE PATRIARCH MODESTUS

The greatest difficulty presents itself in any attempt to bring the ancient wall (1) into any usual harmony of design with the colonnade (2) in front of it. The wall has all the appearance of being the original Roman work of the fourth century. The largeness of parts, the scale of the masonry, and the evidence of the dowel holes, which correspond with the statement of Eusebius about the marble on the external walls of the Martyrion, are all characteristic of the period. But the colonnade is on a very different scale and evidently belongs to the poor rebuilding of the seventh century by Modestus and St John Eleemon. The two oldest representations of the basilica hitherto discovered—the apse mosaic of St Pudenziana, Rome, and the rude attempt to show the buildings on the famous Madeba floor mosaic—clearly give the impression that the Martyrion was originally designed without any portico covering the great eastern doors. This must have been added in the seventh century, and within a few years the Caliph Omar appropriated this new feature in the buildings for his mosque. (*Vide infra.*)

The existing base of a wall of great stones in which the three doorways of the basilica are traceable extends in a line from south to north from the corner within the new Russian church, for a distance of 100 feet, the northern portion being buried within the substructures of the Coptic convent. The central doorway [see fig. 12] was laid bare in the autumn of 1907, but it has since been covered up with modern additions so that it is difficult to appreciate its proportions. This central doorway is the only one of the three which has any architrave mouldings cut in the stone jambs [see fig. 13], and from this circumstance we must conclude that the wall has been in some manner rebuilt, and that the central door was re-erected or restored under the circumstances. As already remarked, the wall within the Russian church appears to be *in situ* covered with dowel holes, and has been pared down to receive marble slabs, and the doorway which occurs in this portion may have been furnished with a marble architrave, but in that case the central doorway must belong to the rebuilding of the seventh century, as it seems hardly probable that the builders would give it a mere stone architrave in the centre of such a very important façade decorated with marble. The fact that this central doorway has no apparent cill and is consequently at a lower level than the door in the Russian church harmonises with the idea of its belonging, together with the colonnade, to the seventh century. To the rebuilding of this century also belongs the lowering of the rock platform in front of the three doorways to almost the level of the Suk-el-Amud of modern days.

If the above theory be correct, the fragment of wall within the Russian church may be considered to belong to the fourth century, and the central doorway with the colonnade to the period of rebuilding after the first destruction of the basilica by the Persians in 614.[1]

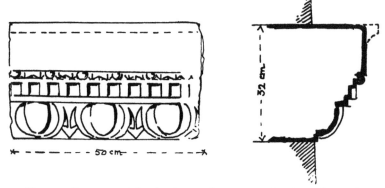

Fig. 19. Fragment of Cornice (stone) formerly *in situ* (?) at the north end of the Basilica Wall. Now destroyed.

[1] A series of nine much mutilated Corinthian capitals of a debased character, possibly of the seventh century, have recently been found during the demolition of the Muristan ruins, adjoining the Holy Sepulchre. They are of a plan combining a column attached to a square pier, suggesting a cornice with projections over the columns in the later Roman or Byzantine manner. These capitals, which have all the appearance of having formed part of such a façade as once existed at the east end of the Basilica, are now stored in the entrance to "Abraham's Convent." The capitals (Corinthian) are of an inferior workmanship, but of the usual design with small volutes. They measure 2 feet 10 inches in height by about the same in width, and would fit on to the usual columns of about 2 feet diameter. It should be noted that the average width of column fragments found in these ruins is about 2 feet [figs. 17, 18].

In 1894 the present writer observed a fragment of cornice with egg-and-dart ornament [fig. 19], evidently of the same date as the central doorway, which looked as if it was *in situ* on the top of the great stone courses within the Coptic convent. This fragment has been since destroyed. Its presence seemed difficult to explain, and it may have merely formed part of some accidental feature of which no other record now remains.

One of the most interesting discoveries connected with the monument was made in May 1897. One of the large stones in the basilica wall, at a height of about 15 feet, at a point a little to the south of the central door, which had become exposed during the repairs to the Coptic convents, was found to be inscribed with a large panel of elegant Cufic. The inscription runs in the formula: "In the name of God, Merciful and Compassionate. From the Exalted Majesty. It is commanded that this mosque is to be guarded, and that none of those under our protection (*i.e* Jews and Christians) be permitted to enter it, either by payment or under any other pretext, &c., &c."[1] The name of the Caliph, and the date, are unfortunately omitted, but it is doubtless of the period of Omar and Sophronius. This most interesting memorial of the foundation of the first Moslem mosque in Jerusalem was immediately, on being found, sent to Constantinople, where by this time it is probably lost; a photograph of the stone appears in *P.E.Q.S.* for 1898 (p. 86). In this inscription we have an additional identification of the seventh-century colonnade of the east front in which the mosque was established by the Caliph in 637. Here it may be permissible to suggest that the very rudely executed column base, the northern of the two within the Russian church, may belong to some alteration or subsequent rebuilding of this portion of the colonnade when in use as a mosque. According to Arculf the early Moslem settlers in Jerusalem were content with very poor makeshift buildings for their mosques, the great mosque of the Haram being a mere adaptation of the ruined temple of Jupiter.

---

[1] Cufic Inscription: found May 1897, in a stone about 1 metre 10 cent. square *in situ*, at the side of the roadway leading to the Coptic convent. *P.E.Q.S.*, 1897, p. 302.

See also M. C. Ganneau's remarks on above in *P.E.Q.S.*, 1901, p. 246.

See also *P.E.Q.S.*, 1898, p. 86, for photo of stone, by Dr Van Berchem.

Remains of the earlier Byzantine period in the history of the Holy Sepulchre Church, excepting those above described, are comparatively difficult to trace. On the south side of the parvis of the Crusaders' building are the evidences of an arcaded construction, uncertain both in design and in date, which, to judge by the remaining wall-respond which still stands at its western extremity, may also be of the period of Modestus. This wall-respond or wall-shaft (about 2 feet in diameter) has the curious basket-shaped capital so characteristic of early Constantinople work. Several bases of columns belonging to this arcade may be traced along the south side of the parvis or piazza, but it is difficult to imagine what purpose such an arrangement served unless it reproduced to some extent the colonnades surrounding Golgotha described by Eusebius and the earlier pilgrims. A similar arcade on the north side of the church, occupying a position close against the front of the north transept, seems to represent the corresponding cloister on the opposite side of the buildings. The basket-shaped capital above referred to has a very early character; but still both these arcades may very possibly be no older than the much later rebuildings after the great destruction by El Hakim in 1008, and the northern arcade has evidently been completely rebuilt long subsequently even to the latter period.

The Church of St Mary the Latin[1] was a building of the Byzantine and Romanesque period, within the limits of the southern arcade above described. Its position was clearly defined for the first time by the present writer in 1895. De Vogüé had a general idea on the subject which was correct, but he seems to have missed seeing the still well-preserved apse of this ancient church which is visible enough to anyone passing through the parvis; and indeed its large wide arch resting on capitals built up in the flat wall on the east side of the little piazza is almost intrusive on the sight. This apse is now used as a Holy Site by

---

[1] It is evident that the Church of St Mary the Latin built by Charlemagne was one of several churches dedicated to the B. V. M. which, at different periods, appear to have occupied much the same site. In one of these churches the stone of the Anointing seems to have been first placed, and the church was also known as that of the "Ointment-bearers."

the Armenians. The church to which the apse belonged is completely swept away, but the pathway down to it shown on the plan of Arculf is still preserved in the long straight staircase within the Greek convent of the Trinity[1] on the western side of the parvis [*vide* plan fig. 21].

Of this earlier period a much mutilated fragment probably survives in the new Russian church in the form of an archway about 15 feet high. It has, however, been very much altered and rebuilt at different times, so much so that its present position and condition hardly afford even a subject for speculation. Where the present new Russian hospice and Greek shops stand was formerly a bazaar which may have perpetuated the existence of a mediæval market—perhaps the "Malcuisinat" of Crusading times where the pilgrims found their miserable cookshops and restaurants of the period. The Byzantine-looking archway now within the Russian premises may have been built in connection with this market.

The later Byzantine buildings are again somewhat problematical. The well-known description of the Rotunda by Sæwulf the Englishman, with its side chapels extending southwards in such a way that "all the churches were visible to a man standing in any one of them," would lead us to suppose that the line of three chapels known at the present as those of St John the Divine, the Trinity, and St James is identical with what Sæwulf saw. These three chapels with the chapel of St Mary (now called "of the Apparition") on the opposite side of the church may probably occupy the exact sites of a more ancient date, but such architectural features as they possess give an impression of a much later style than the pure Byzantine. The chapel of the Trinity had at one time a dome, no longer in existence, the pendentives of which remain with some traces of mediæval painting on them.

---

[1] This "Convent of the Trinity" (of which no Latin records seem to remain) was probably the headquarters or Monastery of the Orthodox during the period of the Latin Kingdom. Its three chapels have very much the appearance of the contemporary small Orthodox churches in Cyprus.

CHAPTER II

THE CHURCH IN ITS PRESENT CONDITION

WITH that romantic sentiment which marks the nineteenth century, M. de Vogüé expresses the feeling of a visitor to Jerusalem in the days when Gothic architecture meant so much to the enthusiastic student of history: "Je retrouvais avec bonheur, au temps désiré du pèlerinage ces formes communes qui me rappelaient la patrie, et qui mêlaient aux glorieux souvenirs qu'elles évoquent les douces pensées du clocher domestique." At the present day these charming sentiments would perhaps be less keenly felt by the tourist who has visited many other lands where the remains of Gothic architecture survive in the midst of alien surroundings. The distinguishing characteristics of Gothic art are well enough pronounced in the buildings of the Holy Sepulchre, but they are certainly not so well preserved as in the cathedrals of the neighbouring island of Cyprus. The churches of Nicosia and Famagusta, the immediate successors of the Jerusalem monuments in point of date, are singularly untouched except for the removal of all Christian emblems, and this of course is due to their conversion into mosques. Far different has it been with the Church of the Holy Sepulchre, owing chiefly to the great fire of 1808, and to the subdivision of the interior into the tenancies of the different sects of Christendom.

The study of the existing group of buildings is complicated by many remarkable circumstances. The visitor to the Holy City is confronted by the appearance of the half-ruined, half-rebuilt remains of one of the grandest monuments of the Middle Ages, tenanted by representatives of every branch of existing Christianity except the Protestant;[1] and these various sects

[1] The German "Johanniter Orden," which occupies a portion of the north-east corner of the area, possibly within the ancient precincts, may perhaps be considered to represent the Protestant section.

occupy the place as the tenants of Mohammedan owners of the property.

As a consequence of this anomalous condition of affairs, the different tenants seek every opportunity to gain an advantage over each other, but up to the present time their mutual rivalries have only resulted in maintaining the property, as far as its structure is concerned, in very much the condition in which it was first handed over to the Mohammedans.

The sects at present occupying the Holy Sepulchre buildings are: Latins, Orthodox Greeks, Armenians, Syrians (Syriac Jacobites), Copts, and Abyssinians. At the time of the Latin kingdom of Jerusalem the then dominant Latin Church appears to have permitted the presence of the above-mentioned sects, together with others which have since become absorbed into the larger communions or have died out. At the time of Ludolph von Sudheim's pilgrimage (c. 1350) the Georgians were in possession of the key of the Holy Sepulchre itself, and the Nestorians, "*pessimi heretici*," and some mysterious sect distinguished by a "cauterised" cross on the forehead, impressed with a hot iron, are mentioned.

Whatever may have been the circumstances under which the different sects obtained possession of their distinct properties, and rights to the usage of those nominally belonging to other forms of Christianity, the settlement of the present day must evidently date from 1810, the year when the rebuilding of the Anastasis is considered to have been completed.[1]

---

[1] As an illustration of the existing conditions under which the Holy Sepulchre is held, the following extract from correspondence presented to the English Parliament in 1854 may be quoted: "After the Corban Bairam festival, the Commissioner Afif Bey, with a suite of local effendis, met the three patriarchs, Greek, Latin, and Armenian, in the Church of the Resurrection, just in front of the Holy Sepulchre itself, and under the great dome; there they were regaled with sherbets, confectionery, and pipes, at the expense of the three convents, who vied with each other in making luxurious display on the occasion. M. Botta, the French consul, was the only consular person present." On other occasions, especially of late years, the Moslem landlords have been called upon to settle disputes amongst their tenants, and hold meetings within the sacred precincts of a less genial character. All transactions between the Moslem owners of the property and their Christian tenants, whether in settlement of disputes, the gathering

In attempting to describe the buildings as they stand at the present moment it is perhaps best to follow the custom of the mediæval pilgrims, who invariably begin their accounts with the Anastasis, and then follow the course of the daily procession which is still conducted to the different stations in a certain order by the Franciscan monks, who in a sense act as *ciceroni* of the monuments for the pilgrims and tourists of modern days coming from the West—from Europe and America.

In following this order it is well to begin with the plan and general design of the twelfth-century church; then the Rotunda, and the Tomb, in their modernised condition; the "Chorus Dominorum" and N. Transept; the S. Transept; the Chapels on Calvary; other holy sites within the church. The Augustinian Convent, and the traces of St Mary the Latin, although intimately associated with the buildings and forming part of them may be considered under separate heads.

The modern ritual arrangements and furniture of the chapels belonging to the different sects are without any kind of interest. The "Chorus Dominorum" of the Latin Crusaders has been fitted up by the Orthodox as their "Metropolis" or "Catholicon," and is precisely like any other nineteenth-century Greek church with its deplorable architecture and gaudy painted woodwork of the most tasteless description. As far as such details are concerned, there is probably not one item which could by any stretch of the definition be considered a "work of art" in the whole building. Even the icons and wall paintings are the poorest of their kind.

THE PLAN

At the present day we possess the general plan and proportions (both very remarkably preserved in spite of past vicissitudes), a very great part of the decorative architectural details, and much mutilated sculpture, of the original *new* building of the twelfth century. The once splendid mosaics are,

of taxes, or other matters of the kind, seem to be carried on in the church itself, and every day the Moslem custodians solemnly lock and unlock the great door, and only entrance, of the church, with three great fetter locks as in the Middle Ages. The great door is still only open in the daytime during certain hours.

Fig. 20. Upper Story of the South Transept Front, Church of the Holy Sepulchre. From a photograph, made in 1860, kindly lent by the Palestine Exploration Fund.

unfortunately, entirely gone, and the Rotunda and eastern apse are rebuilt in the Turko-Greek style of the nineteenth century on the ancient lines and proportions [see fig. 21].

The design of the new church was very imposing and, considering the period and conditions of artistic development, on a very large scale. Few buildings of the twelfth century rivalled it in size. Perhaps the only churches resembling it of equal or greater proportions, at that time in existence, would have been Santa Sophia, Constantinople, or the older rotundas of the Pantheon and San Stefano, Rome; and certainly none other excelled it in boldness and novelty of construction. The great Basilicas of Rome, the wonder and admiration of an earlier period, were of so utterly different a style as to admit of no comparison with the new church of Jerusalem and its Gothic vaults and domes of an unprecedented fashion.

The Crusaders evidently carried in their train many master-masons and architects who belonged to that expiring school of Romanesque art of the twelfth century, the monuments of which are scattered over the south of France, Provence, Savoy, the greater part of Italy, and in fact all round the littorals of the Mediterranean and Adriatic. The artists and artizans of the period who followed the Christian armies were naturally drawn from the nearest European shores, whilst their masters and employers were Normans, Flemings, or even in some cases Englishmen. As a consequence the Provençal style of art is particularly pronounced, the great domical churches of France seem peculiarly akin to many of the principal crusading monuments of the Holy Land, whilst the sculptors of Arles or Pisa are represented in their decorative carvings. Saint-Front, Périgueux, which has often been compared with the Holy Sepulchre Church as an example of the pointed domical style, was burnt in 1120, and its reconstruction was contemporary with the new building in Jerusalem. It is therefore of special interest to find that the two buildings resemble each other in some particulars. At the same time it is curious to observe how much advanced the Church of the Holy Sepulchre appears to be in the Gothic style of plan and detail when compared with the French example.

Nearer the Levant, the churches of Venetia, St Mark's,

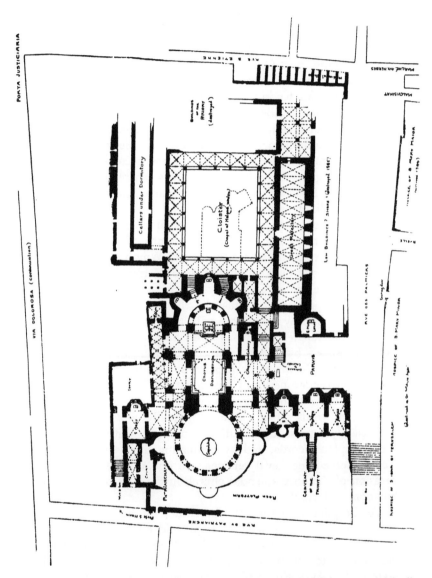

Fig. 21. Plan of the Holy Sepulchre Church and Augustinian Convent as originally built in 1150. Traced from the Ordnance Survey Plan of 1864. Scale, $\frac{1}{1200}$.

Venice, Sant' Antonio, Padua, and a host of other examples originally of. the twelfth-century Italian style, display the same domical-pointed arch construction, but have less organic character, and less of that vitality of design which was becoming evident in the early Gothic architecture of France. The prevailing architecture of North Italy was also in brick and marble —materials unknown in the Holy Land. The mosaic decoration which seems to have been lavished on the interior of the Holy Sepulchre Church certainly suggests a strong Italian influence in the design—an influence which may be traceable to the inevitable employment of Italian artists for the decorative details, although the general construction and masonry remained in the hands of the French architect—whose name has been handed down by tradition as " Jourdain."

Two of the most graphic accounts of pilgrimages in the twelfth century giving careful descriptions of the buildings then recently consecrated are by John of Wurzburg (1150) and Theodoric (1175), both supposed to be of German origin. These stories of travel, along with many others of contemporary date, have been reprinted in English by the English Palestine Pilgrims' Text Society, connected with the Palestine Exploration Fund. Unfortunately, in many cases books of this kind have been translated by persons imperfectly acquainted with the topography of the places in question or with technical terms in use at that remote period. Consequently it is necessary in the following extracts to suggest some slight differences in the reading of words which, although literally correct, may not very clearly represent the author's meaning. With the aid of these graphic records, and by comparing them with the still well-preserved mediæval remains, we obtain a very fair impression of the once splendid church in the days of the Latin kingdom of Jerusalem.

To the pilgrim of the twelfth century the new building of Jerusalem appeared a novel and splendid revelation of architectural art. More especially would a German or Englishman accustomed to the ponderous character of the round-arched style of Northern Europe be impressed by the comparatively lighter and more elegant forms of the earliest pointed architecture.

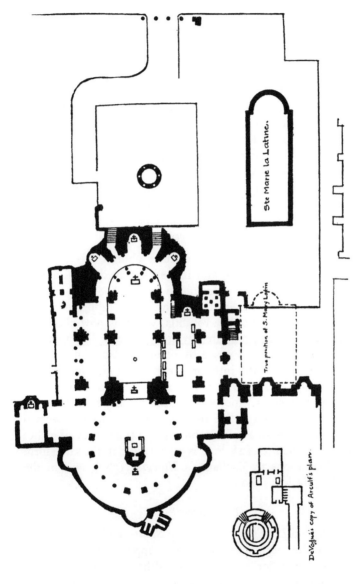

Fig. 22. De Vogüé's plan of the Holy Sepulchre Church, with the position of Sta Maria Latina, as corrected by G. Jeffery. This plan made by De Vogüé in 1860 seems to have been copied from the plan made by Mr Scoles in Williams's *Holy City*, II, p. iii; see p. 177 of *Les Églises de la Terre Sainte*.

John of Wurzburg (1150) gives the following description of
the interior of the church:—

Columns, eight round and eight square, are arranged in a circle;
but now on their eastern side their number and arrangement are
altered, because of the new church which has been built on to them,
the entrance to which is at this point. This new building contains a
spacious Choir of the Canons and Sanctuary, and a high altar
dedicated in honour of the Anastasis, that is of the Holy Resurrection,
as is shown by a picture in mosaic-work above it. Outside this
Sanctuary and within the cloister is contained a space sufficiently
wide in all directions both through the new buildings, and through
the old building round about the aforesaid monument, to be suitable
for a procession (*i.e.* an ambulatory is carried all round the new
church as well as the old circular building), which takes place every
Sunday night from Easter to Advent at Vespers, to the Holy Sepulchre with the respond *Christus Resurgens*.

It will be noticed that the old circular church was carefully
retained by the Crusaders, and indeed survived in an almost
intact condition until the unfortunate fire of 1808.

The ambulatory referred to by John of Wurzburg seems to
be the encircling aisle of the rotunda, which is now closed up
with partitions and appropriated by different sects. When merely
divided from the central space by open arcades, it must have
added immensely to the interior effect of the circular church.
The curiously preserved " tomb of Nicodemus " would be
entered, as at present, from a little apse or chapel on the west
side of this ambulatory. The rotunda seems to have possessed
this ambulatory, with a gallery above and a third story of niches
over all, until the fire of 1808. It is represented in the same form
in the illustrations to Zuallardo's *Viaggio* (1586), and in the
other old pilgrims' books.

The Rotunda

De Vogüé, in *Les Églises de la Terre Sainte*, gives a restoration
on paper of the rotunda as it must have appeared in the Middle
Ages. His restoration seems sound, although the number of
columns does not agree with the older descriptions [see fig. 22].

Theodoric (1175), speaking of the rotunda, says:—

The church is vaulted both above and below like the Church at Aix-(la-Chapelle). It is supported in the same way by eight piers and sixteen columns. The lower stringcourse which runs round the whole church glows with mosaic work of incomparable beauty. On the wall itself rests a leaden roof supported by rafters of cypress wood, having a large round opening in the midst.

This account is a little vague, as it is evident that the rotunda of the Holy Sepulchre could never have resembled, except in a very general way, the famous circular church of Charlemagne, a building of much smaller area and of a completely different method of construction. Quaresmius mentions the mosaic figures around the rotunda, representing SS. Constantine and Helena, Thomas, James, Philip, Matthew, Bartholomew, Simon; and the Prophets Ezekiel, Daniel, Hosea, Joel, Amos, and Abdias. He also notes the various texts attached to the mosaics. On the great arch of the choir appear to have been representations of the Annunciation and the Ascension. The great mosaic of the Resurrection in the apse seems to have been extant in his time, and similar pictures in mosaic in the choir and transepts, but their ruined condition prevented his copying the mutilated inscriptions.

The diameter of the rotunda appears to be 66 feet, and the height of the dome inside must be about 90 feet. But as originally built, with an open arcade, the circular church measured 115 feet in diameter, according to the plan of the Ordnance Survey.

In the old illustrations of the church before the fire of 1808 the covering of the rotunda is invariably shown as a straight-lined conical roof. The straight beams of the original construction show as a ceiling within the church. In Zuallardo's picture of the south front, however, the roof of the rotunda appears as an ordinary hemispherical dome.[1] The reconstruction of the covering in the nineteenth century after the fire of 1808 very probably resembled that of the great wood dome of the neighbouring "Kubbet es Sakhra" in the great mosque enclosure of the Haram. The Levantine builders have displayed considerable

---

[1] This may be a mere concession to the fact that in Zuallardo's days roofs over circular buildings were usually of a distinctly domical form.

ingenuity in covering over large areas with wood roofs, *e.g.* the roof of the Basilica of Bethlehem, constructed in a manner unlike any European method of carpentry. There are not wanting traditions of much earlier times, when strange *tours de force* in carpentry were executed in the Levant, such as the Odeium of Herodes Atticus in Athens, the cedar covering of which remains a puzzle in construction to modern engineers.

After the fire of 1808, which calcined and destroyed the encircling arcades with their columns, and consequently reduced the surrounding galleries to a complete ruin, the rotunda was reconstructed *de novo*. The outer semi-circular wall, following the rock cutting of the earliest period, seems the only part to have been retained.

The style of the rebuilding was poor in the extreme, and closely resembles the usual mosque-building of that period, than which nothing could be much more inartistic, or at least merely utilitarian. In the new rotunda there is not a single attempt at artistic expression. The domical covering was carried on a wall pierced by narrow arched openings about fifty feet high in place of the triple arcades of the former building. The divisions between these openings have the appearance of square piers or pilasters with a connecting wall behind them. At the level, apparently, of the ancient triforium a similar gallery was arranged for the convenience of spectators during the ceremonies of Easter, and also for the customary vigil of the Latins and Armenians. Above this triforium in the position of the former panels containing mosaics a second gallery was substituted. The appearance of the interior was completely altered by this rebuilding, although the general proportions and dimensions seem to have been adhered to with Chinese exactness. Even the new Russian dome, constructed about 1870 in place of the wood covering of 1810, is evidently confined within the exact limits of its predecessor.

In this connection it may be observed that no such remarkable case of restoring an ancient building has ever taken place before or since the rebuilding of the Holy Sepulchre rotunda. The Christians were permitted by their Turkish landlords to rebuild the premises, but doubtless with the most stringent regulations and restrictions, and, fortunately for history, these peculiar circumstances involved the most scrupulous reproduction in dimensions of all that had been burnt.

The studied simplicity, or rather baldness, of design in which the great square pilasters carrying the dome are executed, and the absence of any architectural detail or moulding, have a depressing effect upon the beholder, more especially when it is remembered that they replace a mediæval building of great beauty and originality. The ugly square pilasters, by the immense size of their parts, detract from the apparent size of the interior, and serve to dwarf the central monument.

The dome of the rotunda as it existed during the earlier part of the nineteenth century.—Under the date 4th May 1852, Dr Robinson, in his *Biblical Researches*, p. 196, states that "the great dome over the sepulchre was covered only with boards, and these again with lead. The lead was now in great part stripped off, and the boards rotten, so that in winter the rains fell thick and heavily within the rotunda below." It is singular that the work should have become so decayed in the course of only forty-four years.

In Dr Schick's model of the church now preserved in the library of St George's College, Jerusalem, which was probably made about the middle of the century, the dome is represented as constructed of sixty-five curved ribs meeting in a circular curb round the central opening, while a large purlin connects them together half-way between the central opening and the wall plates. It appears as if Herr Schick had the intention of copying something at one time in existence, and which he had actually seen. The Holy Sepulchre was evidently covered with an ordinary-looking hemispherical wooden dome with an opening in the middle, in place of the straight-sided conical covering destroyed by the fire of 1808.

The present hemispherical covering is constructed with iron lattice girders converging to the central opening and braced together, with an external covering of lead and a plaster ceiling beneath them. The latter is now in a dilapidated condition and the decoration of gilded stars on a blue ground is peeling off. The central opening is covered over with a common glazed skylight; the whole effect is poor and modern to an extreme.

The Tomb

In the centre of the rotunda stands the Tomb, the central object and shrine of the whole group of buildings. No longer

Fig. 23. The Tomb in the Rotunda.

exposed to the possibility of destruction by alien fanatics, nor likely ever again to be injured by such an accident as overwhelmed it in 1808, this remarkable object will remain sacred in the eyes of a large proportion of humanity for ages to come, and the true condition of what remains behind or underneath the deplorable-looking stone and native marble casing with which it was covered over in 1810 must continue a mystery.

As an example of the peculiar taste of the Orthodox Church at the beginning of the nineteenth century it possesses but trifling interest. Its chief curiosity consists in its close resemblance to what may be termed the Turkish style of the great Constantinople mosques, a sufficient evidence perhaps of its present ownership and of the nationality of the architect or mason to whom its design is due. The same large clumsily moulded panels of stone divided by slender marble columns, the same exceedingly coarse attempts at cornices and other blundered architectural details, impress the European visitor with repugnance—a repugnance heightened by the presence of the tawdry rubbish of modern ecclesiastical art (!) with which the monument is covered. The internal chambers of the Holy Sepulchre are lined with decorations of a taste which is even more deplorable—if possible—than the exterior.

Fig. 24. The Holy Sepulchre as represented by Amico, 1596 (from De Vogüé).

Fig. 24 gives some idea of the appearance of the Tomb as restored by the Franciscans in the sixteenth century.

In describing the structure and appearance of the tomb, M. de Vogüé says:—

L'œuvre des Croisés, plusieurs fois endommagés par les Barbares et particulièrement par les Kharismians en 1244, fut refait au XIIIe et au XIVe siècle. Le nouvelle forme, en juger par le dessin de Breydenbach (1480), ne différait pas sensiblement de celle qui fut donnée au Saint-Sépulcre pendant le siècle suivant. Cette dernière décoration qui dura jusqu'à 1808 fut exécutée en 1555. Elle est représentée dans les ouvrages de B. Amico, Le Bruyn, Pocock, et beaucoup d'autres.

Le système adopté était, au lieu d'un porche à jour, on trouvait devant la porte du S. Sépulcre une petite chambre carrée à une seule entrée voutée d'arêtes. Cette petite pièce simulait le vestibule antique qui dans l'origine précédait la chambre sépulcrale. Extérieurement le rocher était couvert d'un revêtement de marbre, orné d'un arcature ogival—l'art de la renaissance n'avait pas encore pénétré en Terre Sainte.

Quaresmius a conservé la lettre par laquelle le P. Boniface décrit ses travaux et raconte comment, après enlevé le revêtement de marbre primitif, il met à nu le saint rocher, et le touche de ses mains.

Quoique cette petite construction eut très peu souffert lors de l'incendie de 1808, les Grecs la refirent en entier afin de se donner le plaisir d'effacer les inscriptions latines qui on y trouvait. *Les Églises*, p. 185.

The raised floor in front of the tomb is shown on the oldest illustrations, and on it, under the great arch of the Chorus Dominorum would seem to have been an altar, which is mentioned by Zuallardo (1587) as used by the "Goffiti Indiani." The choir-arch also accommodated a "lutrin" or Rood-screen, frequently referred to, and in this position at the present day there is a somewhat similar screen of marble and iron, an enclosure for the modern use of the choir by the Greeks as their "Metropolis."

The "Chorus Dominorum" and Transept

The ancient choir of the Crusaders, measuring 110 feet by 42 feet, is now occupied by the Orthodox as their "Metropolis." Not a trace of any of its ancient decorations survives, and merely the bare outlines of its Gothic construction appear through the dirty plaster and whitewash of its interior. The eastern apse was entirely rebuilt in 1810, without any regard to its ancient design, although, as in the case of the rotunda, its dimensions seem to have been most scrupulously preserved; the central dome seems to have escaped untouched.

The pointed arches supporting the central cupola spring from square pilasters with a plain moulded architrave, and the windows are simple pointed arched openings with wide splays. The vaulting over the transept is of particular interest on account of its being constructed with the earliest example of the diagonal rib, a feature which differentiates pure Gothic from the earlier Romanesque. At the time when the Holy Sepulchre was being erected in Jerusalem the great cathedrals of Europe were also being planned, and the work in Jerusalem coincides in date with the early Gothic churches of Saint-Denis (1144), Chartres (1145), Noyon (1152), &c. It is of particular interest to remember that the same French king and queen—Louis VII and Eleanor of Aquitaine—were present at the consecrations of Saint-Denis and the church in Jerusalem.

Our own English cathedrals of the eleventh century were also rising in all the majesty of their massive "Norman" naves at this period. Canterbury, Peterborough, Oxford, Norwich, Ely, &c. were almost completed as we see them at the present day. Durham Cathedral has a special interest for English architects on account of its ribbed vaultings, which are considered as the earliest attempts at such a system of construction—a system which became in after ages the particular characteristic of the Gothic style. According to many authorities, the "ogival" or ribbed vault certainly owes its origin to English mason-craft, although the use of the pointed arch may have been first adopted in France and Italy. In Jerusalem we see one of the first instances of this element in construction but recently introduced into French art from the English Norman style.

The design of the capitals of the aisle arcades, several of which remain in fair preservation in the interior of the church, recalls the usual type of French work of the period, but with a suggestiveness of Byzantine tradition in sculptured details. The plain unmoulded arches of the north transept, instead of springing direct from the capitals, are carried on a moulded architrave which also serves as a stringcourse. This is, of course, one of the characteristic features of Provençal work as well as that of the Levant.

With the exception of the moulded rib to the vaulting, all the arches of the twelfth-century interior are of a square section in different orders, starting from square piers or columns. The effect is bare and poor under the all-prevailing coat of dirty whitewash, but of course in the Middle Ages the surfaces were completely painted where not covered with mosaic [see fig. 25].

The masonry of the vaulting over the transepts and in other parts of the buildings, which survive intact from the twelfth century, is of the somewhat rough description always intended to receive plastering; the courses of stone being horizontal in the French manner, and not in the Anglo-Norman fan-style; the vaulted ambulatory around the high altar is now an odd botch of the remains of the old groining and its ribs and a rebuilding in conn_ection with the arcade of the great apse which was entirely rebuilt after the fire of 1808.

The rough rebuilding by the Greeks of the early nineteenth century bears no resemblance to any kind of European mediæval work. It was in the style practised by the natives of the Levant of the present day; and although this modern pointed vaulted work has a curious resemblance in some respects to the true mediæval type, the principles of con-

Fig. 25. N.W. angle of the North Transept.

struction are really quite different. The common domical vault of Jerusalem, still used by the builders of an inferior class of houses (superior modern buildings being constructed with imported iron girders and cement for concrete floors and roofs), is a mass of small stones and mud mortar moulded on a centering of earth and brushwood, and covered on the outside against the weather with a surface of small slabs of stone, very carefully laid with a pointing of cement composed of lime and broken potsherds. This domical system sometimes takes the form of a simple hemisphere on pendentives of different types, or more commonly it assumes the outlines of a regular groined vault, (but of course without any groining-ribs,) in which the keystone is somewhat higher than the points of the arches against the side walls. An interesting thing to note about this modern method of building is that in all probability it owes its origin to the genuine vaulted structures erected all over Palestine in the twelfth century by European masons.

Above the Chorus Dominorum is a dome of a very interesting character, as it seems to have escaped untouched the rebuilding of 1810, and appears to be exactly in the condition as shown by Zuallardo and the early delineators of the church. Even the old spiral staircase on the outside can still be traced, in spite of its being broken away (*vide* frontispiece).

This dome is of very considerable size—some 35 feet or 40 feet in diameter, carried on an arcaded drum, which is supported on pendentives. The interior design is elegant: the arcade is of pointed arches on columns with carved capitals, sixteen in number, eight of the interspaces being filled with single light pointed arch windows, the others being blank. The construction of the dome on a high drum, and without the usual Byzantine method of resisting lateral pressure by carrying up the walls above the spring of its curve, recalls the well-known Aquitanian domed churches of the same date (1150).

This dome is probably the largest of its type ever built in Palestine; it seems to be on the true domical principle, a sufficient proof of which is its present preservation. There is little doubt that from this masterpiece of some twelfth-century Perigordian mason the natives of the Levant derived the idea of constructing similar domes, although none exist in Cairo or elsewhere of so early a date.

Standing under this dome the visitor to Jerusalem is irresistibly reminded of St Front, Périgueux, and in this reminiscence must be included the thought of the intensely and exclusively European character of its surroundings in as far as they are monumental.

The Abbey of St Denis is probably the earliest dated example of the mediæval pointed-arch style as defined by the presence of the diagonal vaulting-rib, or ogive of the French architects. This diagonal vaulting-rib, although not an indispensable part of vaulted construction, usually adds very much to its stability, and as a decorative feature may be considered one of the most important elements in the development of style and character. According to Viollet-le-Duc it was evolved out of the domical type of vaulting—or rather the combination of dome and pendentive—by the Angevin and Anglo-Norman builders of the eleventh century. Although made use of at an early date in England it was most quickly developed amongst the masonic schools of the N.E. of France, where the cathedrals of Sens (1170), Laon (1195) and Paris (1223) are amongst the most famous and most perfect examples. It is a curious thing that in the earlier developments of the style, what is known as the sexpartite vault is almost invariably made use of to span the wider spaces of the nave and transept whilst the aisles are covered by quadripartite groining. The sexpartite plan—i.e., in which the two compartments against the side walls of the nave or transept are sub-divided by an additional transverse arch, thus making with the two undivided compartments an arrangement of six parts, two large and four small—had some advantages over the simple quadripartite vault. It carried the total weight of the construction on to six points of support instead of four, and at the same time linked the nave and aisles together into a more harmonious design. It has been supposed with much probability that the vaulting-rib owed much of its popularity in an age of great economy to its serving as an easy and permanent substitute for a large amount of heavy wood centering; its later developments are as a rule merely decorative.

In the case of the Holy Sepulchre Church the plain square or quadripartite vault over the north transept is the best preserved portion of its roof construction. A heavy vaulting-rib of circular section springs from a square shaft in the angle of the compartment, harmonizing with the square profiles of the arcade below, and rises to the keystone in a slightly domical outline, as is usual in the French vaulting of the period. The effect is curiously archaic or at least primitive.

The capitals of the main arcade in the north transept still retain some traces of their sculpture: De Vogüé describes the great capital of the isolated column as "corinthien sans volutes," that of the engaged column "se compose d'une petite figure couronnée, assise entre deux feuilles d'acanthe, sous une arcade flanquée des petites tourelles à jour. Cette fois il faut reconnaître un de ces capitaux historiés dont nos églises romaines offrent de si nombreux exemples, et auxquelles l'art byzantin n'a aucune part." Another of these capitals is evidently by the same sculptor who carved the remarkable lintel of the south front; the curious interwoven pattern with heads interspersed is very western in style.

The external wall of the ambulatory surrounding the "Chorus Dominorum," with its three small *chevet* chapels, remains intact. This portion of the building is of the simplest construction, the chapels forming square recesses with apses of a semi-circular plan covered with simple hemispherical semidomes. The wall of the ambulatory has eight attached circular wall shafts, which once carried ribs in the vaulting, but the vault has been destroyed in the course of rebuilding the great apse in 1810. The capitals of these wall shafts are of the same "Corinthian" type as those in the arcades dividing the north transept from its aisles. The east aisle of the north transept forms the entrance to the "prison"; it is covered by a plain square vault without ribs.

An interesting architectural detail may be discovered by mounting on to the outside of the aisle roofs, which extend in flat paving after the usual Jerusalem manner all round the central portion of the church. Here the windows of the north and south aisles of the ambulatory, above the level of the semicircular portion, may be discovered. They are much mutilated and blocked up; that on the south side retains its Gothic arch with mouldings similar to the work on the south front, and supported on "Corinthian" capitals in the jambs. All the windows in the buildings with the exception of those of the clerestory have been blocked up with masonry, which accounts for the singularly dark condition of the interior. This is more especially noticeable in the ambulatory of the "Chorus Dominorum," where the light is so deficient as to completely prevent any view of the three apsidal chapels or of their contents. The windows of the apsidal chapels have been walled up, and the only one which can be seen from the outside with its pointed arch and moulded dripstone is that of the central chapel.

Considered in a general way and as a twelfth-century design, the interior of the Holy Sepulchre Church strikes the visitor as bold and original. The spanning of the arches is on the largest scale, and the effect of spaciousness with nobility of proportions is the work of a trained architectural genius. A certain severity in detail, or rather an absence òf detail verging on poverty, is perhaps a characteristic of this style of architecture, and may be noticed as much in the great churches of the South of France as in the huge interiors of North Italy of the same period. Denuded of all artistic decoration in colour and mosaic, the interior now seems a great contrast with the richly decorated façade of the south front. One can, however, see through all the rubbish and frippery which now fill the place that at no period would the interior have appeared of the richness of carved and moulded detail to which we are accustomed in the later examples of the style. The fine effect of the interior is produced by those principles of design which were beginning to be displayed in the great cathedral architecture of Central France during the twelfth century.

It is an interesting problem to imagine what the arrangement of the Holy Sepulchre Church may have been in the days of the Latin Kingdom, fresh from the hands of its designers and builders.

In its present condition, divided amongst all the sects of Christendom, with all their distinguishing marks and divisions obtruded upon the view, there is of course very much to prevent the ordinary observer from realizing its original condition. At the same time it must be remembered that the interior would have been almost as full of screens and side-altars, &c., as at present, only they would have been representative of the Latin Church alone.

In every Christian church built before the period of the Reformation, the idea governing its plan was the provision of a specially screened off space constituting the Choir in front of, or around, the altar. This choir, or sanctuary, had various significations and developments, but its chief meaning was to represent the permanent living Christian organization divided off from the outside world, which was established for perpetual service at the altar. In the West no church could be designed without the initial conception of this central feature, for which the building was merely the shell. The nineteenth century critics of our old churches, accustomed to their denuded interiors, imagined that a Roman basilica or a French cathedral without its rood-screen, stalls, &c., was to be regarded as a completed design, and compared with others of a similar class. But as a matter of fact the pre-reformation church has frequently lost more than half its original design, and all its beauty and interest, by the destruction of its furniture.

The above remarks apply to the Western church; in the East, or more properly speaking in the Levant, the primitive Byzantine churches followed the early Roman type of sanctuary as the centre of their design, but at a later date the interior was much modified by the rood-screen being placed on the east side of the choir, and afterwards developing into the solid erection of the iconostasis. Another peculiarity of the East, which very much influenced the planning of churches, was the custom of the faithful to perform acts of worship by the osculation of sacred pictures and relics. For this particular purpose the iconostasis, or picture-stand, had another and particular meaning as well as that of acting as the enclosure of the altar and its ministers.

In the case of the Holy Sepulchre Church the object of the circular enclosure of the tomb was obvious from the beginning, and has always remained so. The "Chorus Dominorum" of the eleventh century had however a very different appearance from what that part of the building now has. Across the western arch of this choir was a large rood-screen, probably of marble, and the eastern or sanctuary end was filled with an altar of large proportions under a baldachino or canopy. On either side, north and south, would be ranged the carved wooden stalls for the immense body of clergy attached to the new foundation. At the backs of these stalls would be probably screens on a large scale, occupying the space now filled up by a modern wall. The interior would have been very much less obscure when this wall had no existence than at present; its space would have been occupied by the row of royal tombs shown in the old illustrations, and which remained until the end of the eighteenth century.

We have a very interesting record of the appearance and arrangements of the "Chorus Dominorum" at the time of the Latin Kingdom in the description by the German pilgrim Theodoric (1175), whose account of the architectural design and construction of the Rotunda has already been quoted. With characteristic German prolixity he gives a longer catalogue of all that was to be seen in the new building at the time of his visit than any of the other contemporary pilgrims. After describing the Rotunda, he continues:—

Moreover there adjoins this church a sanctuary or holy of holies of marvellous workmanship, which was subsequently built by the Franks. The Canons hold prebends, and half the offerings of the Holy Sepulchre are assigned to them for income, and half is appropriated for the use of the Patriarch. The high altar is to the name and in honour of our Lord and Saviour, and behind it is placed the seat of the Patriarch, above which hang from the arch of the sanctuary a very great and adorable picture of Our Lady, a picture of St John Baptist, and a third picture of Holy Gabriel her Bridesman. In the ceiling of the sanctuary itself is represented our Lord holding a cross in His right hand, bearing Adam in His left, looking royally up to heaven, with His left foot raised in a gigantic stride, His right still resting on the earth as He enters heaven, while the following stand around: His Mother, St John Baptist, and all the Apostles. Under His feet a scroll reaching from one wall to the other contains this inscription: "Praise Him crucified in the flesh, glorify Him buried for us, adore Him risen from death." Beyond this on a higher scroll drawn across the same arch is the Scripture: "Christ ascending on high hath led the flesh captive and hath given gifts to men."

The apse wall on which these decorations appeared in the Middle Ages, and until the appropriation of the "Chorus Dominorum" by the Greeks, was completely pulled down after the fire of 1808 and rebuilt in a very different style.

About the middle of the choir is a small open altar of great sanctity, on the flooring whereof is marked a cross inscribed in a circle, which signifies that on this place Joseph and Nicodemus laid our Lord's body to wash it after it had been taken down from the cross.

This would seem to be the "Holy Site" afterwards called the "Stone of Unction" which now occupies the centre of the floor in the south transept.[1]

[1] The small open altar in the middle of the choir here referred to is probably the "centre of the world" stone of an earlier period, which the German pilgrim has confused with the "Stone of Unction."

Before the gate of the choir is an altar of no mean size, which is however only used by the Syrians.

No trace of such an altar now exists; the presence of such a feature in such a position is strange, but it continued to exist until the time of Zuallardo, who shows it on his plan of the church, 1586. Theodoric continues:—

On the west side of the church (*i.e.*, towards the north), near the door from which one mounts more than thirty steps up from the church to the street, in front of the door itself is a chapel dedicated to St Mary, which belongs to the Armenians.

This evidently refers to the "Chapel of the Apparition" (as it is now called), at present belonging to the Latin Franciscans.[1] The chapel is apparently of ancient construction, and the one mentioned by Sæwulf as belonging to the eleventh-century period of the church's history. The arched doorway at the top of the steps leading down to this chapel from Christian Street is still in existence, although the way down is blocked up and diverted. This arched doorway appears as if it had also originally formed the entrance to the Patriarchate, of which the façade with its massive buttresses seems still to survive in remarkable preservation fronting the Rue du Patriarche (modern Christian Street). The doorway is of the same curious design as the great front of the south transept. A square opening with two Romanesque columns is surmounted by a pointed arch treated in the "expanded concertina" design, over which is a moulded drip-

"The middle of the world" is described with drawings of the present vase-shaped monument. *P.E.F.Q.S.*, 1888, p. 260. Abbot Daniel states that in his time this spot was covered by a small domical building adorned with a mosaic.

[1] According to Fra Bernardino Amico the Franciscan friars were first established in the Church of the Holy Sepulchre at the expense of Queen Sanchia of Sicily, in 1336, by a Bull of Clement V, "Gratias agamus gratiarum." The queen's husband, the famous Robert the Good, king of Sicily, was brother to the celebrated Franciscan bishop St Louis. Close to this chapel is preserved the ancient quatrefoil font, evidently used formerly in the great church of the Latins. It would seem that the Moslem landlord had turned the Armenians out of this chapel, and permitted the Franciscans to occupy it during the period of revolution succeeding the Kharismian invasion of 1244.

stone. It is still sometimes known by the name of "St Mary's Gate."

The Cartulary of the Holy Sepulchre is a collection of ancient documents published at the Imprimerie Nationale, Paris, in 1849. It contains a series of charters signed by various Popes and Patriarchs of Jerusalem[1], which are particularly interesting as throwing considerable light on the plan and arrangements of the church during the twelfth century.

One of the most important of these charters was given by Amabric, Patriarch of Jerusalem, in the year 1169, and confirmed in the following year by Pope Alexander III, in which "the High Altar within the Choir; the Prison, and its altar; the altar of SS. Peter and Stephen; the altar of the Invention of the Cross; the parochial altar within the *Chevet*; and the Patriarchal Throne behind the High Altar" are mentioned in connection with certain offerings made at these Holy Places. The place called *Compass* in the middle of the Choir is also referred to.

All the places above mentioned with the exception of the Throne are on the north side of the Choir, or in the north choir aisle, a portion of the church but recently finished building in the middle of the twelfth century.

It will be noticed that the Patriarchal Throne is clearly described as standing behind—or to the east of—the High Altar, in its arrangement resembling the eleventh-century churches of the north of Italy, and not the mediæval plan of the French cathedral. On either side of the throne would doubtless be the usual raised platform of the presbyterium, whilst the stalls of the canons and other clergy of the church extended along the sides of the choir beneath the dome.

The processional paths of the Patriarch, and of the Prior and Canons, would be along this north side of the church; the Patriarch coming from his palace at the west side of the Holy Sepulchre, whilst the Canons and choir approached from their cloister by the door-way now walled up at the N.E. corner of the Choir.

The "Porte Ste Marie," which appears to have been an entrance into the church at the side of or through the Patriarchate, has been walled up for ages; in the seventeenth century the area

[1] For list of Patriarchs see p. 28.

which it forms at the side of the Franciscan Convent was a source of constant trouble to the friars who were exposed to insult and annoyance by the Moslem tenants of the property which lines one side of this area at its upper level. Over this entrance, or near by, according to John of Wurzburg, the following lines appeared engraven on the wall:—

QUID MULIER PLORAS? EN JAM QUEM QUERIS ADORAS
ME DIGNUM RECOLI JAM VIVUM TANGERE NOLI.

The name of "Porte Ste Marie" is therefore an ancient one, and together with the neighbouring chapel of the "Apparition" refers to the meeting in the garden of Christ and St Mary Magdalene. It is in fact suggestive of the idea of the garden gate, near which the Magdalen mistakes Christ for the gardener, a subject for many old Italian paintings with the title of "Noli me tangere."

The only evidence of an Italian interest in the fabric of the Holy Sepulchre Church during the earlier period of the crusading kingdom, is in a record that a tablet setting forth the privileges of the Genoese Republic in Jerusalem was set up in the sanctuary wall by king Baldwin I, but removed by king Amaury in 1167. (*Lib. jur. Respub. Gen.* Turin, 1854, t. i.)

The northern side of the church seems to have been much altered at some time subsequent to the Moslem occupation of Jerusalem in the thirteenth century. Theodoric states:—

Also on the left-hand side of the church, towards the north, is a chapel dedicated to the Holy Cross; and this chapel belongs to the Syrians. Also on this side, opposite this chapel towards the east, is a chapel of peculiar sanctity, wherein is a most holy altar of the Holy Cross, and a large piece of the blessed wood. The Christians are wont to carry this holy symbol against the pagans in battle. Near this chapel, on the east, one enters a dark chapel by about twenty paces; in this chapel our Lord is said to have been imprisoned.

These two chapels of the Holy Cross no longer exist. They must have stood at the side of the present Khankah mosque, which was evidently built partly for the purpose of overawing the Christians with its tall minaret, whence the Saracen soldiers could command the turbulent crowd beneath. The minaret of the small mosque of Omar on the opposite side of the church served the same purpose for the *parvis* of the church.

Behind this chapel (the "Prison") is an altar dedicated to St Nicholas (now known as the chapel of St Longinus). Beyond this is the gate of the Canons cloister, which stands round about the sanctuary.

A rudely rebuilt (?) arcade which passes outside the whole width of the north transept apparently dates from the time when the modifications were made to chapels and to the front of this transept; and the large latrines constructed for pilgrims passing the night within the church probably occupy the sites of the two chapels of the Holy Cross described by Theodoric This arcade has at times been called the "Arcade of St Mary."

THE SOUTH TRANSEPT FAÇADE AND CALVARY

References to the southern or entrance front of the church— its only external architectural feature of importance—are rare in the pilgrims' books of the twelfth century. Perhaps this south transept façade appeared but insignificant in those days to Europeans accustomed to the magnificent cathedrals then coming into being in all the countries of the civilised world.

Theodoric (1175) is one of the few mediæval pilgrims who give some description of this façade. He says:—

Outside the doors of the church, in the space between the two doors, stands the Lord in a saintly garment as though risen from the dead.

The general design of the south transept façade is somewhat remarkable if not unique. Such an arrangement of two stories of large pointed arches of the same dimensions, the lower forming a double portal, the upper enclosing windows, does not recall any well-known European building, although the detail of the architecture is purely Occidental. The great arches are built in a very singular manner, with an outer order of voussoirs cut with rounded bevelled edges; the effect is somewhat like that of an extended concertina of gigantic proportions, or of a starched frill. Such a treatment of arch stones is characteristic enough of Renaissance Art, but in early transitional from the

Romanesque to Gothic it can only be taken as one of the many varieties of the "chevron" decoration so common in twelfth-century buildings.

The lower, or portal, arches have a heavy dripstone cornice above the outer order. This cornice terminates in a very small corbel or boss over the central springing stones where the two arches meet above the central column. Possibly the figure of our Lord referred to by Theodoric may have been merely a painting on the wall between the two arches. In the sketch of this front

Fig. 26. Sketch (assisted by a photograph) showing the south side of the church as it existed in the twelfth century.

(traced from a photograph) showing its appearance in the twelfth century the figure of Christ is represented in the usual position occupied by such a statue on the *trumeau* of a cathedral door [fig. 26], but it may have stood at some period on the column built against the steps up to Calvary.

The general character of the carving on the front is that of the south of France of the period. A character common to both the Romanesque and Byzantine styles in the early ages of Christian Art makes it somewhat difficult at first sight to distinguish between what is really eastern from what is essentially western. The " Corinthian " capital, the dentil and console cornices and the familiar egg-and-dart mouldings continued in use under various modifications in all the provinces of the vanished Roman Empire until the coming of the genuine Gothic style. There is little to distinguish between the Romanesque

Fig. 27. Earliest woodcut representation of the Church. "Viaggio da Venezia al S. Sepolcro." R. P. Noe, 1500.

churches of Spain and France, of Lombardy, Venetia or Tuscany and the far south of Italy, and the earlier buildings of the crusaders in the Levant. The stilted arches carried on well-proportioned nook shafts with " Corinthian " capitals of the Holy Sepulchre recall such contemporary work as the churches at Arles, Tarascon, and elsewhere in Provence. The chief difference in the development of the style consists in the arches springing direct from a slight architrave moulding placed on the abacus of the capitals, instead of the usual intervening frieze and cornice which survives in many Provençal buildings.

Two finely carved stone panels of great width span the double portals of this front. These are also exceedingly suggestive of the famous front of the Abbey of Saint Gilles in Provence. The western of these two lintels is covered with a bas-relief representing the triumphal entry of Christ into Jerusalem riding on an ass. The effect of these small figures treated in a pictorial manner is precisely similar to the French work of the same period. The carving is excellent and full of vigour. Over the eastern doorway (now closed) the lintel is treated in a very different manner, as a panel of elaborate intertwining scroll leafage. This also is beautifully carved, but with somewhat more of a Byzantine character.

The tympana of the portals seem to have been decorated at some period with a geometrical pattern or diaper executed in cement, the foundation probably of some mosaic decorations; and the whole front would undoubtedly have been treated in colour in the style of the period to form an appropriate background to the figure of Christ between the doors as described by Theodoric.

The elaborate bracketed cornices to both stories of the façade covered with egg-and-dart mouldings are thoroughly Provençal in style and give a singular richness to the design.

De Vogüé says that at one time the words "Iordanus me fecit" were to be seen inscribed on the south transept front.

The columns of the doorway are of foreign marble, and the capitals are of very varied design; the inner series being of "Corinthian" style, whilst the outer ones have the curious treatment as of foliage brushed aside by a strong wind—a treatment very reminiscent of the façade of St Mark's, Venice.

In both stories of the façade the archivolts are decorated with mouldings which correspond to the orders of capitals, but without carving. A heavy dripstone, continued as a stringcourse across the façade, is elaborately carved, but in a singularly crude and "dry" manner; the design of the simplest—a mere succession of foliated scrolls.

The cornices which decorate this front are of the almost classic style of the earliest Provençal work.

A voir la pureté de ses lignes, à voir les palmettes, les oves, les billettes qui le décorent, les modillons feuillagés qui le supportent, on serait tenté de le croire arraché à quelque édifice romain. De même, l'entablement qui couronne toute la façade est conçu suivant le goût antique: cette disposition s'accorde bien avec la forme horizontale des combles. (De Vogüé.)

Perhaps certain processional regulations for the entrance and exit of pilgrims—referred to by Idrîsî in 1154—may account for the very marked difference in the decorative details of the twin portals of the great façade, differences which it is otherwise difficult to account for.

The tympanum on the east, as already stated, was filled with ordinary mosaic, the cement for which still adheres to the walling and also to the inner order of the arch. The western tympanum seems to have been similarly treated in mosaic, covering a pattern of squares and hexagons cut on the stone surface.

The apparent lintels supporting these tympana are in reality mere slabs of fine white stone or marble carved on the outer face and secured by iron clamps to flat arches behind. This Italian method of construction is ornamented with sculpture of very Provençal character.

The western lintel slab is carved with the "Resurrection of Lazarus," the "Entry of Christ into Jerusalem," and the "Last Supper." The first two subjects are treated in two scenes each, the last occupies a small corner of the panel on the right.

The lintel of the eastern or right-hand door is treated in an altogether different and very remarkable manner. An interlacing scroll of acanthus foliage of Byzantine type encloses small figures of naked men, a centaur with an unstrung bow, and a winged bird-like figure with a woman's head. The whole composition is a mystical curiosity of the period, and the workmanship is of the very finest, worthy of the best Italian school, and superior perhaps to its companion panel.

In the mediæval "Bestiary" books, of which this carving evidently forms an illustration, a centaur represents pride and arrogance, the bird with a woman's face and dragon's feet is a syren or harpy, doves suggest the simplicity of the Holy Spirit, and the horned bird or "Calandre" figures Jesus Christ. The scroll evidently represents the "peredixion" or tree of life. In

Fig. 28. The Great Façade: Decorative Details of Lintel over the Eastern Portal.

the present case the human figures are perhaps represented as protected by the shadow of the "peredixion," whilst fantastic birds and monsters occupying the lower part of the composition

7—2

are evidently watching for their prey. The animation of the figures and the refinement of workmanship of this twelfth-century sculpture are very remarkable.

The platform on which the Moslem guardians of the church have been accustomed to sit for centuries is referred to by Fra Bernardino Amico as the "Poggetto che sta avanti la porta," where on cushions and carpets these tax-collectors sat "con magnificenza, e quanto maggior numero vi è di Peregrini, tanto più allegri si dimostrano, perchè da ciaschedúno di nostri pigliano nove zecchini." In the days of the Christian Kingdom of Jerusalem "Custodians" or guardians are mentioned who probably occupied the same position for keeping the motley crowd of pilgrims in order as the Moslems of the present day (*vide* p. 27).

The external staircase leading up to Calvary is a noticeable feature of the transept front to which it is attached and of which it forms a part. The loggia, with its three open arches, is ornamented with precisely the same cornices, columns, and carved arch mouldings as the rest of the front.

Theodoric (1175) describes the external entrance to Calvary:

It remains now to speak of Mount Calvary. Before the doors of the Church, which are covered with bronze and of a double form, one mounts by about fifteen steps to a small chamber, which is railed and adorned with paintings. Here, at the top of the steps, stand guardians watching the entrance, who only allow so many pilgrims to enter as they choose, lest by excessive pressure, as often happens here, crushing and danger to life should occur. From this vestibule one ascends by three steps through another door into the chapel of Calvary.

The external staircase, with its open loggia at the top, remains much in the condition as seen by Theodoric, but half-way down the stairs a column is built into the side wall, the use of which is not very evident. It looks as if designed to sustain a statue, or some heraldic badge. It is just possible that this column may have been the pedestal supporting the figure of Christ referred to by Theodoric as "between the doors," *i.e.* the doors of Calvary and the Sepulchre.

Here a note may be made on the means taken in a few instances to assist in preserving the fabric of the church. Two heavy iron straps may be noticed banding together the sides of the external walls of the vestibule where the arches have perhaps shown some little disposition to spread. Nothing could be more satisfactory than to see such evidences of a desire to keep up the ancient building without any pretence at "restoration." The cupola covering the chamber is doubtless a mere modern invention put up at the time the vestibule was converted to its present use and when it was strengthened with the iron ties.

The alterations to the Calvary chapels necessitated by the change in their approach—inside staircases being substituted for that on the exterior—are not of ancient date. In Zuallardo's picture of the two chapels viewed from the transept, he shows in his time the approach to have been by a staircase in the south choir aisle. After passing the Chapel of the Crowning with Thorns (a dedication older than the sixteenth century) Zuallardo remarks:

Di là nel medemo lato circa otto o dieci passi si monta per diecinovi scaloni, in due volte (dei quali una parte è di legno et nel portico proprio, che va intorno al choro, et l'altra di pietra, si truova nel concava del muro), al monte Santo di Calvario.

John of Wurzburg states that over the entrance to the Calvary chapels were written these lines:

HIC LOCUS INSIGNIS CALVARIAE SANCTUS HABETUR
PRO DUCE PRO PRETIO PRO CRUCE PRO LAVACRO
NEMPE JESU CRUOR ET TITULUS SACRA CORPORIS UNDA
NOS SALVAT REDIMIT PROTEGIT ATQUE LAVAT

Quaresmius gives some fragments of inscriptions which survived upon the vaults of these chapels in his time: De Vogüé has pieced together these fragments with the description by John of Wurzburg, and produced the following result:

EST LOCUS ISTE SACER SACRATUS SANGUINE CHRISTI
PER NOSTRUM SACRARE SACRO NIL ADDIMUS ISTI
SED DOMUS HUIC SACRO CIRCUM SUPERAEDIFICATA
EST QUINTADECIMA QUINTILIS LUCE SACRATA
(SUB BALDEUUINO) A FULCHERICO PATRIARCHA
CUJUS TUNC QUARTUS PATRIARCHATUS (ERAT ANNUS)
. . . . ET SEMEL UNUS AB URBE
QUAE SIMILIS PURO (FULGEBANT)
ET ORTU DOMINI NUMERABANTUR SIMUL ANNI
UNDECIES (CENTUM QUADRAGINTAQUE NOVEMQUE)

The present staircases to Calvary and the rebuilding of the arcade over the entrances of the church date from after the fire of 1808.

Theodoric (1175) describes these chapels as follows:

"Upon the west side of Calvary" (meaning perhaps on the western arches or vaulting of the chapel, as there has always been a sort of triforium arcade where the modern inside staircase exists) "there is a picture on the wall in which these verses may be seen in golden letters:

> This place was hallowed by Christ's blood before,
> Our consecration cannot make it more,
> Howbeit the buildings round this stone in date,
> Were on July fifteenth consecrate,
> By Foulcher Patriarch in solemn state."
>
> *Pal. Pil. Text Society's translation.*

The upper chapels of Calvary would appear to have been untouched, as far as their decorations are concerned, since De Vogüé's visit in 1860. He states that he discovered the remains of the mosaic figure of Christ on the ceiling. At the present day all the chapels and rooms connected with the "monticulus" of Calvary have been embellished with the usual rubbish and frippery of Levantine ecclesiastical art, and any vestige of antiquity is very difficult to trace in the profound obscurity. The chamber contiguous to Calvary marked on De Vogüé's plan as "débris de l'église de Modeste" can no longer be identified under such a name.

The mosaic work on the walls and vaulting of the Calvary chapels were the last surviving decorations of the interior, and the texts which served as commentaries on these pictures have been preserved by Quaresmius. According to the assiduous Guardian of Mount Sion, there were two figures on the outside of the arcade towards the transept representing St Helena and the Emperor Heraclius, the vaulting of the chapels was covered with scrolls of foliage, a small fragment of which still survives in the tympanum of the archway which communicates with the former external porch of Calvary. The style of workmanship and design—a very conventional vine-leaf pattern—recalls the twelfth-century mosaic work of Italy. In the centre of the vault of the Latin chapel, within an oval frame of modern plasterwork, is an oddly preserved fragment of these mosaics—once the gorgeous decorations of the most famous church in Christendom: it is, as far as can be discerned through the dirt and cobwebs, a figure of Christ in the small cube glass mosaic of the thirteenth century.

The Latin Calvary chapel contains the débris of an ancient mosaic pavement in the Italian style, with the usual design of a large circle of marble within a square, and four smaller discs in the four angles. The interspaces are filled in with minute patterns in coloured marbles of different designs. This chapel being considered a Latin property has escaped the general wreck of the rebuilding by the Greeks in the beginning of the nineteenth century.

En étudiant les fragments transcrits par Quaresmius, j'ai reconnu qu'ils appartenaient à des vers rimés, formant un morceau complet sur la Passion. A ce titre on les lira, je pense avec intérêt; on y reconnaîtra sans doute la poésie du xiie siècle, telle que nous l'avons vue souvent se dérouler, en longues lignes autour des sculptures et sur le portail de nos églises romanes. (De Vogüé.)

Processional Paths. In the earliest accounts of ritual at the Holy Sepulchre we hear of the crowd of worshippers flowing into the Basilica in the early morning after a vigil spent on Olivet, and visiting the various Holy Sites within the enclosure. The regulation of a vast crowd of pilgrims must have been a matter of some concern to the ecclesiastical authorities from the very beginning, and more especially when we consider the varied nationalities, their contentious characters and frequently savage manners and customs. The precincts of the church have been at all times in past history the scene of turbulence and bloodshed, and with a view to mitigate these accompaniments of religious fervour the designers and planners of the great mediæval church have evidently prepared a very large number of entrances and exits—all of which were closed up after the Moslem occupation of Jerusalem in 1244.

The mediæval custom for solemn processions was for the entrance of clergy and people to take place by the north-west door of the church, thence to pass up the north aisle, and where a structural ambulatory existed to continue behind the High Altar, and so down the south aisle, and then up the central nave into the choir, the people remaining outside the gates of the rood-screen, whilst the clergy and their attendants took their seats within the stalls surrounding the altar.

Processions have always been a remarkable feature and accompaniment of religious observances all over the world, and even in the reformed branches of Christianity such customs have been retained. Jerusalem has always been a place for religious processions of the most dramatic character; even in the fourth century St Silvia of Aquitaine found them well established as part of the attractions for her pilgrimage.

It is difficult to trace the course of the longer ritual processions from the Mount of Olives to the Holy Sepulchre, referred to by St Silvia, owing to the alterations in the eastern wall of the city. It is probable that a city-gate stood in early times much in the same position as the present "St Stephen's Gate" to account for the presence of the Roman Arch which spans the modern "Via Dolorosa." The "Golden Gate" of the Haram enclosure is undoubtedly "Byzantine," and in all probability was built in connection with the vanished church of St Sofia, or the "Pretorium"; its double form may possibly be accounted for in the same way as the double entrance of the Holy Sepulchre Church —the necessity for regulating the motley crowd upon this famous processional path. As mentioned elsewhere in referring to this gateway, it appears to have remained open until the Turkish occupation, and was even used for a commemorative procession on Palm Sunday by the Franciscans. This usage of so late a period as the sixteenth century suggests a survival from primitive times and throughout the middle ages; in the same way as the Franciscans represented Christ's entry into Jerusalem by their Superior riding on an ass, so the Bishop of St Silvia's period (possibly Cyril) was led by the crowd, mounted on a donkey: "in eo type quo tunc Dominus deductus est." In the fourth century this Palm Sunday procession terminated at the Holy Sepulchre, but in the sixteenth century it was merely so far as the "Golden Gate."

The original design of the tower is preserved in the woodcut of the transept façade in Padre Noe's guide book (1500). It possessed two stories above the high ground floor, which latter constitutes a chapel, forming one of the series of three on the west side of the *parvis*. These three stories of the square portion of the tower were crowned by a fourth stage, of an octagonal plan, covered by and terminating in a pointed dome of a specially German character, a character which is represented in the towers of the Apostles' Church, Cologne, and other Rhenish examples of the eleventh and twelfth centuries.

Although the terminal octagonal stage had this German character, which in Germany is usually accompanied by the round arched style, the masonry of the lower part of the tower (the portion which survives at the present day) is of a very ordinary thirteenth-century Gothic pointed-arch detail. The two remaining upper stories of the tower have arcaded sides; arches with roll-mouldings and dripstones carried on short columns with square abaci to the capitals decorate the present top story facing the parvis.

Massive buttresses at the angles of the tower give the full character of perfected Gothic construction, although they were not apparently planned with a clear conception of the purpose in view. The whole design has an ill-planned, accidental appearance, and is very much out of harmony with the venerable façade to which it is clumsily attached, and which it partly conceals.

The absence of any carved detail about the tower prevents a very clear impression of its exact date, but the general design and character of the work clearly point to the very last years of the Christian occupation of Jerusalem.

As already remarked, the lower part of the tower forms a small chapel, which is dedicated to the forty martyrs, a dedication which perhaps dates from the time of the Patriarch Thomas (813), who instituted a commemoration of his remarkable dream by erecting an altar somewhere within the precincts of the Holy Sepulchre. In one corner of this chapel is preserved a large sarcophagus said to contain the bones of certain patriarchs. This chapel was originally dedicated to St John, or at least a chapel which occupied the same position, and is one of those mentioned by Sæwulf. These chapels seem to have changed names at different periods; in Murray's handbook for Jerusalem, 1858, they are described as "built before the Crusades." The first is dedicated to St James, of whom tradition says that he celebrated mass and was consecrated there. The second was originally called the Chapel of the Trinity, and Beugnot remarks that all the women of the city were married, and all the children baptized, in it. It is now named the Chapel of the "Ointment-bearers" —that is, Mary Magdalene and her companions—and is the parish church of the Greeks. There is another small chapel, dedicated to St John, in a line with the above, on the basement story of the great tower.

THE HOLY SITES WITHIN THE CHURCH

It is a little singular that most, if not all of the "Stations" or Holy Sites which constitute the object of religious pilgrimage to the Holy Sepulchre Church, appear to be of considerable antiquity. And at the same time the different sects of Christians seem to agree at least in recognising the sites belonging to rival religions as equally authentic.

The Holy Sepulchre itself seems to be in the custody of a general committee of the sects under the auspices of the Turkish Government, which appears to regulate its use according to circumstances.

At the west end of the Holy Sepulchre (on its outside) is a little chapel now belonging to the Copts. This seems to have been in existence formerly on the east side of the sepulchre under the arch dividing the rotunda from the great choir. It was re-erected in the modern taste, after the fire of 1808, in its present position.

One altar or Holy Site alone seems to have been reconstituted at the restoration of the buildings in 1810. This was an altar in the middle of the great choir which occupied the "Centre of the World" of an earlier period. A stone column now marks this place called "Compass" in the remote period of Arculf and Abbot Daniel (see note on p. 90).

The tombs of six, or perhaps seven, Latin Kings of Jerusalem were swept away after the fire of 1808. The tombs were of Godfrey de Bouillon, Baldwin I, Fulk (?), Baldwin III, Amaury Baldwin IV, and Baldwin V. The first three were buried within what is now the Chapel of Adam; the other four lay in a row across the south transept arch of the choir. No trace remains of

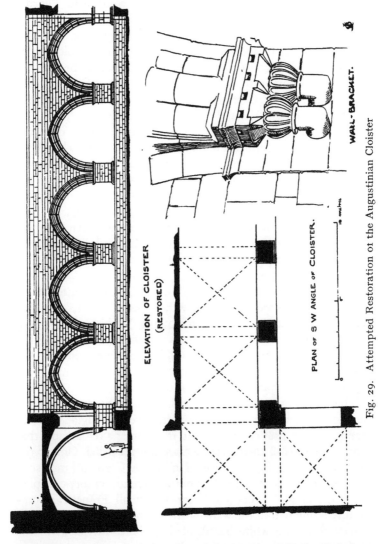

ELEVATION OF CLOISTER
(RESTORED)

WALL-BRACKET.

PLAN OF S W ANGLE OF CLOISTER.

Fig. 29. Attempted Restoration of the Augustinian Cloister

their monuments, and the site of the tomb of Fulk of Anjou, pointed out as the grave of Melchisedec (!) during the nineteenth century, has since disappeared.

The marble circles in the flooring at different points within the church have a certain antiquity, dating at least back to the Crusades. The Stone of Unction, the Crowning with Thorns, the Division of the Garments, the Apparition of the Gardener, the Column of Flagellation, the "Stabat Dolorosa," are all probably of that period: at least, they appear in the old guide-books, such as Sigoli (1384). The three chevet chapels of the "Chorus Dominorum" are respectively identified with the "Crowning," the "Casting Lots for the Garments," and the "Column of Flagellation."

The Chapel of Abraham, a curious upper story over the Chapel of Calvary, appears to be of the twelfth-century building, and its window forms part of the great façade. It is merely a square chamber without architectural character beyond some marble and mosaic decorations designed by the present writer, and executed at the expense of certain English clergy, in 1893. The greater part of these decorations have since been removed by the Greeks. This chapel is shown on Zuallardo's plan of the church. It is approached through the Greek "Convent of Abraham," and not from inside the church.

At the entrance of the "Prison" chapel, on its south side, is a perfectly enclosed chamber, without light or air, in which according to Fra Bernardino Amico (1620) "abito un devoto di Christo molti anni." This is perhaps a survival of the legend that a Count of Poitou—Guillaume VIII—for some time in the thirteenth century inhabited an "in pace" within the church (see *Légendes de S. Sépulcre*, Couret, 1894).

The idea of living as a hermit within the precincts of the Holy Sepulchre would be irresistibly attractive to religious mono-maniacs of the past centuries, and it is perhaps remarkable that more evidences of their presence are not recorded. One of the most picturesque figures of this kind is the German Franciscan "Father John," who at the close of the fifteenth century occupied the position of "procureur" for the small Franciscan community living within the walls of the church. A tall bald-headed man with a long white beard, clad in the brown cloth of the Order, he seems to have been credited with supernatural powers by his contemporaries who speak of his conversations with de-parted spirits amongst the shadows of the gloomy interior. In any case he exercised the important office of conferring the knighthood of the Holy Sepulchre upon many distinguished pilgrims of the period, dubbing them with the reputed sword of Godfrey de Bouillon within the Tomb, in accordance with a ceremonial of rather an obscure origin. This sword and the other paraphernalia which he used still lie within the Franciscan sacristy—but legitimate Knights of the Holy Sepulchre have long since ceased to be made. Father John, according to one legend, was a scion of the Hohenzollern princes driven by remorse for the part his family had played in the Lutheran Reformation to atone for their crimes by a life-long repentance.

The presence of individual recluses in such a place as the Holy Sepulchre precinct has always been somewhat difficult in the face of pilgrim crowds, and contending factions; this may account for their absence in the past.

In Fra Bernardino Amico's description (1620) several of the Holy Sites are said to be without "offitiatura," *i.e.* disused, and the altar which still stood in front of the east end of the Sepulchre was only used by the Greeks for the ceremony of the Holy Fire. At this time the mosaic pictures on the walls of the church representing the apostles, prophets, and Constantine and Helena were much decayed, "son consumati in maniera che a pena si veggono."

CHAPTER III

THE AUGUSTINIAN CONVENT

THE ruins of the Augustinian Convent of the Holy Sepulchre are of great interest. The remains which exist *in situ* are the north-west and south-east corners of the great cloister, the greater part of the Refectory on the south side of this cloister, and the undercrofts of the Dormitory on its north side. At the south-west corner of the cloister some portions of the vaulting may also be observed.

De Vogüé was led into a strange fancy of identifying the remains of the cloister, with its pointed arches and clumsy egg-shaped ornaments, with the work of the fourth century—a strange error for an architectural student to commit.

Plans and details of the existing remains and of the general design of the cloister are shown in figs. 29, 30 and 31.

The Order of Canons Regular of St Augustine, founded in the eleventh century, obeyed a rule which was almost identical with that of St Benedict, and as a consequence the arrangements of the convent enclosure followed the usual regular plan of a western monastery. The very exceptional nature of the site occasioned a slight divergence from the more usual monastic plan in as far as affected the relative positions of the different portions. During the twelfth century the cloister-garth of a monastery was more usually built against one side of the nave of a great church, but in the present instance the circular form of the Anastasis and the nature of the site in the midst of a crowded city obliged the placing of the conventional buildings around the east end of the new choir of the church. Such an arrangement, although very exceptional, is not altogether unknown elsewhere; for instance, the famous church of St Francis Assisi has the cloister in a similar position.

Amongst the numerous descriptions of the mediæval buildings by pilgrims of the twelfth and thirteenth centuries occur such entries as:

The Canons' cloister which stands round about the sanctuary.— Theodoric, 1175; *P. P. T. Soc.*, 1895.

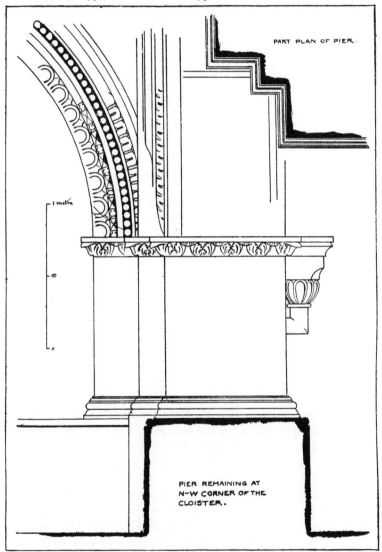

Fig. 30. The Cloister of the Augustinian Convent. Details.

On issuing by the Canons' door from the Church of the Sepulchre, on the left hand is the Dormitory, and on the right hand the Refectory and also the Mount Calvary. Between these two divisions of the convent are the cloister and cloister-garth. In the middle of the garth its a grea opening, through which may be seen the chapel of St Helena, which is below.—Ernoul, *Le Citez de Jherusalem*, 1231; *P. P. T. Soc.*, 1895.

After one has made the circuit of the cloister, and is re-entering the church from the other side (the south), one notices a figure of Christ on the cross painted above the doors of the cloister so vividly as to strike the beholder with great remorse. Round it this verse is inscribed:

> "You that this way do go
> 'Twas you that caused My woe;
> I suffered this for you
> For My sake vice eschew."

To the eastward of this one goes down into the venerable chapel of St Helena.—Theodoric, 1175; *P. P. T. Soc.*, 1895.

The entrances, both north and south, into the cloister from the church have been walled up. The Canons' door, on the north, was conveniently planned in relation to the Dormitory so that the monks might descend direct into the church for their night offices. The continuation of the staircase up to the now vanished Dormitory may probably be traced in the entrance of the large Coptic convent of modern times, built on the north side of the ancient precincts.

The building lining the north side of the cloister is no longer the original structure of the Middle Ages, although its walls may in part survive within the later construction. The general plan of this portion of the convent may, however, be detected in the undercroft or cellarage which formed its ground floor, and which is still fairly well preserved. Here it may be noted that in the later developments of monasticism the dormitory or general sleeping apartment of the Benedictine rule, whilst being retained in theory, was often divided up into cells by low partitions, as at the Premonstratensian Abbey of Bella Paise in Cyprus, or in many of the Dominican convents of Italy. No indications remain of the actual size of the Dormitory.

The Refectory on the south side of the cloister is partly preserved. Two bays of its vaulting at the west end still stand

Fig. 31. Attempted Restoration of the Cloister of the Augustinian Convent. View from the eastern side.

intact, the space beneath them having been converted into a
church by the Greeks at some period. The area of the Refectory

seems to have been about 33 metres by 9 metres, proportions which appear to have been common in buildings of this type. It was covered with either six or seven bays of simple cross-vaulting without cross-ribs. Each bay was lighted with a window on either side, of a single light with pointed-arch head, and sides and sill deeply splayed in the thickness of the wall. These windows occupy the wall space between the apex and the spring of the arches above a string-course which serves to unite together the pilasters which carry the pointed groining.

The whole of the south wall, with ruined vaulting, also stands intact. The Refectory was of a simple architectural character, the vaulting of pointed arches without rib mouldings starting from square pilasters with a plain bevelled string-course cornice. At the east end of the Refectory, where in all probability stood the conventual kitchen, all traces of the mediæval buildings have now been completely removed in building the new Russian church. At this point (probably in some connection with the doles from a conventual kitchen) stood the entrance to a covered street or bazaar traditionally known as "Malcuisinat," or the street of poor cookshops, where the poorer classès of pilgrims obtained their food.

The eastern part of the Refectory is almost completely lost in the ruins which are now inhabited by the Abyssinians, or which have been pulled down in the course of constructing the new Russian premises on the site. The eastern side of the cloister is also missing, and nothing resembling the architectural building of the twelfth century can now be detected in the squalid modern buildings which cover the site of the Basilica. A row of ancient shops fronting the Bazaar (formerly Rue Saint-Etienne), and forming, doubtless, the boundary of the Holy Sepulchre property on its eastern side, still survives. To judge by some traces of a sculptured string-course at their southern extremity, these interesting relics of ancient commerce must be contemporary with the Priory buildings.

The Canons' doorway, leading from the cloister down into the church at the north-east angle of the "Chorus Dominorum," is one of the few surviving ornamental features of the interior. A chevron-moulded arch above a square lintel is carried on two Romanesque columns as nook shafts in the style of the great façade of the church. The passage and staircase leading down through this doorway are now walled up.

In the centre of the cloister-garth stood (and still stands) the unusual feature of a cupola lighting the underground chapel of St Helena. The present octagonal erection which answers the purpose has the appearance of being a rebuilding of the original out of old materials, and doubtless belongs with the chapel of St Helenà below to some period of squalid restoration after the events of 1244.

The cloister-garth and the greater part of the Refectory are now occupied by Abyssinian monks, who have built their mud huts amongst the ruins, whilst the east and north walks of the cloister, long since destroyed, have become a crooked lane leading to the chief Coptic convent.

In this connection perhaps a reference may be made to the probable continuity of such an important foundation as the Augustinian Convent of the Holy Sepulchre in the history of the Levant subsequent to the loss of Jerusalem. The great Abbey of Bella Paise in Cyprus was doubtless a daughter house of the great convent in Jerusalem. Its origin is obscure, but it was at first a convent of Canons Regular of St Augustine, and subsequently, in 1206, passed under the reformed rule of Prémontré. It became the representative of the Augustinian Order in the Latin kingdom, transferred from Jerusalem to Cyprus, and as the finest monastic building remaining in the Levant it is a worthy successor to the great church of Jerusalem. It carries on the tradition of fine architecture by being in the more perfected style of geometrical pointed art.

St Helena's Chapel.—This venerable-looking but squalid underground chamber appears almost too poor a structure to belong to any period before the general destruction of the Priory buildings which were built above and around it. It was probably rebuilt in its present rude and clumsy manner at the end of the thirteenth century, when the Priory was given over as a quarry for second-hand building materials. Four roughly constructed pointed arches, eight cross-vaults, and a central cupola are carried on four ancient granite columns with capitals and bases which have no pretension to fit their present purpose. The capitals, which are too large for the shafts on which they stand, are so mutilated as to be unrecognisable in style, but they certainly have nothing to do with the fine architecture of the twelfth century.

The "Cross-finding" Chapel, an ancient cistern at the southeast corner of St Helena's Chapel, is described at p. 52. It possesses nothing of architectural character.

The doorway leading down by a staircase from the ambulatory of the "Chorus Dominorum" into St Helena's Chapel seems to have been rebuilt. Instead of corresponding in design with the Canons' door on the opposite side of the church, it is now a mere square opening formed with a straight lintel without architectural treatment.

The gloomy, squalid interior of this strange underground shrine is one of the most impressive and at the same time picturesque examples of the kind in existence. It must be remembered that such an effect is due to dirt and decay, combined with historical associations, and has nothing to do with any artistic or archæological features—the only parts of the structure which are probably of great antiquity are the two side-walls on north and south. These two side-walls—the east and west ends and the stairs down from the church have evidently been much modified in later ages—are doubtless the same which formed the enclosure of a crypt beneath the famous Basilica to which references occur in the earliest accounts of the Holy Sites.

STA MARIA LATINA[1]

A venerable monument of a particularly interesting period of history may still be traced within the much-altered surroundings of the Holy Sepulchre Church. Although the circular church of the Anastasis survives in a miraculous manner—as far as plan and arrangement are concerned—very much as it stood sixteen hundred years ago, its surroundings have changed hands over and over again in the course of those centuries. One of the few portions of these surroundings of a remote antiquity still traceable is the church of the Latins—Sta Maria Latina.

The common history of its origin is to the effect that about

[1] This church is, to a certain extent perhaps, represented at the present day by the "Chapel of the Apparition," see p. 91.

the year 800 a Benedictine monastery was founded on the south-east side of the Anastasis, and remained in existence on that site until the coming of the first Crusaders under Godfrey de Bouillon. Gibbon in his turgid manner describes how:—

the zeal of the Christian sects was embittered by hatred and revenge; and in the kingdom of a suffering Messiah, who had pardoned His enemies, they aspired to command and persecute their spiritual brethren. The pre-eminence was asserted by the spirit and number of the Franks; and the greatness of Charlemagne protected both the Latin pilgrims and the Catholics of the East. Haroun-er-Raschid, the greatest of the Abbasides, esteemed in his Christian brother a similar supremacy of genius and power: their friendship was cemented by a frequent intercourse of gifts and embassies; and the Caliph, without resigning the substantial dominion, presented the emperor with the keys of the Holy Sepulchre, and perhaps of the city of Jerusalem.

The last paragraph is in the Gibbonian style, but as an historical statement is somewhat doubtful, and still more as regards an annual fair on Mount Calvary:—

In the decline of the Carlovingian monarchy, the republic of Amalfi promoted the interests of trade and religion in the East. Her vessels transported the Latin pilgrims to the courts of Egypt and Palestine, and deserved by their useful imports the favour and alliance of the Fatimite Caliphs: an annual fair was instituted on Mount Calvary; and the Italian merchants founded the convent and hospital of St John of Jerusalem, the cradle of the monastic and military order which has since reigned in the isles of Rhodes and of Malta.[1]

This page of history assumes, perhaps, a rather more interesting form under the pen of the Abbé Vertot (*History of the Knights of Malta*, English translation, London, 1728, p. 7):—

Another modern writer, learned in our antiquities, in the thirty-seventh book of the annals of his order, tells us of one Bernard, a French monk who lived in A.D. 870, and who in his account of a voyage to Jerusalem relates that he found there an hospital for the

---

[1] Gibbon's *History of the Crusades*, Chandos Library edit., p. 361.

Latins, and that in the same house was a library, collected by the care and at the expence of the emperor Charlemagne.[1]

But after the death of the caliph Aaron and his first successors, as those of Charlemagne did not come up to him either in power or reputation, the French lost the regard that had been formerly paid them in Palestine. They were no longer allowed to have any house of entertainment in Jerusalem;...differences in point of discipline having, in a manner, put an end to all union between the Greek and Latin Churches, our European Christians were scarce less odious to the Greeks than they were to the Arabians and Saracens of the East.

In the middle of the eleventh century, some Italian merchants, who had experienced the inhumanity of both the one and the other, undertook to provide an asylum for the European pilgrims, in the very city of Jerusalem, where they might have nothing to fear from the false zeal of the Mahometans, or the enmity and aversion of the schismatical Greeks. These pious merchants were of Amalphy, a city in the kingdom of Naples, but at that time subject to the Greek emperors of Constantinople.

The governor, by the order of the caliph Mostanser-Billah, assigned them a piece of ground, on which they built a chapel, and dedicated it to the Blessed Virgin, by the name of St Mary ad Latinos, to distinguish it from the churches where divine service was celebrated according to the Greek ritual: some monks of the Benedictine order officiated in it. Near their convent they built two houses of entertainment for the reception of pilgrims of both sexes, whether in health or sickness, which was the chief view in this foundation; and each house had afterwards a chapel in it, the one dedicated to St John the Almoner, and the other to St Magdalene.

Some lay persons from Europe, full of zeal and charity, renouncing the thought of returning into their own country, devoted themselves in this religious house to the service of the poor and pilgrims, and were subsisted by the monks above mentioned; and the merchants of Amalphy, out of the alms which they collected in Italy and either

---

[1] "De Emmaus pervenimus ad S. Civitatem Jerusalem et recepti sumus in hospitale gloriosissimi imperatoris Karoli in quo suscipiuntur omnes qui causa devotionis illum adeunt locum, lingua loquentes Romana. Cui adjacet ecclesia in honore S. Mariæ, nobilissimam habent bibliothecam studio prædicti imperatoris cum duodecim mansionibus, agro vineis et horto in valle Josophat."

brought or sent regularly every year to the Holy Land, supplied the wants of the pilgrims or sick.

Yet this pious and useful foundation had like to have been ruined in its very infancy, and it had hardly subsisted fifteen years when the Turcomans conquered Palestine, surprised the city of Jerusalem, and cut the caliph of Egypt's garrison to pieces. The inhabitants and Christians scarce met with a better fate: numbers of them were butchered; the hospital of St John was plundered, and these barbarians, fierce and cruel in their nature, would have destroyed the Holy Sepulchre had not their avarice restrained their impiety. The fear of losing the revenues raised upon the pilgrims of the West preserved the tomb of our Saviour. " Soli etiam dominici sepulcri templo, ejusque cultoribus christianis parcebant propter tributa quæ ex oblatione fidelium assidue eis fideliterque solvebantur, una cum ecclesia Sanctæ Mariæ ad Latinos quæ etiam tributaria erat."— *Alb. Aquensis*, i. 6.

Amongst the references to St Mary the Latin in writers on mediæval history may be quoted Baronius, who under the year 800 (Eginhard, 799) speaks of the Patriarch George sending monks of Palestine to the court at Aix begging aid and protection for the Christians of Jerusalem. Baluse (*Capitularies* I. p. 473) gives the capitularies established by the Western Emperors for regulating the alms collected for the support of the Convent and Hospice of St Mary the Latin and for the benefit of Latin Christians in the Holy Land (Eginhard: *Vita Caroli*, c. 27).

In Muratori, *Ann.* III. p. 577, will be found an interesting account of the Carlovingian policy with regard to "Outremer," and of the taxation imposed on the Holy Roman Empire by Louis le Débonnair for the benefit of the Jerusalem Hospice. The famous hospice on Mont Cenis is also said to have been founded, partly for the purpose of facilitating the passage across the Alps in connection with pilgrimages to Jerusalem, by the Emperor Louis II. (See also *The Monk of S. Gall.* II. c. 14.)

During the first years of the twelfth century the Convent of St Mary the Latin continues to be mentioned. In the *Assizes of Jerusalem*, II. section 4, Charter 51, the Benedictine Abbey of St Mary returns fifty sergeants to the Royal service. The oath of fealty from the Abbot to the Patriarch is given, and the right of the Abbot to wear mitre, cross, and ring is mentioned. John of Wurzburg mentions that the relic of St Philip's head was preserved in the chapel of the convent.

The convent is apparently referred to under the names of "Sainte Marie la Latine et Marie Cleophe, La tirerent leur chevaux," by William of Tyre in the middle of the thirteenth century, and Philip Musquet, in his rhymed chronicle of 1241, evidently refers to the chapel as

> U Madame Sainte Marie
> La Mere Dieu s'estoit marie
> Et la Marie Cleophè
> Od la Marie Salomè.

It is mentioned in *Les Pelerinages por aller en Jherusalem*, c. 1250:—

Par devers midi pres d'iluec (S. Sep.) est l'yglise de Nostre Dame de la Latine, la premier yglise qui onques fust des Latines en Jherusalem et por ce a nom la Latine. Et est de moines noires.

The earliest plan of the Holy Sites—the famous drawing attributed to the French bishop Arculf—shows the church of St Mary Latin as evidently forming a component part of the group of buildings; his description also implies that the square church of St Mary adjoined the round church of the Anastasis. But in the later plans of Jerusalem, of which many versions remain from the thirteenth and later centuries, the "Ecclesia Latina" is clearly enough marked on the opposite side of the street known as "Vicus ad Templum Domini," or "Rue des Palmiers."

From the foregoing it is evident that the church founded by the Emperor Charlemagne under such romantic circumstances was removed from the site which it first occupied in front of the south entrance to the Holy Sepulchre to some distance further off in the same direction. This removal must have taken place in connection with the building of the new south transept of the Crusaders' church in about 1130.

The church known traditionally as Santa Maria Maggiore, the ruins of which, after forming a part of the "Muristan" of Jerusalem, and subsequently a tannery, have in recent years been rebuilt as the German Lutheran Church of the Redeemer, would apparently be the St Maria Latina of the twelfth and thirteenth centuries. The position of this building corresponds as far as may be with the mediæval plans and descriptions, and its ruined precincts still contain the cloister and a few chambers of a small religious house. The surrounding premises towards the south-west constituted the hospice accommodation, and seem to have been contiguous with the two other hospices mentioned in the chronicles as St John and St Mary Magdalene or St Mary the Less.

Of the church rebuilt by the Germans in 1896 nothing now remains *in situ*, but some arch stones have been re-used in the principal entrance which have the usual character of French transitional sculpture of the period. They represent the signs of the Zodiac.

Fig. 32. The Apse of St Mary Latin, now used as an Armenian chapel, in the parvis of the Holy Sepulchre.

De Vogüé in his plan of the Holy Sepulchre Church (*Les Églises de la Terre Sainte*) has guessed at the probable position of Charlemagne's church, but at the same time has shown a singular want of perception in failing to recognise its actual situation by the apse which still survives on the east side of the present parvis.

This apse is sufficiently evident to the most casual passer-by. Its wide pointed arch is supported on two capitals of the usual Byzantine style of carving, as far as can be seen, embedded as they are within the wall which has been built across the apse and which has converted the interior, covered by its semi-dome, into a small chapel now in the occupation of the Armenians. The outline of this apse arch can be easily seen in the photograph [fig. 32].

The flight of steps which still serves as a means of communication between the modern Greek convent of Constantine and the parvis is evidently in the same position as the approach of a similar kind shown upon the plan of Arculf as a walled or enclosed passage [see fig. 33]. The date of the buildings forming three chapels on the west side of the parvis is very obscure. These chapels are evidently in the position described by Sæwulf, but at the same time their architectural character appears of a later date. It seems possible they may have been built or rebuilt at the period when St Mary Latin was pulled down and the new church of St Mary Major took its place.

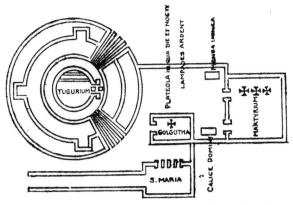

Fig. 33. Plan of Bishop Arculf, *c.* 700. Reproduced in the MSS. of Bede, *Hist. Eccl.*, and elsewhere.

It seems more than probable that the three chapels described by Sæwulf as forming a continuous line or perspective view with the rotunda of the Anastasis must have at one time formed the western end of St Mary Latin of the ninth century, because they are described as being in existence long before the destruction of St Mary Latin. We may perhaps therefore consider that the east end, and possibly the west end, of this ancient church survive, whilst the central portion or nave has quite disappeared, and its site is now occupied by the open *parvis*. It will be noticed that the three chapels in their rebuilt form have very much the appearance of a nave with side aisles, the centre one being the widest. [See plan on p. 73.]

The apse of this ancient church—now turned into a small shrine of the Armenians—is much altered internally by arrangements intended to give it a more usual parallelogram form, but the semicircular plan and the pointed semi-dome which covers it are still easily detected.

The Benedictine Abbey of the ninth century would presumably have occupied the area of the small modern Convent of Abraham, part of which, until within a few years back, was the site of a tannery, and at one time seems to have been built as a bazaar. This bazaar would probably have come into existence at a time when the Benedictines were transferring their premises to the other side of the main road called "Rue des Palmiers," and when the Augustinians were enlarging their boundaries around the grand new convent of the Crusading epoch.

The site of the bazaar is now completely modernised, with new European shops and the new Russian hospice. Within the latter, close to the rock-cut steps supposed to be those of the ancient pretorium, is a singular and quite inexplicable fragment of an arched porch or doorway to some building of presumably Byzantine age. Nothing has been discovered throwing light upon this fragment.

The Palace of the Latin Patriarch.—Although so important a dignitary of the church as a Patriarch of Jerusalem must have been surrounded by a regular court during the palmy days of the Latin Kingdom, there are few if any references in the pilgrims' books to his palace, which still stands on the east side of the Rue du Patriarche. The interior of this building is now practically inaccessible. The upper stories seem partly disused, and approached from other neighbouring property, and the ground floor is cut up into small shops, which may or may not be of some antiquity. Its massive external wall with square buttresses and small splayed windows with pointed heads is the only interesting feature remaining.

NOTE ON THE TOMBS OF THE KINGS SAID TO HAVE BEEN DE-
STROYED AT THE TIME OF REBUILDING THE ROTUNDA AND
THE EAST END IN 1810

A screen dividing the southern transept from the Chorus
Dominorum, as at present, appears in the old plans, and on the
south side of this screen the area of the transept seems to have
constituted the royal burial place of the Latin kings of
Jerusalem.

On either side of the entrance to the Chapel of Adam were the
monuments of Godfrey and Baldwin I. The inscriptions on
their tombs have been preserved in various authors:—

✠ HIC JACET INCLYTUS DUX GODFRIDUS DE BULION QUI TOTAM
ISTAM TERRAM A(C)QUISIVIT CULTUI CHRISTIANO. CUJUS
ANIMA REGNAT CUM CHRISTO. AMEN. ✠

    ✠ REX BALDUINUS JUDAS ALTER MACHABAEUS
    SPES PATRIAE VIGOR ECCLESIAE VIRTUS UTRIUSQUE
    QUEM FORMIDABANT CUI DONA TRIBUTA FEREBANT
    CEDAR AEGYPTI DAN AC HOMICIDA DAMASCUS
    PROH DOLOR IN MODICO CLAUDITUR HOC TUMULO. ✠

Baldwin II and Foulques d'Anjou were buried within the
Chapel of Adam as well as Godfrey and Baldwin I. The tomb of
Foulques was long pointed out as that of "Melchisedec" by
the Greeks, after they had obtained proprietorship of this chapel,
but at the present day only a couple of stone seats against the
walls, one on either side of the entrance, serve to represent the
monuments of the first Christian kings of Jerusalem.

De Vogüé has discovered in the Bibliothèque Imp. MS.
Lat. 5129, what he supposes to be the original version of the
inscription on the monument of king Godfrey in a style of ver-
sification more in conformity with that of the thirteenth century
than the above inscription. He supposes the epitaph usually
noted by the mediæval travellers to have been a later composition
engraved upon the tomb, probably after the profanations committed by the Kharismians in 1244. This version runs as
follows:—

    MIRIFICUM SIDUS DUX HIC RECUBAT GODFRIDUS
    EGIPTI TERROR ARABUM FUGA PERSIDIS ERROR
    REX LICET ELECTUS REX NOLUIT INTITULARI
    NEC DIADEMARI SED SYON SUA REDDERE JURA

CATHOLICEQUE SEQUI SACRA DOGMATA JURIS ET EQUI
TOTAM SCISMA TERI CIRCUM SE JUSQUE FOVERI
SIC ET CUM SUPERIS POTUIT DIADEMA MERERI
MILICIE SPECULUM POPULI VIGOR ANCHORA CLERI

The four last Latin kings of Jerusalem who resided in the
Holy City were interred within the Holy Sepulchre Church in
tombs placed in the usual mediæval fashion along the side of
the choir. Their epitaphs have been lost owing to mutilation in
subsequent ages, with the exception of that on the boy-king
Baldwin V. Quaresmius the sixteenth-century antiquary of
Palestine and "Guardian of Mount Sion" has preserved this, at
that time still extant, example in the *Elucidatio*, as follows:—

SEPTIMUS IN TUMULO PUER ISTO REX TUMULATUS
EST BALDEVINIUS REGUM DE SANGUINE NATUS
QUEM TULIT E MUNDO SORS PRIME CONDITIONIS
UT PARADYSIACE LOCA POSSIDEAT REGIONIS
(Quares. *Elucid.* II. p. 482.)

All these sepulchres were probably of the same plain and un-
ostentatious design which may be made out in the rude copperplates of Zuallardo and other pilgrims' books. They consisted
of simple coped blocks of stone like the covers of sarcophagi,
raised on short columns, and with panelled sides. No sculptured
figures or armorial bearings appear to have been displayed upon
them.

A few examples of this same type of tomb survive in Cyprus,
such as the tombstone of Adam d'Antioche in a church near
Nicosia. (See Enlart, *L'Art Gothique en Chypre*, p. 486.)

By a strange chance, owing to its having been covered over
by a stone platform ever since the Moslem occupation of the
city until quite recent years, a solitary tombstone of a crusader
still lies *in situ* before the south-transept entrance. The grave
looks as if it had never been disturbed, so that the body possibly
still lies untouched below. The person commemorated in the
inscription on the stone is a certain Philip d'Aubigni, Governor
of the Channel Islands, one of the Councillors of King John at
the signing of Magna Charta, and tutor of the young king
Henry III. He visited Jerusalem in the train of Emperor
Frederick II, 1229, and died there in 1236. F. Gough Nichols,
F.S.A., in *Proceedings of Archæol. Inst.* (Lincoln) gives the text

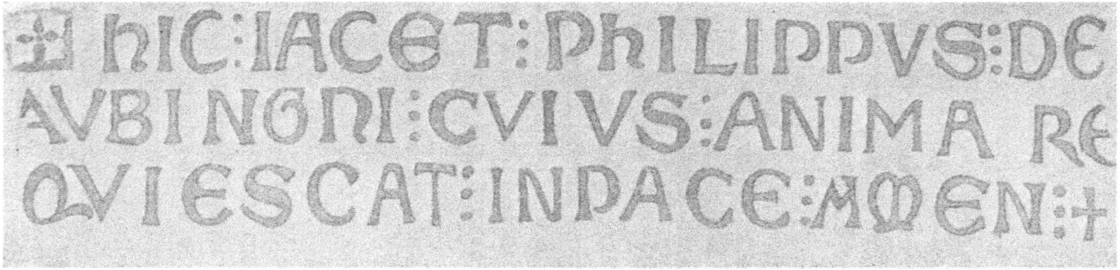

Fig. 34. Inscription on Tomb of Sir Philip d'Aubigni, at the Entrance to the Holy Sepulchre Church.

Fig. 35. Inscribed on a tombstone of the twelfth century which was found on the site of Christ Church (English) and presented to the Mediæval Collection at St Anne's by Bishop Gobat about 1850.

of a letter from Philip d'Aubigni to the Earl of Chester on his arrival in Jerusalem. Two Acts of Assizes held by him in Jersey are sealed with the same coat-of-arms as on the grave-stone in Jerusalem—four fusils in fess.

It would appear that the knight reached Acre at the moment when the Emperor Frederick II was beginning his diplomatic crusade of 1229.

M. J. Havet, in his researches into the history of the Wardens and Lords of the Channel Islands, *Bib. de l'École des Chartes*, 1876, p. 170, has discovered references to this personage in the Chronicle of Matthew of Paris:—

Philippus de Albineto, postquam militaverat Deo in terra sancta, peregrinando pluries, tandem in eadem die claudens extremum et finem faciens laudabilem, sanctam meruit in terra sancta, quod vivus diu desideraverat, sepulturam.

Philippus de Albineto, miles strenuus ac morum honestate commendabilis, regis Anglorum magister et eruditor fidelissimus, iter Hierosolymitanum arripiens, illuc cum prosperitate ac sine rerum diminutione pervenit.

M. Havet states that the "faithful teacher" of the young king Henry III is also mentioned in the preamble to Magna Charta, amongst the "nobiles homines" whose council the king (John) declares that he has taken. At this time he was Warden or Bailiff of Jersey, Guernsey, Alderney and Sark, the only portions of the Duchy of Normandy remaining to king John. Upon his departure for the Holy Land in 1222, these islands passed to the government of his eldest son, also named Philip.

The name of Philip d'Aubigni occurs in the Chancellor's Rolls of the reigns of John and Henry III.

PART III

LESSER SHRINES
OF
THE HOLY CITY

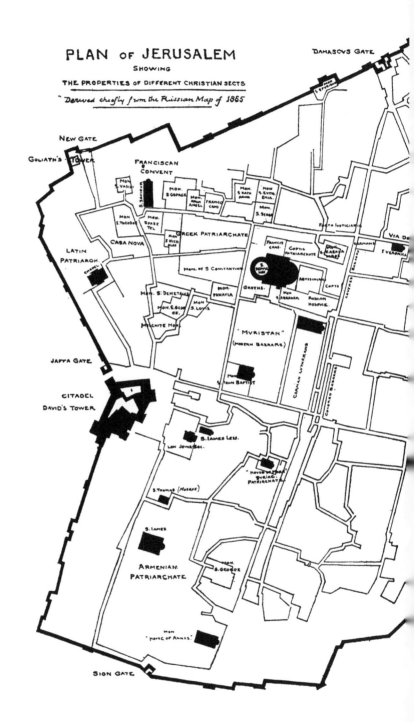

PLAN of JERUSALEM

SHOWING

THE PROPERTIES OF DIFFERENT CHRISTIAN SECTS

Derived chiefly from the Russian Map of 1865

DAMASCVS GATE

MON. S SPYRIDION

NEW GATE

GOLIATH'S TOWER

FRANCISCAN CONVENT

MON. S VASILI

MON. S GEORGE

MON. S GEORGE

MON. S KATH ARINA

MON. S EVTH. EMIA.

FORTA IVSTICIARIA

VIA DO

MON. S ANGEL

FRANCI CANS

MON. S SEGO

CASA NOVA

MON. S THEODOR

MON. SPASE TEL

GREEK PATRIARCHATE

MON. S NICH OLAS

FRANCI CANS

COPTIC PATRIARCHATE

MON. S KABARA OARE

BAZARS

BAZARS

S VERONICA

LATIN PATRIARCH.

CHAPEL

MON. OF S CONSTANTINE

S SEPVLCHRE

GREEKS.

ABYSSINIANS

COPTS

COVERED BAZARS

MON. S DEMETRIVS

MON. PANAYIA

GREEKS.

MON. S ABRAHAM

RUSSIAN HOSPICE

MON. S GEOR GE

MON. S LOVIS

MELCHITE MON.

"MVRISTAN"

(MODERN BAZARS)

GERMAN LUTHERANS

JAFFA GATE

MON. S JOHN BAPTIST

COVERED BAZARS

CITADEL

DAVID'S TOWER

S IAMES LESS.

LON JEWS SOC.

"HOUSE OF THE SYRIAC. PATRIARCHATE"

S THOMAS (MOSQVE)

S IAMES

ARMENIAN PATRIARCHATE

MON. S GEORGE

MON. "HOUSE OF ANNAS"

SION GATE

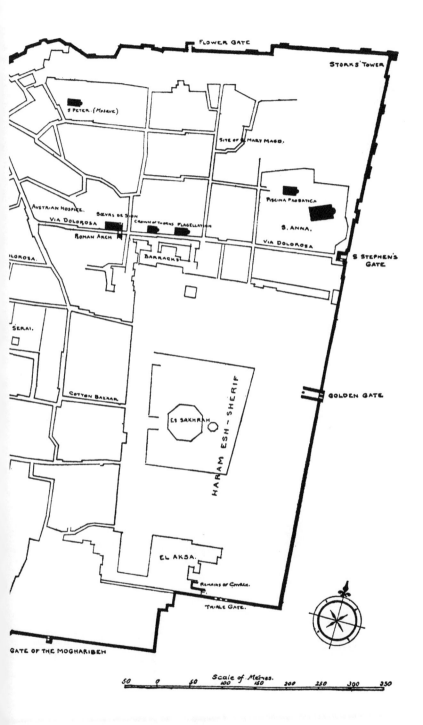

FLOWER GATE

STORKS' TOWER

S. PETER. (MOSQUE)

SITE OF S. MARY MAGD.

PISCINA PROBATICA

AUSTRIAN HOSPICE.

SŒURS DE SION

VIA DOLOROSA

CROWN OF THORNS FLAGELLATION

ROMAN ARCH

S. ANNA.

VIA DOLOROSA

S STEPHEN'S GATE

...LOROSA.

BARRACKS.

SERAI.

COTTON BAZAAR.

GOLDEN GATE

ES SAKHRAH

HARAM ESH – SHERIF

EL AKSA.

REMAINS OF CHURCH.

TRIPLE GATE.

GATE OF THE MOGHARIBEH

Scale of Metres.

50   0   50   100   150   200   250   300   350

CHAPTER I

CHURCHES WITHIN THE WALLS

THE great church of the Holy Sepulchre is the most remarkable and interesting monument of twelfth-century art and history in the world—the secondary churches of Jerusalem, chiefly built by the Crusaders, also attract the attention of the architectural pilgrim.

De Vogüé, in his *Églises de la Terre Sainte*, 1860, gives a description and plans of nearly all of these remains of the wonderful crusading kingdom, and such few monuments as escaped his notice have since been planned and fully investigated by more recent visitors to the Holy City. The following notes are now offered as a résumé of the past fifty years' studies on the subject, and as a means of affording some idea of the present condition and probable future fate of these most interesting monuments.

Our principal source of information as to the condition of the monuments of Jerusalem at the time of the Crusades is the laborious description of his pilgrimage written by John of Wurzburg, at the beginning of the twelfth century. Although considered of no great importance by the historians of the Crusades, he certainly gives the most interesting account of the mediæval Holy City.

THE HARAM

The ancient churches of Jerusalem are mostly the property of the different Christian sects, or have been turned into mosques. The great and famous mosque of the Haram esh-Sherif (the Noble Sanctuary) is in a sense the most important of these ecclesiastical monuments, although its Christian character has been but of the most evanescent and transitory kind at different periods of its history. It in fact owes its world-wide interest to having been the great Holy Site revered by Jew, and Moslem, and Christian, without counting the religious interest of a pre-historic period, or its brief glory as a Roman acropolis crowned with a classic temple and colossal statues. At the present day it remains hardly second in the religious estimation of the whole Moslem world, and of course to the Jew it represents the last stronghold of his strenuous faith, but occupied, alas! by aliens.

As we see the Haram at the present day we probably look upon the design of the master masons employed by Selim I and Solyman I in 1530, when the new Turkish masters were setting in order their recently acquired provinces and the government of the chief cities of Islam. Its numerous Saracenic monuments are as varied in age as they are in size or use, but they all appear to have undergone a certain amount of "restoration" at the hands of the sixteenth-century Turks, and they have all been rebuilt or repaired with a *cachet* betraying the Turanian race of the designers.

"Restoration" is a word fraught with evil associations in any land; how much more so in a country—a "Holy Land"—where every ruin and almost every stone possesses associations with an historic past which have no equals in the world. The restorations of nearly 400 years ago are in themselves of a certain venerable antiquity at the present day in other countries, but in Jerusalem they seem but of yesterday. The general appearance of the Haram enclosure is not particularly venerable, whatever its associations may be; the different monuments, small and large, are built up of ancient second-hand materials, but this seems their chief antiquity. The clearing away of mediæval remains, and the substitution of new shrines and buildings, must have been far greater in the sixteenth century than is usually supposed. Taking the several separate monuments of the area in rotation, the most important from all points of view is the

Kubbet es Sakhrah.—This famous shrine was very much "restored" and embellished with fresh decorations in the sixteenth century. The main parts of its construction are doubtless old, such as the double arcade of the interior, and the general design of the great dome covered with lead. But the outside casing of the walls and certain details of interior decoration, stained glass, etc., are entirely Turkish. The tile-work and marble *placage* added in the sixteenth century are remarkable for beauty of colour at the present day, whatever the effect may have been when the work was new. The tile covering to walls, external and internal, seems to be specially associated with the sixteenth century. To this period belong the tile-covered minarets and mosques of Damascus and Asia Minor, and the equally extensive decorations of Sicilian and Neapolitan buildings. The churches of Jerusalem are full of these famous "Persian" tiles which give such a brilliance and colour to otherwise most dingy interiors, and the Kubbet es Sakhrah is certainly a very splendid example of their external application after the Turkish occupation.

With some little effort of the imagination it is easy to picture the appearance of the Haram as it must have appeared in the twelfth century. The Kubbet es Sakhrah, which had been built for the Moslem Arabs nearly 500 years previously, was known as the fourth "Templum Domini," and its building was very correctly attributed to a Moslem prince of the Arabs, Abdelmelek Ibn Merouan, seventh Omayyad Caliph, in 691. This remarkable piece of architecture is thought by some to represent an attempt on the part of the early Caliphs to remove the centre of the Mohammedan faith and pilgrimages from the primitive Mecca to the more convenient Jerusalem—an idea which was never carried out.

No alterations were made by the Crusaders in the structure of the Kubbet for the purpose of fitting it up as a Christian church; the only matter of importance in this respect was the covering of the Sacred Rock, above a Sacred Cave, supposed to be the "threshing-floor of Araunah the Jebusite," with a marble platform upon which rested the High Altar, and the stalls of the ritual choir of the Augustinian Canons serving the church. This marble platform was removed by the Moslems when they resumed possession of the building in 1187, leaving the rugged rock surface in its present bare condition. The church does not seem to have been fitted with an east-end choir like the somewhat similar rotunda of the Holy Sepulchre, a door on the east side being mentioned by John of Wurzburg. The ritual choir was above the "Rock" under the centre of the dome in a way which is represented in certain early churches in Italy copied from the "Templum." At Pisa is a particularly interesting example of such a copy; a small octagonal church, traditionally built for the Templars by the early architect "Diosisalvi" (who has left his name inscribed at the base of the campanile) in the twelfth century, exactly reproduces this arrangement. In this case also there is no eastern choir but the altar stands under the central cupola on a raised platform—it is remarkable that such an example should survive at the present day.

A very curious fact may here be noted: although the Kubbet es Sakhrah was clearly an entirely Moslem building in origin (built in all probability by Greek masons for their Moslem rulers), about the years 688–691 (A.H. 68) it became the model for innumerable Christian churches all over Europe, which were supposed to be copies of the "Templum Domini" in Jerusalem. The circular plan of church which had been common in primitive times, but had fallen into disuse during the earlier Middle Ages, was revived under the impression that the ancient Jewish Temple, now once more in favour as a Holy Site amongst Christians, was of a circular form! Long after the abolition of the Order of the Temple by the Popes the popular idea of a circular Jewish Temple survives in the pictures of Perugino and Raphael.

The "Templum Domini" was constituted, according to William of Tyre, a collegiate church of the Augustinian Order by King Godfrey in A.D. 1100. The names of four of its Priors are preserved by De Vogüé:—

1112, Achard. 1138, Geoffroi. 1169, Raymond. 1176, Roger.

Beyond a mere general outline the Kubbet es Sakhrah can bear little, if any, resemblance to its appearance in the Middle Ages, when it served as the "Templum Domini" of the Crusaders and was surrounded by the usual buildings of a collegiate church with its Prior and chapter of canons of the Augustinian Order. Discoveries of its original design, as to wall construction and fenestration, were made during some repairs about thirty years ago, and the facts then recorded were published in the *Survey of Western Palestine*, 1881.

The elegant wrought-iron screen encircling the sacred rock, which closely resembles the ironwork dividing the choir from its aisles in Lincoln Cathedral, is presumably mediæval, and a few fragments of mediæval carving may also be discovered within the interior. A few traces of mediæval fresco decoration have been detected on its inside walls, but nothing remains of the lengthy inscriptions which John of Wurzburg copied down with so much care, and which accompanied the mural paintings. In converting the Kubbet into a monastic church, the Crusaders are said to have left untouched the Arabic inscriptions which they found within it, in the same way that the Spanish knights have left the Hebrew texts upon the walls of their chapel in Toledo, but the Moslems have generally swept away all traces of Christianity in those churches which they have appropriated in different parts of the Levant.

The exterior of the Kubbet during the Middle Ages was covered with a placage of marble, probably in the style of the Tuscan baptisteries, above which was a deep frieze of mosaics enclosing Arabic inscriptions. William of Tyre says that he saw and understood this inscription as mentioning the name of the Prophet Omar, son of Katab, second successor of the Prophet, as the builder, with the expenses of the work, and the dates of its commencement and end. He also speaks of two such inscriptions, one on the exterior and one inside the building.

The Fatimite Caliph Zahir is also said to have been commemorated by another inscription dated 1022.

John of Wurzburg gives a detailed list of the Latin inscriptions on the exterior, which were apparently additions also in mosaic. The four sides of the building presented the following texts:—

W. PAX AETERNA AB AETERNO PATRE SIT HUIC DOMUI
BENEDICTA GLORIA DOMINI DE LOCO SANCTO SUO
S. BENE FUNDATA EST DOMUS DOMINI SUPRA FIRMAM PETRAM
BEATI QUI HABITANT IN DOMO TUA IN SECULA SECULORUM
LAUDABUNT TE
E. VERE DOMINUS EST IN LOCO ISTO ET EGO NESCIEBAM
IN DOMO TUA DOMINE OMNES DICENT GLORIAM
N. TEMPLUM DOMINI SANCTUM EST DEI CULTURA EST DEI
AEDIFICATIO EST

Over the entrance doorway on the west side was to be seen a figure of Christ with the following inscription:—

HAEC DOMUS MEA DOMUS ORATIONIS VOCABITUR

The decorations of the Kubbet in their mediæval style have entirely disappeared from the exterior, although their general design and arrangement may be represented by the Turkish tile-work which occupies the position of the mosaic inscriptions, and possibly the marble placage is to a great extent the original much "restored."

The mediæval descriptions of the interior of the edifice are less easy to understand than those of the exterior. John of Wurzburg states that the following inscriptions were at a height encircling the interior:—

AUDI DOMINI HYMNUM etc.

RESPICE DOMINI etc.

and on a lower line in golden letters were the verses of the hymn:—

URBS HIERUSALEM BEATA etc.

The positions of these inscriptions are difficult to identify because we do not know how the great wooden dome was finished internally before its modern decoration. It doubtless had some kind of wooden ceiling, and the inscriptions were painted and gilded upon it in the usual twelfth-century style of Europe.

No trace remains of the marble floor with which the famous rock covering the sacred cave was made level to accommodate the circular choir and altar space that possibly represented to mediæval eyes a realisation of the arrangements of the ancient temple of the Jews. But the doorway which still leads down to the cave or crypt beneath, with its moulded pointed arch and side columns, may possibly belong to this marble sheathing.

As already remarked, the exterior of the Kubbet es Sakhrah must be entirely unlike anything with which the Crusaders were familiar in the twelfth century. In addition to the covering of brilliant tiles[1] and the large porches over the doors, the alteration of the windows, etc., the removal of contiguous buildings would tend to alter its appearance considerably. John of Wurzburg mentions the buildings of the canons' residences as attached to the Temple of the Lord, and he also refers to the

---

[1] "Persian" faïence was known in Persia in the thirteenth century, but it did not become popular in the Mediterranean countries until about two or three hundred years later.

arcaded entrances, which are presumably the same that still stand in a curiously isolated manner at the four cardinal points or sides of the raised platform. These now detached arcades have all the appearance of having at one time carried on a continuous cloister surrounding the Kubbet. At least such a design seems to suggest itself as being usual in buildings of this character, even if it was never actually carried out. These four arcades are of a "fragmentary" style (merely built of old fragments), and may really belong to any period as far as we can see them at the present day. The Dervish huts and tombs which now surround the raised platform probably replace the canons' residences, the refectory, and other buildings of the college which was dedicated by the Cardinal legate Alberic, Bishop of Ostia, on Easter Day 1136.

The different levels of the platforms constituting the Haram enclosure are defined to a great extent by the presence of the rock surfaces which appear at different points, culminating in the central "Sakhrah," round which so many associations linger. The retaining walls which surround these platforms have been rebuilt at different periods, and with the exception of the great outer enceinte, which evidently dates from an early period with Roman and Byzantine additions, there is no very precise history. The upper platform on which the Sakhrah Kubbet is built owes its present irregular form doubtless to the demolition of the cloister and buildings which once surrounded it.

Upon the platform of the Kubbet es Sakhrah stands one other ancient monument which may, or may not, be of the crusading period. This is the Kubbet es Silsileh, an octagonal structure supported on a double arcade with ancient columns, but evidently completely reconstructed in 1530, and covered with the same beautiful tile-work as the great Kubbet es Sakhrah.

This Kubbet, or some building exactly occupying its side, was known to the Crusaders as the Chapel of St James, situated at the east door or side of the "Templum Domini." To them it commemorated the martyrdom and casting down from the acropolis height into the adjacent Valley of Siloam of the Apostle James (of Alphæus, or "brother of the Lord") and round its walls (it has none at the present day, being an open arcaded structure) ran the long inscription, preserved by John of Wurzburg:

JACOBUS ALPHAEI DOMINI SIMILIS FACIEI
FINIT PRO CHRISTO TEMPLO DEPULSUS AB ISTO
SIC JACOBUM JUSTUM PRAEDICANTEM PUBLICE CHRISTUM
PLEBS MALA MULCTAVIT FULLONIS PERTICA STRAVIT
JACOBUS ALPHAEI FRATER DOMINI NAZAREI
PISCATOR VITA VERE FUIT ISRAELITA
DE TEMPLO PINNA COMPULSUS FRAUDE MALIGNA
AD CHRISTUM LAETUS MIGRAVIT RECTE PEREMPTUS

The present Kubbet es Silsileh cannot resemble the mediæval chapel of St James as it has no walls on which the above inscription could have been written.

The rich blue colour of what, seen at a distance, was supposed to be the stone with which they were built attracted the notice of the pilgrims, such as Stochove and Sandys, in the sixteenth century to these monuments on the highest platform of the Haram. The tile-work was no doubt then of a remarkable brilliance; it would appear to have been made in Jerusalem, as the parts which follow the lines of arches or their spandrels, etc., are all exactly modelled and painted to suit the exact positions which they occupy. This is more especially noticeable in the smaller of the two shrines. At the present day there appears to be nothing in the shape of a fabrique of pottery or porcelain in or near Jerusalem; the ancient and very beautiful art is quite extinct in Palestine, but perhaps lingers in Asia Minor.

The lower area of the Haram must have been much altered and rearranged by the Turks in 1530. The defences towards the Valley of Jehoshaphat were rebuilt in conformity with the rest of the city wall, the ancient Byzantine gates were walled up, and the modern minarets erected. Many of the extraordinary caverns or reservoirs with which the area is honeycombed were probably more exposed to the upper world than they are at present; this would account for Holy Sites mentioned by John of Wurzburg, spoken of as caves or grottos, which have since been covered up. The enclosing walls and arcades on the south and west are possibly of the date which is inscribed over the central gate, the Bab-el-Katanin (or Cotton Bazaar), A.H. 737 (A.D. 1336).

De Vogüé in his *Églises de la Terre Sainte*, 1860, gives some interesting views and details of the Haram as it appeared more than fifty years ago. These drawings were made from photographs taken at a great distance, as Christians and Europeans were prevented from visiting the sacred enclosure in those days. Such records have a particular interest at the present day as showing how very little has been altered within the Sanctuary during the past half century. Some twenty years ago the German Emperor William visited Jerusalem, and the Haram was treated to a sort of whitewashing and painted decoration, but these disfigurements have almost entirely disappeared.

In 1825 the buildings of the Haram were repaired by the Ottoman Sultan Mahmud II, but with this exception they seem to have been little interfered with or added to since the days of Solyman the Magnificent.

The Golden Gate.—This remarkable Byzantine monument remains at the present day in an interesting state of preservation. Its debased Classic architecture, with its Levantine peculiarities, seems intact. It was walled up by the Turks in 1530, and the ancient wood doors removed at this time were presented to the Franciscans of the Cœnaculum, to be placed amongst their relics in the Church of the Holy Sepulchre. At the same time the annual commemoration of Christ's entry into Jerusalem from Bethphage, which was celebrated by the Franciscans with a procession headed by the Padre Guardiano riding on a donkey across the Valley of Jehoshaphat, was necessarily discontinued (*vide Liber de perenni cultu Terræ Sanctæ*, by Fra Bonifazio Corsetto, 1553). Although apparently quite disused at the present day, this peculiar structure has received some attention in the way of support. The western side showing a tendency to settlement, two very ornamental flying buttresses have been erected against it in the form of archways. This addition, made about 1880, is in very good taste, and harmonises with the original building.

The "Stables of Solomon."—These immense substructures of the Haram main platform have excited astonishment at all periods. As we see them at the present day we look upon a style of construction of no very great antiquity. The vaults and arches are built of small stones, and with the general shape and proportions of what is recognised as "Crusaders' work." The square piers supporting this vaulting, of evidently much older materials re-used, have the venerable appearance of the outside wall of this part of the enclosure. The place has evidently been used as a stable, because the curious holes cut through the angles of every "coign of vantage" for the purpose of tethering animals are a sufficient proof. Doubtless we are looking therefore upon a genuine untouched portion of the Crusaders' arrangements of the twelfth century. The entrance into these stables would be through the triple gateway in the south wall of the Haram. There would seem to have been a passage, now walled up, between the stables and the long corridor beneath the Aksa, where a doorway opening eastwards shows in the wall.

In the fifteenth century, before the occupation of Syria by the Turks and the great wars between the Ottoman Empire and the European States, the Haram was perhaps a little less jealously guarded by the fanatical Moslems than at subsequent periods. Francesco Suriano, Guardian of Mount Sion in about 1480, has left some interesting notes upon this subject. He says:—

Soto el tempio è vacuo, facto tute a volta sopra colonne altissimi... Soto queste volte credo che tenevano li animali offerti al tempio... e quando bisogna a fare da novo o reparare el vecchio alcuna cosa mandano per li nostri frati in Monte Sion.

The latter statement of the Padre Guardiano is very remarkable. It implies that the Christians and Arab Moslems were on such good terms that the Latin monks with their superior technical ability were habitually employed whenever repairs to the monuments of the Haram were necessary. After the coming of the Turks and a great many other revolutions in the affairs of Jerusalem, these amicable relations between Christian and Moslem ceased, and from the middle of the sixteenth century to the middle of the nineteenth the Haram enclosure was closed against all Europeans under penalty of death. Dr Eli Smith, the first editor of Murray's *Palestine*, states that the Haram was opened to European travellers in 1856 on payment of £1 each.

It is supposed that a much larger extent of these vaulted chambers really exists than is now accessible, but the Palestine Exploration Society does not seem to have cleared up this part of the matter at present.

The triple gate entrance into these stables must evidently belong to the period of their construction, or reconstruction, and may possibly be mediæval.

The Vaulted Corridor beneath the Aksa.—This evidently Byzantine fragment of somewhat obscure origin and significance is clearly identical in date with the Golden Gate. The same design and detail is to be found in both.

It is difficult to realise what may have been the plan and use of the double gate in the south wall of the Haram. It has evidently been very much changed in its plan and position with regard to the successive superstructures reared above it. Presumably it was intended to form a grand approach to the Kubbet es Sakhrah or the Roman temple which previously occupied that position. But the Kubbet es Sakhrah, as known to history, is a Mohammedan building, not older in any case than the traditional date of its foundation by Abdelmelek in 686, whilst this mysterious passage entrance looks of a different style, and if it should belong to the buildings of Justinian, as has often been supposed, it would be about a century older than anything we see on the Haram excepting the "Golden Gate." If it has any connection with the Church of the "Presentation," said to have been built somewhere about this site, its position is all the more remarkable and difficult of explanation as part of any regular design, unless we suppose the original Byzantine portion of the construction to stop at the flight of steps leading up from the actual entrance, with its famous column 6 feet 6 inches in diameter, and the long double tunnel leading to the Kubbet to be some later modification of its use.

The Church of the "Presentation," erected by Justinian, is described by the pilgrim Antonio of Piacenza as being built between two hospices (each of which accommodated 2500 pilgrims), disposed in the form of a hemicycle in front of its entrance. Such a group of large buildings may have occupied the southern part of the Haram in the sixth century, but it is difficult to imagine its plan or any connection with this long underground passage nearly 300 feet in length. In any case there can be little doubt that the long tunnel (which is only double for a certain distance) has been lengthened at some period in order to carry its upper entrance outside the confines of the subsequently built mosque. It is unfortunate that Procopius should have been so unintelligible in his descriptions of Justinian's works on this acropolis.

El Aksa.—This large and imposing building, although somewhat resembling a church in appearance, was built by Moslems as a mosque, and is therefore on that account rather outside the scope of the present volume. That it should ever have been regarded as possibly a "restoration" of the Church of the "Presentation" of the sixth century can only be attributed to the confusion of ideas about all the historical sites of the Holy Land which characterises the pilgrims' accounts of the Middle Ages. Even Fra Francesco Suriano, who professes to have often visited its interior, and who consequently ought to have known better, states:—

Presentatione.—Questa gloriosa chiesia è facta al Italiana ed è in sete navate cum sete porte principale...de dentro tuta è foderata de tavole de marmaro...le quále ho tute vedute e più fiate.

The mosque El Aksa is generally considered to owe its present form to the munificence of the Baharite Memluk Sultan Nasir Mohammed Ebn Kaláuon, after his victory over the Tartars in 1303. There is said to be an inscription within it recording Sultan Kaláuon as its founder in 1327, which may very well be correct, as this Sultan did not die until 1341 under the name of Bihars II [fig. 36].

The only interesting portion of this immense building, with its seven naves and numerous dependencies, to the Christian ecclesiologist is the fragment of a mediæval church which may be found on the east side near the south end, used up as part of the outside walls of the mosque[1] [fig. 37].

This fragment is apparently the west end of a twelfth-century church, with its doorway decorated with the characteristic cushion voussoir moulding, and a large well-preserved circular window above. The doorway is now walled up, and the window is unfortunately covered over by a ruinous fragment of lath and plaster filling-in; but so far as can be now seen the gable-wall must have been the west end of an important church with an open space in front of it. This open space would be just above the great Byzantine entrance with double arch of the south wall,

[1] I am indebted to the Rev. Canon Yarborough, Vicar of Christchurch, Hants, for permission to use some sketches of these details made by him at my request on a recent visit to the Haram esh-Sherif.

and is the area within the present mosque called the *Jami' al Arbein* (Mosque of the Forty).

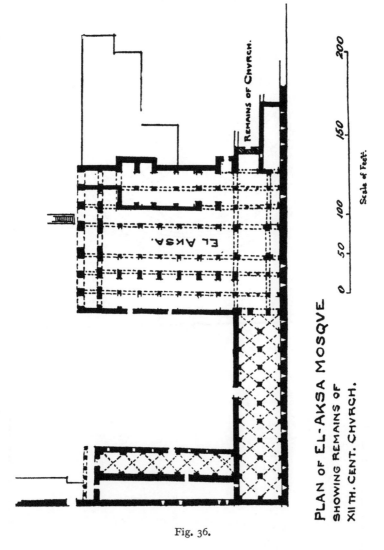

Fig. 36.

This singularly situated relic of the Crusading period (which seems hardly to have been noticed by any visitor to the Haram

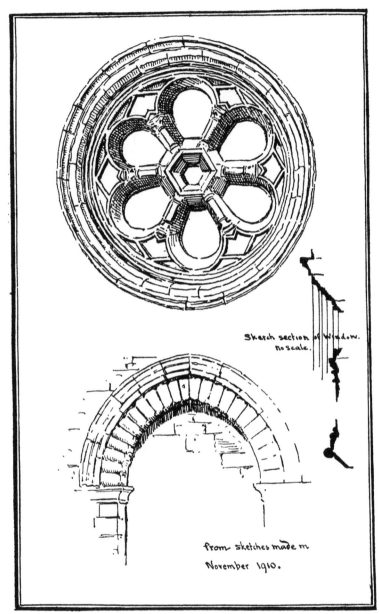

Fig. 37. Fragments of the twelfth century now built into the east wall of the El Aksa Mosque, originally the west wall of a Christian church, viewed from inside the mosque.

until the present writer described it in the *Journal of the R.I.B.A.* in 1911) may very probably be part of the church which the Templars erected on the site of the Basilica of the Presentation: *i.e.* on the traditional site over "Solomon's Stables." Its position would exactly correspond with such an idea, and it would certainly be consonant with the sentiments of the period for such a memorial of an important Basilica to be so erected. In assuming that the rose-window with a door beneath it once belonged to a church, no proof can be advanced beyond the fact of its answering all the conditions of an ordinary twelfth-century design for such a position. Circular windows of the same kind are also found in refectories and other parts of a monastery of the period; but in any case this fragment is clearly *in situ*, and undoubtedly formed part of the Convent of the Temple, or of the adjacent premises of the Royal Palace, or "Palatium Solomonis."

At the taking and sack of Jerusalem by the Kharismian tribes in 1244, it is probable that the "Palatium Solomonis," as the residence of the Frank kings was called, situated at the south end of the Haram, was destroyed. Part of its ruins, in a rebuilt state, may survive in the long two-aisled building which extends along the western part of the south wall, and is known as the Bakáat al Baidha, or Mosque of Abu Bekr (El Munsoor Abu Bekr, son of Nasir Mohammed Ebn Kaláuon, who succeeded his father in 1341). At the end of the thirteenth and the beginning of the fourteenth century the condition of Jerusalem must have been deplorable; warfare between Saracens and Latin Christians had culminated in the massacre of Acre, and the enemies of the Christians now allied with their former adversaries, the Mongols, were in possession of the whole eastern littoral of the Mediterranean. Ricoldo di Monte Croce, the Dominican monk of Santa Maria Novella, Florence, was one of the earliest visitors to the Holy Land after the events of 1291. In his *Itinerarium* he describes the devastation of Jerusalem, but he does not appear to have visited the Haram. Ludolph von Sudheim, another early visitor (1337), does not mention very much, although by this time: "Templum autem, quod nunc est, non habet tecta atria; sed in circuitu est ambitus non tectus et in pavimento albo marmore bene structus." By the beginning of the fourteenth century the unsightly ruins of the Christian occupation of the Haram had probably been completely cleared away or had been readapted to Moslem requirements. The range of buildings which extended along the southern boundary of the Haram is repeatedly referred to in mediæval documents as "the Temple" (distinguished from the "Templum Domini"), the palace or the portico of Solomon, but without definite description. In the plan of Jerusalem of 1170, now at the Hague, the "Claustrum Solomonis" is perhaps shown as the southern end of the west wall, above the present "Jews' wailing place"; and the "Templum Solomonis" is a building of imposing proportions but indefinite character. All that we can really know about these very interesting edifices once occupying the south end of the Haram is that within the "Templum" or "Palatium" the Latin kings lived and held their court, and that in the adjoining buildings the Order of the Temple was installed, with presumably the lodgings of the Grand Master.

Abdelmelek (685) is said to have restored the church of St Mary (or of the "Presentation"), with the removal of certain ruins on its eastern side, and to have furnished it with silver-gilt doors. But forty years afterwards, the church was again ruined at its east and west ends, and the silver-gilt doors had to be sold to pay for its repair. In 775 it was again rebuilt with many alterations, and once more in 1061, just before the Crusades, after centuries of use as a Moslem mosque, the roof fell in and necessitated another complete rebuilding. After such vicissitudes it is not surprising that Justinian's church should have wholly disappeared leaving not a trace behind; this is all the more probable considering the precarious nature of the site.

A propos of this subject, although not a Church, it may be as well to recall the pre-crusading aspect of the Haram, at a time when the first Mohammedan occupation of the site was drawing to an end. Mukaddasi (*c.* 1000), a Moslem native of Jerusalem, describes the mosque as follows:—

The Masjid el Aksa (the Further Mosque) lies at the south-eastern corner of the Holy City. The stones of the foundations (of the outer wall) are ten ells or a little less in length, which were laid by David. They are chiselled, finely faced and jointed, and of hardest material. On these the Khalif Abdal Malik subsequently built, using smaller, but well-shaped stones, and battlements are added above. This mosque is even more beautiful than that of Damascus, for during the building of it they had for a rival and as a comparison the great church belonging to the Christians at Jerusalem, and they built this to be even more magnificent than that other. But in the days of the Abbasides occurred the earthquakes which threw down most of the main building; all, in fact, except that portion round the Mihrab. Now when the Khalif of that day obtained news of this...he wrote to the Governors of Provinces and other Commanders, that each should undertake the building of a colonnade. The order was carried out, and the edifice rose firmer and more substantial than even it had been in former times. The more ancient portion remained, even like a beauty spot in the midst of the new; and it extends as far as the limit of the marble columns, for, beyond, where the columns are of concrete, the later part commences.

The main building of the mosque has twenty-six doors. The door opposite to the Mihrab is called Bab en Nahâs al Atham; it is plated with gilded brass, and is so heavy that only a man strong of shoulder and of arm can turn it on its hinges. To the right hand of the great gate are seven large doors, the midmost one of which is covered with gilt plates; and after the same manner there are seven doors to the left. And further, on the eastern side are eleven doors, unornamented. Over the first mentioned doors, fifteen in number, is a colonnade supported on marble columns, lately erected by Abdallah ibn Tahir (Governor of Khurasan, 828–844 A.D.). In the court of the mosque, on the right-hand side, are colonnades supported by marble pillars and pilasters; and on the further side are halls vaulted in stone. The centre part of the main building of the mosque is covered by a mighty roof, high pitched and gable-wise, behind which rises a magnificent dome. The ceiling everywhere, with the exception of that of the halls on the further side of the court, is formed of lead in sheets, but in these halls the ceilings are faced with mosaics studded in. (Le Strange's translation. Palestine Pilgrims Text Society, 1886.)

From the foregoing description it must be evident that few, if any, traces are to be found of this earlier mosque amongst the comparatively modern buildings occupying the south end of the Haram, and perhaps the only fragment of a monument of the period of Latin occupation is the hitherto unnoticed west end of a church, which may be the one dedicated at Easter 1136 by the Cardinal legate Alberic, Bishop of Ostia, in the presence of Guillaume, Patriarch of Jerusalem, and numerous chevaliers, on this site. The Order of the Temple had been founded in 1128; John of Wurzburg speaks of the magnificent buildings and of a church in course of erection in 1170. How these buildings, comprising a royal palace and the military convent of knights, could have been arranged on such a site is for the present an unsolved mystery. All that we can know, from such trifling explorations of the buildings at the south end of the Haram as different Palestine Societies have been permitted to carry out, is that nothing which can be identified with the royal hall of a mediæval palace or with the usual conventual buildings of a monastery can now be traced on the site.

The mosque of El Aksa, as rebuilt by the Memluk Sultans of the fourteenth century, may perhaps be an attempt to reproduce the older mosque (possibly unconsciously) as described by Mukaddasi at the beginning of the eleventh century.

The vanished church of the "Presentation."—According to generally received traditions and such scanty history as is available the Acropolis of the Temple was found covered with ruins and debris at the time of the Moslem conquest in 637. A church of St Mary is mentioned as existing near by, or on the site, but whether this was the church of the "Presentation" built by Justinian in the middle of the sixth century (about seventy-five years previously) is not very clear. It is very singular that a building of so very much architectural importance as we may suppose one of Justinian's erections to have been—and as it is also described by the magniloquent Procopius—should have attracted so little consideration at the time of the Moslem seizure of the site, and should have so completely disappeared. Procopius states that the church of the "Presentation" was built partly on the rock, and partly in the air, as the eastern and southern sides of its emplacement were insufficient for the plan proposed. This would of course agree very well with the idea of its having occupied a position at right angles to the nave and aisles of the present mosque of El Aksa. The flank or south side of the church would stand on the vaults of "Solomon's Stables," and the sanctuary towards the east would have stood over a spot now known as the "Cradle of Jesus." The remains of a small

Crusaders' church of the twelfth century *in situ*, built up into the east side of the mosque, possibly represent the recovery of the traditional site of the more ancient church (*vide supra*).

The vast substructures of the Aksa have never been very fully explored. If the foundations of the "Presentation" church remain amongst the vaulted corridors of "Solomon's Stables," they perhaps account for the filling in of certain parts of these chambers with masonry. In this case the church would have occupied a most prominent position overlooking the valley of Jehoshaphat, and possibly the curious double gate below would have formed a stairway approach to its west door; the whole of the Christian church being outside the area of the present mosque in the open space at the south-east corner of the Haram, where Abdelmelek is said to have cleared away the ancient ruins "on the eastern side."

The much rebuilt mosque of El Aksa survived, in possibly a ruined condition, into the days of the Latin kingdom, and its remains immersed in the new buildings of the Templar Convent are mentioned by the pilgrim Theodoric.

The Order of the Temple, an essentially military organisation, was recognised by Pope Honorius II in 1128. It seems to have constituted a sort of bodyguard to the kings of Jerusalem, and hence it took its name from the "Templum Solomonis" or "Palatium," in part of the buildings of which palace it was installed by Baldwin II in 1131. To accommodate this important body of monastic soldiers the buildings must have been sufficiently imposing, and so they are described by the pilgrim Theodoric in 1172. He mentions the main hall of the convent as resembling a church with a central dome, and the appearance of a rounded sanctuary or apse at the end. But this building was not used as a church—it was doubtless the Moslem mosque of the Aksa, and may have been in ruins at that time. On the western side of this old building the knights were erecting in 1172 "a new church of wonderful size and workmanship," possibly the church above described as surviving in a fragment built into the walls of the modern Aksa. "Also on the western side of the palace the Templars have erected a new building with its cellars, refectories, staircases, and a roof rising with a high pitch, unlike the flat roofs of that country." Moreover they were building a new cloister in addition to the old one existing in another part of the premises.

The "Stables of Solomon" (so named even in the twelfth century) were a remarkable feature of the Crusading fortress of the period, and probably the triple gate entrance to them was an arrangement made by the knights for their cavalry horses to pass through.

The "Frères de la milice du Temple" came into existence ten years before the official recognition of the Order by Honorius II at the Council of Troyes in Champagne in 1128. The Rule was composed by St Bernard of Clairvaux, who had so much to do with the earlier crusades. The Grand Masters are usually catalogued as follows:—

1118.	Hugh de Payens.	1168.	Philip de Milly.
1136.	Robert de Craon.	1171.	Odo de S. Amand.
1147.	Everard de Barres.	1179.	Armand de Toroge.
1149.	Bernard de Tremelay.	1184.	Thierry.
1158.	Bertrand de Blanchfort.		

THE CHURCHES IN THE JEWISH QUARTER (ADJOINING THE HARAM)

The "Juiverie" of the crusading period in Jerusalem history was the north-east quarter of the city, which, in more recent times, has become exclusively Moslem. The modern Jewish quarter extends over the west side of the town, between the great Armenian convent and the Haram enclosure. Within this latter district almost all traces of churches once existing have entirely disappeared. St Giles in the Tyropœan, St Marie des Allemands, St Peter, and St Martin are mere names in ancient records.

St Thomas is a small church of no architectural character, close to the Armenian property, which has been abandoned to ruin, apparently for centuries. Some attempt to restore it about 1850 seems to have failed, and whether for Christian or Moslem use is not very apparent. There would seem to be some legend current about treasure buried within the ruin, which may account for its appearance of "being in Chancery." Not mentioned by De Vogüé.

Not far from the ruin of St Thomas, and adjoining the old

Anglo-German "Christ Church," is a very complete little Crusaders' church, dedicated to *St James the Less*. It only measures 10 m. by 6 m., and is covered with a barrel vault, and possesses a sort of choir recess with an apse. It is entirely without architectural character, but has an appearance of belonging to a later period than the twelfth century. De Vogüé states that in his time it was owned by the Syrians, but at the present day it is occasionally used as a stable or sheepfold by its Moslem owner. Like many of the small chapels of Jerusalem —even those built by the Crusaders—it possesses but small interest, historical or artistic.

The adjacent *English church*, now belonging to the London Jews' Society, was originally built for the use of the Anglo-German Missionary Societies, and as the Cathedral of the Anglo-German Bishops of Jerusalem during the latter part of the nineteenth century. Since the abolition of the Anglo-German arrangement, which came to an end about forty years ago, the little church has ceased to be used for the latter purpose. This insignificant building has a certain interest as representing the taste of the period—of a very characteristic English kind—and on account of its having been erected under considerable difficulties. It was designed by a young English architect named Hillyer, who died during the progress of the work in 1845, and was buried on Mount Sion. A clerk of works named Crutchlow, who was assisting Mr Hillyer in Jerusalem, carried on the building, which was finished and consecrated in 1846. The foundations are said to go down to a depth greater than the height of the building, through the enormous collection of rubbish and débris on which modern Jerusalem is built. The design of the little church hardly calls for remark, but every English visitor is vividly reminded of his native land at the sight of this familiar "carpenter's Gothic" chapel of the early Victorian era.

The *House of St Mark* is the residence of the Syriac Bishop in Jerusalem, and is the traditional scene of St Peter's visit after his miraculous release from prison. The church is of twelfth-century type, but built, like most of these smaller shrines, in so plain and unarchitectural a manner as to be difficult of identification. The main entrance to the building is also in the ancient style, but, although ancient in general appearance, such a building may be but another example of the small native church imitating the older models of the crusading epoch.

Here it may be interesting to note that the native Christians of the Levant had, until quite the middle of the nineteenth century, the custom of building their small unpretentious churches in a very fair traditional style of mason craft based on the surviving remains of the crusading epoch. It is often difficult to be sure of the century when some village church of Syria or Cyprus was actually built. An illiterate peasantry can hardly be expected to leave inscriptions or dates on monumental buildings although evincing a certain amount of artistic feeling in their erection.

The Hospital.—Within recent years the traces of this famous institution have been growing fainter, and some of the last surviving of its long pointed-barrel vaults have been pulled down by the German Lutherans who occupy the eastern half of the site to enlarge their premises.

The Order of St John, founded in 1048 by the Amalfitans, occupied a vast enclosure situated in the centre of Jerusalem, on the south side of the Holy Sepulchre, and bounded on all sides by rows of bazaar shops, above which the buildings were carried as a second story. This enclosed area is almost a square, formed by the Rue du Patriarche on the west, the Rue David on the south, the Rue des Palmiers on the north, and on the east the still unchanged covered bazaar. There was also a narrow lane called "Ruelle," which penetrated this enclosure on the south, also full of small shops. De Vogüé supposes this area to have been filled with numerous cloistered courtyards in the style of Eastern *khans*, in two stories, and in some accounts no less than 180 marble columns are mentioned. These structures were completely ruined at the fall of the Latin domination in the Holy City, but according to Medji-ed-Din, writing in 1495, it was within this enclosure that Saladin took up his abode in 1187, and hence it was afterwards known to the Moslems as the "Hospital of Saladin." Another tradition survives that Saladin here instituted a mad-house for the district—*Muristan* in Arabic—but this may be but a term of derision under the circumstances, like the name of "rubbish heap" applied to the Church of the Holy Sepulchre.

For 300 years the ruins of the "Hospital" afforded shelter to the pilgrims of the Middle Ages. Felix Faber lodged there in 1483. But by the eighteenth century the area had become a mere piece of waste ground in the middle of the city, with unsightly heaps of rubbish and filth, surrounded by tottering walls. The site remained in this condition until the middle of the nineteenth century, when its eastern half was presented, for some unexplained reason, to the then Crown Prince of Prussia, afterwards Emperor Frederick of Germany. The remainder of the land continued unoccupied until the beginning of the present century. It was then taken over by the Greek Convent of the Holy Sepulchre, and turned into a speculative building estate, forming a bazaar of several streets of one and two storied houses, chiefly used as shops for small Jew traders. In the centre of this singularly hideous modern quarter of the Holy City is a strange attempt at a fountain built up of ancient remains found on the site.

The large ruined church situated at the north-east corner of the Muristan, the remains of which are now built up into a supposed "restoration" of the edifice, with the name of the "Lutheran Church of the Redeemer," was known in recent ages as "Santa Maria Maggiore." In reality this church was the re-building of the famous *Sancta Maria Latina*, which had formerly stood on the space of the present *parvis* in front of the Church of the Holy Sepulchre, and as such it is shown on the mediæval plans of Jerusalem under its proper name. This church consequently belonged in date to about the middle of the twelfth century. It consisted of the usual three aisles, each ending in a semicircular apse, and divided from each other by nave arcades of five bays. On the north side was a large porch-like doorway, with a grand and richly decorated semicircular arch, forming a canopy over a double entrance constructed with two small semi-circular arches resting on a *trumeau*. The tympanum of this porch gateway was originally filled with elaborate sculptures, and the outer arch was carved with Zodiac signs in the style of the Provençal churches.

In 1890 the greater part of the lower walls, the nave arcade bases, and almost the whole of the north door of the ancient church remained intact, but within two or three years afterwards the German Lutherans had decided to build their new church on the site, and in so doing the ancient remains were completely pulled down. A clumsy reproduction of the ancient porch was attempted, but the few fragments of sculpture inserted in the new building have a tasteless and ridiculous appearance under the circumstances. In destroying the ruins of this church, the Germans removed one of the most interesting of the long series of shattered landmarks of the great crusading era. De Vogüé gives an excellent drawing of the ruined porch gateway as it appeared in 1860, and as it continued to exist until 1890; in those days the greater part of the Zodiac had disappeared, and only the figures of August and September could be clearly discerned.

The Church of Santa Maria Maggiore is mentioned by the later pilgrims, and in the *Citez de Jherusalem* it is described:—

Au chef des eschoppes (des orfèvres latins) avoit une abaie des nonnains que on apeloit Sainte Marie la Grant.

The convent of Sancta Maria Latina in its later form as Santa Maria Maggiore was perhaps rebuilt and reorganised under the rule of a certain dame Agnes, about 1140, at the time of the great revival or reinstitution of the Order of St John by Raymond du Puy.

The remains of the cloister and its surrounding buildings which adjoined the church on its south side are still preserved to some extent within the modern buildings connected with the Lutheran establishment. The cloister, surrounding a small garth, was of plain and unornamented pointed arches carried on columns with very simple capitals. A large vaulted chamber on the south side of the cloister, which may possibly have been the conventual dormitory, was long used as a Lutheran place of worship, until the building of the modern Church of the Redeemer. All the buildings of this convent, excepting its church, appear to have been of a plain utilitarian character [*vide* fig. 38].

In its original foundation as the successor of the Benedictine Abbey of Sancta Maria ad Latinos, this twelfth-century church and convent of Santa Maria Maggiore would seem to have become the female Hospice of St John's Order. It was divided

by a "ruelle," or narrow lane, from the greater general Hospice
of the Order on the western portion of the Muristan area.

Many revolutions in the general conditions of the western
portion of the Muristan have taken place since the days of

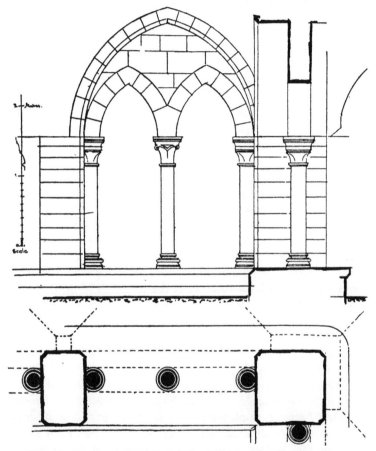

Fig. 38.   Fragment remaining of the Cloister of Sta Maria Latina.

Saladin and of the mediæval pilgrims, and now its very name
has disappeared, and every trace of the "Hospital" has been
clean swept away in the course of covering the site with a
fantastic modern bazaar. A relic of former times, but without
any architectural character to afford identification, has been

permitted to remain at the south-west corner. This is the comparatively modern Orthodox Church of St John the Baptist, with the unusual feature of a large crypt beneath it. This building has been carefully drawn and described by Mr Archibald Dickie in the *Journal R.I.B.A.* for March 6, 1899. In the opinion of the present writer, whatever this edifice may represent or reproduce, it is certainly in itself of no great antiquity. The upper portion of the church is entirely modern (nineteenth century), and the singular undercroft is apparently of the same date, but constructed of old stones—a mere basement to the upper story.

On the north side of the Muristan enclosure, and forming the south side of the *parvis* of the Holy Sepulchre, are two small properties without any special history. The small convent (Orthodox) of Gethsemane is probably a creation of the Turkish period, unless it reproduces a mediæval convent of St Mary the Less, of which there are some documentary evidences and traditions as to existence in this position. The second of these properties is a small mosque which must have been built shortly after the Moslem occupation of Jerusalem in 1244. It has a high minaret, its only architectural feature, rebuilt after an earthquake in 1455. This minaret is curious as having been evidently built, together with the minaret of the Khankah Mosque on the opposite side of the Holy Sepulchre Church, with the intention of serving the purpose of a point of vantage for controlling the unruly crowd of Christians down below by the armed Zaptiehs and Turkish soldiers of former times. This little mosque is known by the name of the "Omeriyia," or Mosque of Omar, and reproduces the original mosque, built by the Khalif in the portico of the Basilica of the Holy Sepulchre after the famous meeting between Sophronius and Omar in 637. The original mosque having disappeared along with the Basilica and its portico, the Moslems, on regaining possession of Jerusalem, having a mere tradition that such a mosque stood formerly in front of the famous church, decided that they must rebuild it in the same relative position, oblivious of the fact that the principal entrance to the Holy Sepulchre was no longer on the east but on the south side.

This little mosque is also called Ed Derkah, and is said by

De Vogüé to have been built by Chebab-ed-Din in 1216, on the site of the original church of the Order. There does not, however, appear to be much more evidence for this latter statement. A few years ago this little mosque having been practically re-built once more, excepting the minaret, a new entrance of a very ornamental description was then added on the west side. During the progress of these works the present writer inspected the lower floor of the mosque, which consists of the wide span pointed vaults built side by side which are always found in Crusaders' buildings. There seemed nothing of any kind which would suggest the presence of any church upon such a site.

Some idea of the importance and magnitude of the Hospital buildings at one time occupying the centre of Jerusalem may be gained in the following abridgment from the Abbé de Vertot's *History of the Knights of Malta*, English version, London, 1728:—

In the eleventh century some Italian merchants undertook to procure an asylum for the European pilgrims in the very city of Jerusalem, where they might have nothing to fear either from the false zeal of the Mohammedans, or the enmity and aversion of the schismatical Greeks....

The governor assigned them a piece of ground, on which they built a chapel and dedicated it to the Blessed Virgin, by the name of St Mary "ad Latinos," to distinguish it from the churches where Divine service was celebrated according to the Greek ritual; some monks of the Benedictine Order officiated in it. Near their convent they built two houses of entertainment for the reception of pilgrims of both sexes, whether in health or sickness, which was the chief view in this foundation; and each house had afterwards a chapel in it, the one dedicated to St John the Almoner, and the other to St Mary Magdalene. This holy house, governed by the Benedictine monks, and which may be looked upon as the cradle of the Order of St John, served afterwards as a place of security and a retreat for pilgrims.

On the 7th June, 1099, the European army of the Crusaders appeared before the walls of Jerusalem, and commenced the famous siege.

The governor of the city shut up the Christians he suspected in different prisons, and among the rest the administrator of the

Hospital of St John. He was a Frenchman and named Gerard, born, as some historians relate, in the island of Martigues in Provence. He had devoted himself long before to the service of the pilgrims, at the same time that Agnes, a Roman lady of illustrious birth, governed the house appointed for the reception of persons of her sex. All pilgrims were admitted into the Hospital of St John, without distinction of Greek and Latin; the very infidels received alms there; and the inhabitants in general, of whatsoever religion they were, looked upon the administrator of the Hospital as the common father of the poor of the city.

After the siege and capture of Jerusalem, the Prince Godfrey visited the Hospital and

was received there by the pious Gerard, and the other administrators of the same fraternity; and there he found a great number of the soldiers of the crusade, who had been wounded in the siege, and carried thither after the taking of the place.

In 1118 the Hospitallers lost the blessed Gerard, the father of the poor and pilgrims. That virtuous man, after having arrived at an exceeding old age, expired in the arms of his brethren almost without any sickness, and fell as we may say like a fruit ripe for eternity. The Hospitallers assembled after his death to choose him a successor pursuant to the bull of Pope Paschal II. There was no division upon the point; all their votes united in favour of brother Raymond Dupuy, a gentleman of Dauphiny.

About the same date (1118) was instituted the Order of the Temple by Hugh de Payens, Geoffrey de St Aldemar, and other gentlemen, all Frenchmen, who formed among them a little society to guard and conduct pilgrims to the Holy City. Brompton, the historian, a contemporary, states that in his time these gentlemen were supposed to be pupils of the Hospitallers, and to have subsisted several years only by relief from them. They retired into a house near the Temple, which occasioned their having afterwards the name of Templars, or Knights of the Temple.

The sudden rise of the two great military religious Orders into the greatest influence and power within the newly instituted Latin kingdom of the Levant was only to be expected under the circumstances; and as a consequence their rivalry and quarrels with the secular clergy might have equally been anticipated. The Templars were eventually crushed by their enemies in Church and State, but the older Order of the Hospital braved and survived many a violent struggle with their ecclesiastical brethren. One of these unseemly conflicts between Christians, which took place in 1154, during the presidency of the first Grand Master, has a bearing upon the architectural history of Jerusalem. After referring to the contentions between the Order and the secular priests, the Abbé Vertot says:—

Besides these general grievances, Foulcher, the Patriarch, complained of one particular relating to himself, viz. that the Hospitallers, whose church and house stood near the Church of the Holy Sepulchre, had erected more magnificent buildings than his own church and palace. The complaints were bitter on both sides, the one founded their claim on common right, the others pleaded their privileges in bar of that right. Invectives and abusive language succeeded reciprocal complaints; and, what is not to be mentioned without concern, they proceeded at last to acts of violence. 'Tis said that arrows were shot from the quarter of the Hospitallers against the priests of the Patriarch. Those ecclesiastics did not return force for force; but out of a more refined sort of vengeance they gathered up these arrows, tied them in a bundle, and, to preserve the memory of so odious an outrage, fixed them up at the entrance of the Church of Calvary. William, Archbishop of Tyre, relates this fact as an eye-witness; he adds, that the cause of these dissensions ought to be laid upon the Popes, who had exempted these military friars from the episcopal jurisdiction.

These unhappy quarrels led to embassies being sent to Rome by both sides, and to further recriminations on either part, the Hospitallers being accused, amongst other things, of ringing the bells of their church whilst the Patriarch was preaching to the people, on purpose to hinder his being heard. From all this it would appear that the church and buildings of the Hospital were of considerable importance in the middle of the twelfth century—buildings of which hardly a trace can be considered to survive at the present day.

Thirty-seven years after the consecration of the Church of the Holy Sepulchre, amidst these jealousies and heartburnings,

Jerusalem was again in the hands of the Moslems. During the period between this event and the cession of the Holy City to Frederick II in 1229, came into existence the famous Teutonic Order of St Mary of Jerusalem. The German Emperors Frederick I and Frederick II were the originators of Teuton enterprise in the Levant, and as such they seem to have come into collision with the more purely Latin interests. Frederick II was an implacable enemy of both the older Orders of Knights. He was denounced in the Papal briefs as the ally of Saracens and Infidels, and as the destroyer of the hospitals and other properties of the Christian religious Orders.

These allegations against the great Emperor Frederick—the man so much in advance of his time—were doubtless dictated to a great extent by the political rancour of the "Guelphs" against the "Ghibellines"; at the same time it is not improbable that amongst the properties which he is accused of destroying, the vast building of the Hospital in Jerusalem may have suffered, whilst the great tower he is supposed to have built on the opposite side of the *parvis* of the Holy Sepulchre was in course of construction. The tentative occupation of Jerusalem by the Christians towards the middle of the thirteenth century was, however, a mere farce, and we have few indications on record of the condition of the city during the period of about fifteen years. Our only conclusions are that the secular clergy took advantage of German, or "Ghibelline," protection to assert their importance in new buildings at the Holy Sepulchre, whilst their rivals, the military friars, who represented the "Guelph" interest, were proportionately repressed.

Christianis odium exhibuit manifestum ad exterminandas domus hospitalis et fratrum militiæ templi, per quas reliquiæ Terræ Sanctæ hactenus sunt observatæ. (Mat. Paris. ann. 1228.)

Elsewhere than in the Holy Land the Order of St John seems to have flourished during these last years of the kingdom of Jerusalem. Their "Commanderies" were established in all the countries of the West, and the fate of the female branch—the Convent of St Mary the Great or the Less—seems to be identified with the foundation of the nunnery of Sixenne, a village situated between Saragossa and Lerida in the kingdom of Arragon.

This royal convent was founded for sixty ladies of noble birth, who were to be admitted without any portion; and such as were of the kingdom of Arragon and Catalonia were to be of an extraction so illustrious and so publickly known, that they should have no need to produce their proofs. Their habit was a robe of scarlet or red cloth with a black mantle *à bec*, upon which was the white cross of eight points directly upon the heart; they had a particular breviary: they wore at church rochets of fine linen, and in memory of the queen, their foundress, they held a silver sceptre in their hands during the office and Divine service. (De Vertot, vol. i. p. 94.)

Small Monasteries surrounding the Holy Sepulchre.—The Convent of Abraham, which may be considered to communicate with the Church of the Holy Sepulchre, is a mass of small chambers and inconvenient staircases of a poor, squalid description, and without any particular interest. The chapels of Abraham and of the Apostles, within the monastery, have already been referred to in speaking of the Holy Sepulchre Church.

The new Russian Hospice and Church of St Constantine and their precious archæological contents belong to the description of the Martyrion (*vide* p. 56).

The Abyssinian village of mud huts, occupying the ancient cloisters of the Augustinian Convent, is naturally more curious than anything else, and the Coptic buildings are modern and entirely without interest beyond the fact of their preserving the former arrangements of historical buildings which once occupied the site.

These properties, mostly of a very squalid and deplorable appearance, are souvenirs of a former age, when every possible coign of vantage was secured by strenuously contending sects of Christians in defiance and in emulation of each other. The names of some of these small monasteries have changed at different periods, and there would seem to have been at one time a small monastery dedicated to the Trinity which occupied the south-western corner of the precincts.

St Anne's

The present church, which is certainly one of the best preserved of the Crusaders' buildings, in spite of a very complete
restoration, is supposed to occupy the site of a much older
building, of which, however, no actual records survive beyond
the cave chapels, forming a kind of crypt of a rock-cut kind.[1]

The history of the present building begins with the year 1104,
when the site on which it stands was secured for the purpose by
Arda, the repudiated wife of Baldwin I. The unfortunate queen
here established a convent of Benedictine nuns, amongst whom
she secured for herself a retreat. We hear of this convent again
as serving for the home of another princess in 1130, when
Judith, daughter of Baldwin II, here took the veil and remained
an inmate, whilst the Abbey of Bethany was being prepared for
her reception by her sister, Queen Milicent. The only name of
an Abbess of St Anne's which survives is that of Sebilla (1157).[2]

After the occupation of Jerusalem by the Moslems in 1187,
the property of the former Benedictine nunnery was appropriated
to the use of a Moslem "medresse," or school attached to the
great mosque of the adjoining enclosure. A long Arabic inscription recording this fact is inserted in the tympanum of the west
doorway of the church. Bohaeddin, the secretary and biographer
of Salah-ed-din, was its first principal. Together with the building of the Abbey, the numerous shops within the covered
bazaars of the city, which still bear on their walls in many places
the name "Sancta Anna" in Gothic lettering, were handed over
to this new foundation. In later times the institution seems to
have decayed, and all the buildings within the convent precincts,
with the exception of the church, became mere ruins. An
attempt at restoration was made by the Turks in 1842, but
eventually the whole property was abandoned and handed over
to Napoleon III in 1856, after being first offered to Lord
Palmerston as a "backshish" at the conclusion of the Crimean
War.

On the French Government becoming the owners of the *ci-
devant* Moslem school, a clearance of the ruins seems to have

---

[1] *Vide* Quaresmius, vol. ii. p. 103.
[2] Pauli, *Cod. Dip.* i. 204.

been immediately effected, and the ancient church, which was in a remarkable state of preservation, was taken in hand by a M. Mauss, "Architecte Coloniale du Gouvernement." M. Mauss was an intelligent and sympathetic worker in the then enthusiastically studied Gothic style, and the restoration of the church could hardly have been entrusted to better hands at that period.

De Vogüé, who was in Jerusalem in 1860, on the eve of this restoration by M. Mauss, seems to have been apprehensive (perhaps justifiably) of the result, and says: "Nous l'aimons mieux pauvre et délabrée, que défigurée," a sentiment worthy of the Society for Protecting Ancient Buildings of the present day. The result has, however, been much better than might have been anticipated, as far as the restoration of 1860 is concerned.

The church, of a cruciform construction, but square in plan, consists of a nave and side aisles, all three terminating in semi-circular apses with a transept, one bay removed from the east wall, over which rises a central dome, the transept and nave vaults being equal in height, and the clerestory occupying the usual position in nave and transept. This type of church seems to have been a common one during the twelfth century; in Jerusalem the Cœnaculum Church seems to have been on the same plan, as was also that of La Madeleine, and very possibly the great Church of St John at Sebaste may have been an enlarged copy of the same plan and construction, although De Vogüé throws some doubt on the presence of a dome.

The architectural details of St Anne's, which are almost entirely confined to the interior, are of the simplest. Pointed arches of square section form the nave arcades and the secondary arches of the barrel vaults, and the only attempt at sculpture or mouldings about the building is confined to the corbels carrying the vaulting and to the capitals of the half-round pier shafts. The vaulting is absolutely plain cross-vaulting without ribs. The general effect of the interior is both imposing and elegant, in spite of its almost meagre simplicity—a simplicity supposed by De Vogüé to be derived from the influence of St Bernard, whose interest in Jerusalem at the time when St Anne's was being built is evinced by his correspondence with Queen Milicent. The Cistercian Abbey of Boschaud in the diocese of

Périgueux (1154) is singularly like St Anne's both in design and detail.

St Anne's may be considered almost as the type of all the genuinely French Gothic churches of Palestine during the twelfth century, and a very good example of the style. That it should become once more the property of the French nation is highly appropriate under the circumstances, and its restoration in the 'sixties of last century was most fortunate. At the present day French architecture in Jerusalem seems

Fig. 39. Capital from St Sepulchre now preserved at St Anne's.

to be at a deplorable ebb, as may be seen by such buildings as St Stephen's or the Hospice of Notre Dame. The same degraded taste has even penetrated the severe and beautiful interior of St Anne's in the form of a miserably designed baldachino over the high altar. This disfigurement to the building was erected in 1895, otherwise the interior seems not to have been touched since the time of M. Mauss.

Fig. 40. Niche of unknown use, now in the garden of St Anne's, removed from the Church of St Sepulchre.

Until the occupation of the property by the French a curious "Holy Site" of early and mediæval interest appears to have been lost sight of. This is the "Piscina Probatica," or Pool of Bethesda. It is an oblong cistern of great depth, which has at one time been covered with a small chapel about 4 by 6 metres in dimension, having a semicircular apse at the east end. The remains of the chapel may be traced in the course of the apse and in the side walls, but nothing of an architectural character survives except some faint traces of a fresco on the west wall. Neither date nor history of this small building seems to have been recovered at the present day.

A curious fancy possessed the pilgrims of the last few centuries that a subterranean passage led at one time down from the Church of St Anne within the walls to the underground Church of the Virgin's Tomb in the Valley of Jehoshaphat. Such an idea originated in the fact of certain blocked-up excavations underneath the Church of St Anne being but partly known. These subterranean chambers have been fully cleared out recently and fitted up as modern "Holy Sites," with different names. In the course of these explorations some traces of a Roman house upon the site have come to light.

The Churches of the Via Dolorosa and of the Moslem Quarter

In 1860 De Vogüé was able to make an interesting series, in his *Églises de la Terre Sainte*, of the small churches of this district, one or two of which no longer exist as he saw them. The church of *St Mary Magdalene* has entirely disappeared, a modern Moslem school occupying its site. In De Vogüé's time the apse and the western end, which were of imposing proportions, remained; and a mediæval legend identified the ruins with the house of Simon the Leper. The neighbouring chapel of the *Nativity of the Virgin*, a small shrine, measuring only 3·25 m. by 5·0 m., was intact in 1860; it has since been completely rebuilt.

Another small chapel, a mere square chamber covered with a pointed dome, but apparently of mediæval construction, is described by De Vogüé as within the Turkish barracks. In the time of Quaresmius this little building was in use as the kitchen of the soldiers; it appears to have been originally dedicated to the *Crowning with Thorns*, a dedication afterwards removed to a chapel within the Church of the Holy Sepulchre, and now once more removed back to a site on the north side of the Via Dolorosa.

On either side of the Via Dolorosa were formerly remains of chapels called the *Pretorium* and the *Flagellation*. The first of these has been completely lost to sight; the second was used until 1838 as a stable for the Pasha's horses, it was then sold to Duke Maximilian of Bavaria together with some neighbouring property, and now serves as a succursale to "Casa Nova." The chapel, which may be a rebuilding of a more ancient structure, is in the poor and vulgar taste of the period. Within the same compound is another small chapel (which has been identified under the name of the "Imposition of the Cross") recently built on the foundations of a mediæval building in a very skilful and tasteful manner, and at a considerable expenditure. The square vaulted interior, with a small central dome, is supported by four monoliths of Bethlehem red stone, and the whole interior is curiously and successfully decorated with stones of local origin and of the most varied colours. The architect is a certain Herr Wenderlin, who has resided for some years past in the Holy Land.

St Peter.—On the height of the Moslem quarter stands a mosque with its minaret, which is in reality a very well-preserved twelfth-century church of the smaller variety. From the extreme plainness of its construction and its good preservation, it has been supposed to be of even a later date than the crusading kingdom, but it closely resembles the smaller of the two churches within the Armenian convent, and the identification by De Vogüé under the name of St Peter is probably correct. From an architectural point of view it possesses but little interest, due to the absence of any carved or moulded detail. It is enclosed within a mass of poor tenement houses—as when De Vogüé saw it in 1860—which prevents any inspection of its outside.

The mere "Stations" of the Via Dolorosa have varied with the lapse of years since it was first instituted. One or two modern churches have been built to enshrine such points as a portion of the "Ecce Homo" arch, the "Porta Judiciaria," etc. The church of the *Ecce Homo* is an elegant little structure in the sober but indefinite style adopted by some French architects of the middle nineteenth century. It was designed by M. Honoré Daumet and was completed in 1875. One of the two lateral passage-ways of the old triumphal arch, which for so many centuries has stood at this point as a famous landmark of the

Holy City, has been ingeniously made to serve as the niche-like east end, containing the high altar of the church.

The old Roman or Byzantine triumphal arch which has thus been used up in the modern church is a singular and unidentified monument of some event in the history of Jerusalem, the memory of which is completely lost. It has been suggested that the famous triumph of Heraclius on his return from the Persian War, bearing the relic of the True Cross, may here be commemorated. The architectural style of the arch is of such a very ordinary and common Roman description that it might belong equally well to any period of the Empire. The high central opening through which the Via Dolorosa passes is now covered by a mere arch reduced to the inner ring of voussoirs, above which has been built a small chamber (shown in the oldest representations). The southern of the three openings has disappeared within the construction of a squalid-looking property at the side of the road which apparently forms part of a convent of Dervishes, and, although the northern of these two passageways is well preserved within the Church of the "Sœurs de Sion," its history is still further obscured by an inscription seeking to identify the relic with some part of the Gospel story, for which there is, of course, no kind of foundation.

In seeking to identify this monument with some historical event in Jerusalem history, it must be borne in mind that such structures do not necessarily commemorate the triumphal progress of an emperor. In the present case the general appearance of the relic suggests the third or fourth century. The remains are too much mutilated to allow of an exact realisation of its original design, which may have been of a somewhat plain description without the usual side columns.

One or two smaller shrines, such as the *House of St Veronica*, whatever their history has been, have passed through such vicissitudes since the Middle Ages, and are now so modernised as to be entirely without interest of an, archæological kind. About midway between the "House of St Veronica" and the "Sœurs de Sion," at a point where the Via Dolorosa makes a sharp turn, is a large modern church built by the Catholic Armenians. It is a building with certain pretensions to architecture which have not been realised in its completion.

THE CHURCHES ON THE NORTHERN SIDE OF THE CITY,
WITHIN THE WALLS

Around the "New Gate," an entrance into the city made
about 1880, are grouped the principal modern Latin or Roman
Catholic buildings of Jerusalem. The large Latin Patriarchate
was built about 1850, and its chapel is a curious monument of
the "Strawberry Hill" Gothic of that period. To give an idea of
its general appearance, one need only say that its windows appear
to be filled with cast-iron tracery painted white, and its vaulted
ceiling is painted with nondescript angels seated on clouds.

The great Franciscan Convent of St Salvador, with its
attached hospices and innumerable dependencies, is, as its
popular name of "Casa Nova" implies, a creation of modern
days. The Franciscans were compelled to abandon their ancient
home on Mount Sion at the beginning of the sixteenth century,
but the church and buildings of "Casa Nova" are evidently not
earlier than the end of the eighteenth century (date on principal
door of church), and it is perhaps singular that no traces of any
earlier building remain about the site, although the property is
said to have been purchased from the Georgians in 1561.

The church dedicated to St John the Divine is a large three-
aisled building of common pseudo-Classic design, gaudily
decorated in the old-fashioned Italian manner with scagliola
and gilding. The whole building, with its very uninteresting
interior, looks quite modern, or a very complete "restoration"
of about 1860. The only curious thing about this church is that
it is built above a high range of vaulted apartments, used as
cellars and offices, so that the visitor has to ascend to the upper
level by an important staircase. This peculiarity, which does
not seem accounted for by the nature of the site, may perhaps
be intended to recall the "Upper Chamber" of the Cœnaculum,
from which the Franciscans were ejected in 1549.

The vast premises belonging to the Franciscans have an air
of modernity, and amongst the busy workshops and educational
institutions of the community it would be vain to look for much
of an archæological character.

The north-west quarter of the city has doubtless always been,
more or less in successive ages, the home of the different

Christian sects which have been allowed to form settlements within the walls. Here the Greek Orthodox may have established their small monasteries at a remote period, naturally selecting the corner of the city nearest the Holy Sepulchre, and farthest away from their doubtful friends and fellow-citizens—the Moslems. There are about twenty small monasteries and hospices belonging to the Orthodox Church within the area of this quarter of Jerusalem, and some of these institutions probably date back to a considerable antiquity.

The small Orthodox monastery, often inhabited by a solitary monk (a true *monachus*) or hermit, is often intended to serve the purpose of a hospice for pilgrims, and in the case of a majority of these institutions in Jerusalem they were built solely for this purpose. Most of them contain chapels or oratories, and although divided up into so many different small properties—mere small private houses to all intents and purposes—they are to some extent under the general management of the Patriarchate. Little if any interest attaches to any of them. They are without any architectural character, and have evidently been built or rebuilt—without exception—within comparatively recent years. Even the residence of the Patriarch, which is surrounded by these small monasteries, contains no feature which could be deemed characteristic or of any historical interest. The private chapel of the Patriarchate, dedicated to St Constantine, is a small vaulted chamber decorated with a common modern iconostasis and perfectly uninteresting.

The artistic efforts of Eastern Christians during the past few centuries hardly call for criticism from a European standpoint. Such poor attempts to build or rebuild churches, which they may have been permitted to occupy after the final Moslem occupation of 1244, are on so small a scale and of so squalid a style as to be beneath notice. Even the furniture and icons of these little buildings impress the visitor with a sense of poverty, both physical and mental, which is really distressing. In hardly one of the native churches of Jerusalem is it possible to find anything which can be deemed a work of art in the ordinary acceptation of the word, or any historical monument of an interesting kind of a date subsequent to the few traces remaining of Crusaders' work of the twelfth century.

Although almost entirely without architectural character the small Orthodox "monastery" possesses a certain interest of its own. Within the contracted space which these buildings always occupy singular little communities have existed for untold ages and their obscure histories would in many cases be worth recording, if only materials were available. But alas! no such records of past history survive. The Greek Orthodox Church takes little interest in mediæval archæology or topography, in singular contrast with its Latin rival as regards such matters. Perhaps the Russian archæologists who now visit Jerusalem in increasing numbers will collect their scanty records before it is too late and publish them in the *Bulletin* of the Russian Palestine Society.

Wedged in between the great Franciscan Convent and a large school also belonging to the Franciscans, in the "haret" or lane of the Khankah mosque, are two small monasteries—one of St George, the other of the Archangel. Both buildings display inconspicuous fronts of rough stone to the narrow lane by which they are approached, and their walls are only pierced by a low arched doorway and a few small grated windows. Within St George's is a rather larger courtyard than is usual in these monasteries, and on its north side is a flight of steps leading up to the church, which like that of the neighbouring Franciscans is built on a high substructure, and to judge by its time-stained walls may be of some antiquity. Nothing of an artistic character about the buildings betrays any real clue to date. Within the church, which is of unusual cross-form, and with a central dome of considerable size, is a richly carved and gilded iconostasis of the usual eighteenth-century type. The Rood and side figures above this iconostasis appear of an older style, but as is usually the case in these churches, the paintings on the screen are so obscured by dirt and tawdry hangings that very little of them is visible. The interior of the monastery of the Archangel does not call for remark; its little church is quite modern or modernised and the courtyard is merely comfortably picturesque.

On the opposite or west side of the Franciscan Convent are two small monasteries—St Basil and St Theodore—both very small and with minute chapels of an oblong plan covered with barrel vaults. Both these monasteries have an ancient air about them, and to judge by fragments of mosaic flooring and other traces they may be mediæval in origin, but their ecclesiastical furniture is entirely modern.

Continuing down the same lane or "haret" of the Khankah mosque a group of three ancient "deirs" or monasteries is found on the left hand about midway between the Franciscans and the "site" of the "Porta Justiciaria" on the Via Dolorosa. They are named after St Catherine, B.V.M. (Sitte Mariam), and SS. John and Euthymius. They all possess traces of

Fig. 41. Deir H. Euthymius, Jerusalem. Interior.

antiquity but the last named is certainly the most picturesque, and its chapel has a venerable appearance, although there is

Fig. 42. Deir H. Euthymius, Jerusalem. Entrance.

nothing about it to afford a date with certainty. In a bastion of the neighbouring city wall is curiously niched a minute monastery or hermitage of modern days dedicated to the favourite St Spyridon —the city walls having been abandoned for defensive purposes long ago.

The Christian "deirs" which lie to the south of the Holy Sepulchre have all been completely rebuilt within the past few years, with a complete destruction of all antiquity and associations.

The Patriarchal "deir," or what is known as the "Greek Convent" where the Orthodox Patriarch resides, is a most curious rambling network of lanes constituting a kind of ghetto or village community within the city: most of its inhabitants are of course priests or monks filling various positions in the household of the Patriarch, or engaged in the mysterious occupation of guarding the Holy Sepulchre.

Some of the whitewashed buildings of the Patriarchate have a venerable appearance, and may indeed be of the Middle Ages, but nothing of an ornamental kind betrays any evidence of date. The principal church within the Patriarchate, dedicated to St Constantine, is quite modern.

A "haret" or lane divides the Patriarchate into two parts, and is perhaps the most picturesque of the Jerusalem highways. On either side project innumerable little bow-windows, whence the inmates of the house can see without being seen. At the bottom of the lane loom up in shadow the remains of the old Latin Patriarchate, a mediæval palace, with its massive buttresses and pointed arches, forming one of the most impressive street fronts to be found in any ancient city.

"Mar Metri," or the monastery of St Demetrius, is an ancient example of these "deirs," situated adjoining the Orthodox Patriarchate and in the lane between the

Fig. 43. Deir el Benat, Women's Hospice, Jerusalem.

Jaffa and New gates of the city. The only portion of the original monastery remaining is the fairly large church described and illustrated by plans in the *P.E.F.Q.S.*, 1900, p. 253 (Dr Schick). This is of some interest owing to its possessing the rather unusual feature of a solid wall occupying the position of the iconostasis, with four doorways in it; the sanctuary or *bema* is consequently a separate apartment from the nave. Orthodox churches in the Levant are frequently provided with a stone iconostasis, but they are not as a rule divided into separate chambers as in this case. The nave of the church is surmounted by a dome 15 feet wide, and owing to the accumulation of earth and débris on the outside of the building (a sign of antiquity in Eastern lands) the only light to the interior comes through the little windows in the drum supporting this dome. The appearance of such a semi-subterranean church is always venerable, even when there is little else to give a clue to date.

The monastery of the Panayia, or "Deir el Benat," as its name implies, is a hospice for women. Its plain stone exterior, with a low arched doorway on the street level, conveys an idea of exclusion befitting its use. Inside it seems to have been re-built and modernised in recent years.

The Churches of the Great Armenian Convent, or Quarters.—The history of this immense institution, the largest enclosure of a conventual kind in the city, is somewhat obscure. It is said to constitute property purchased by the Armenian community from the Georgians in the early part of the fifteenth century. The Georgians were at one time among the wealthiest and most influential of all the Christian sects in Jerusalem; but as the nation declined in its far-distant mountain home, so did also its representatives in the Holy City. The Greeks and Armenians gradually bought up all their convents and property.

The Georgians, or Iberians, were an obscure race inhabiting a region around the south-west corner of the Caspian Sea. They seem to have professed a Christianity very similar to that of the Armenians. They came into prominence as settlers in Jerusalem after the Latin dominion had come to an end, and for about a hundred years they occupied so important a position in the Holy City as to be appointed "Custodians of the keys of the Holy Sepulchre," according to the statement of Ludolph von Sudheim (1340).

At the present day Georgia is a country which has long since been absorbed into the Russian Empire, and its very name has ceased to be geographical.

It would be difficult to identify any of the buildings within the immense compound of the Armenian Convent as Georgian.

Some parts of these rambling premises may be as old as the fifteenth century, but the paucity of architectural detail precludes identification. The two churches—St James the Great and the House of Annas—are certainly mediæval in origin, and retain many portions of crusading building.

St James the Great.— This is a lofty three-aisled building with a central dome or cupola, and a women's gallery constructed in masonry at the west end. The central cupola is curiously constructed of intersecting arches carrying a lantern—in other words, the *construction* is not domical. Into the

Fig. 44. Deir H. Georgios, Jerusalem. View in courtyard.

walls and piers carrying the vaulting are inserted carved capitals of

the twelfth century, evidently re-used from some other building. The walls are covered with the beautiful blue and white faïence usually known as "Persian tiles," a style of mural decoration which dates from the sixteenth century, which is also probably the date of the rebuilding of the church. The flooring in richly coloured local marble and the magnificent screen-work of precious woods,

Fig. 45. Deir H. Georgios, Jerusalem. Chapel.

inlaid with ivory and madrepearl, are all also of this date. There is nothing special in the arrangements or decorations of the church to distinguish it from the usual Armenian style in which it has evidently been rebuilt, but on its south side is a large doorway leading into a vaulted side chapel or narthex, which appears to be of mediæval character. Its richly moulded arch, carried on twelfth-century nook shafts and capitals, is of quite a different style from the main church. This imposing doorway is, however, the only portion remaining from the original building, and it appears to be *in situ* although its position is singular. On the opposite side of the main church is a large vaulted hall or vestry with an altar on the usual platform of the Armenian ritual. This large chamber is especially rich in mural tile decorations of the very beautiful blue and white variety.

As already remarked, this church of the Armenians replaces an older building on the same site of the twelfth century, which must have probably resembled the type of St Saviour's, Beyrout, to judge by the large capitals of square piers with attached shafts which have been re-used in the same position, but on much loftier square piers, to support the vaulting over its three aisles.

The House of Annas, the High Priest.—This traditional site seems to date from the crusading epoch. There is nothing of an historical or early character attaching to the small convent, which has, however, a venerable and picturesque appearance, and one of the prettiest little churches in Jerusalem. Its charming interior of a well-proportioned nave, with shallow side aisles, supported on square piers carrying nave arcades and clerestory, is probably to a great extent modern rebuilding of the same date as the larger Armenian church, but the west door and spacious narthex are apparently mediæval. The characteristic blue-tile mural decoration is lavished on the interior.

This little convent is also known as the " Convent of the Olive Tree," and was used formerly as the female hospice of the Armenians.

In classifying this small Armenian church as a "crusading building" it must be remembered that ever since the twelfth century, when the genuine European Gothic style was introduced into the countries of the Levant, many of the smaller Christian churches of various Eastern sects have been built or rebuilt to meet the requirements of the period. But, as a rule such churches have been built in a style curiously like that of the first Frankish settlers in the land, although many centuries after their time. In this way also additions to genuine crusading monuments are sometimes so much like the original as to deceive even an expert. Certain of the well-known architectural features, such as the cushion-voussoir arch, the elbow-shaped corbel, etc., may be found in Moslem buildings imitated from the twelfth-century style, and naturally such church buildings as the Christians have been permitted to erect during the past centuries are even still more likely to present similar imitated features. The poverty and ignorance of native Christians under Moslem rule have prevented any effort at originality or development, and the idea of emulating the Renaissance or pseudo-Classic movement of Europe was of course quite out of the question, until the modern world of education and more or less political freedom admitted of the atrocious attempts at a kind of "style nouveau" in the very centre of the Jerusalem bazaars. It would be difficult to imagine what the future holds in store as far as the appearance of the native churches is concerned.

CHAPTER II

SUBURBAN CHURCHES

CŒNACULUM.—This very venerable shrine, known in the Middle Ages as "Mater Ecclesiarum" on account of its being considered the house of the Blessed Virgin Mary and the place wherein the first Eucharist was celebrated by Christ Himself, is doubtless a "Holy Site" of the primitive period, if not of the Apostolic age. It is mentioned by Theodosius, *De Terra Sancta*, of the sixth century. Also at the end of the seventh century:—

On Mount Sion Arculf saw a square church, which included the site of the Lord's Supper, the place where the Holy Ghost descended upon the Apostles, the marble column to which our Lord was bound when He was scourged, and the spot where the Virgin Mary died. (*Travels of Bp Arculf,* 700. Bohn's ed. p. 5.)

Bernard the Wise (867) speaks of the church on Sion where the Virgin died as being called the Church of St Simeon, where our Lord washed the feet of the disciples, and where was suspended His crown of thorns.

Benjamin of Tudela's famous story of the discovery of the treasure caves or tomb of King David somewhere on the slopes of Mount Sion is, in all probability, associated with the church in question. A restoration of the building seems to have been in progress, and we have a contemporary description of this building by John of Wurzburg. It appears to have been the usual three-aisled church with three semicircular apses; that on the north, commemorating the death of the Blessed Virgin Mary, possessed a marble ciborium, and was protected by an iron grille; that on the south was called "Galilee of Mount Sion," and was considered the place where Jesus Christ appeared to the disciples after the Resurrection. In the principal apse was the place of Pentecost, and beneath it in a crypt the chamber of the Pedilavium. The upper church was vaulted and with a

Fig. 46. The Cœnaculum or "Upper Chamber."

central cupola (probably resembling St Anne's), and on the south side was the "upper chamber," or upper story of the south aisle, from which a staircase descended into the south apse called the "Galilee of Mount Sion." Chapels of St Thomas and St Stephen seem to have been added in the twelfth century.

During the crusading kingdom a convent of the popular Augustinian canons was established under the name of "Ste Marie de Mont Sion et du St Esprit," and the names of the following priors are preserved:—

Arnold	1117	Enguerrand II	1160
Enguerrand I	1155	Renauld	1169
Gautier	1158		

In 1187 the buildings of the convent and its church were presumably ruined, although within the walls of the city at that date, and so they remained for over fifty years.

"Ecclesiarum mater St Syon" (G de Tyr. I. xv. c. iv.) was the popular name of this church at the period of the Crusaders. All the churches built on this site have preserved the idea of the "upper chamber" in a doubled-storied building, and the earliest representation is that of a simple parallelogram in the travels of Arculf (A.D. 700).

The present remains of the church date from about 1342, when the Franciscans were first permitted to occupy the site. They consist of an upper and a lower chamber measuring 14 metres by 9 metres. Each story is divided into two aisles by an arcade of three arches carried on two columns and two semi-columns in the end walls. The capitals of these columns are in elaborate fourteenth-century foliage, and receive the arches and ribs of the six cross vaults. The capitals of the lower story appear to be uncarved. Three windows exist on the south side of each story, and a staircase at the south-west corner of the monument affords communication between the stories and the entrance courtyard. This church is apparently an example of the later Gothic style in Jerusalem, and was perhaps built by Cypriot masons. The building has suffered much from the ill usage and additions by the Moslems of the sixteenth century.

At the east end of the monument is a small chamber on each floor called the Tomb of David. Below, the "Tomb"; above, a cenotaph.

In Suriano's *Trattato di Terra Santa* (1484):—

Cap. LIX. Qui si nota de la Chiesia de Monte Syon e de la Capella de lo Spirito Sancto.

Da le fondamenta de la chiesia se comprende la sua grandeza la longeza de la qual è cento braza, e cinquanta larga; et era facta in tre navate fodrata tuta de tavole de marmaro finissimo, e lo pavimento era di mosaico. Del qual edifficio nulla vi è rimasto excepto la tribuna del l'altar maior, et el Cenaculo de Christo, ét la Capella de lo Spirito Sancto. La qual capella del mile quatrocento sessanta, a furor de populo fo butata a terra e scarcata e ruinata: la qual fece rehedifficar el magno Ducha (Philippo) de Bregogna che fo tanto bellicoso, e spese quatordece milia ducati d'oro per farla più bella che non era prima. E de questa fino che lui vixe, pigliò el governo et la protectione, tenendola fornita de paramenti de brocato; e dava ogni anno mille ducati d'oro per il vivere de li Frati che officiavano questa gloriosissima capella; e in questa devotione perseverò tuto el tempo che lui vixe. Et quando morite ordino che fosse sparato, e cavato el core, fosse portato e sepellito in questa sua gloriosa capella. E cosi fo facto et cum quello forono portati alli Frati sei millia ducati, e questo fo l'anno.che fo perso Negroponte. Questa adunque capella, tanto bella et tanto ornata, per invidia et in vituperio de la fede Christiana, iterum a furor de populo fo ruinata et insieme cum essa forono scargase e rote tute le camare et celle de lo inchiostro interno dentro del loco. E la cason de questa tanta ruina forono li cani Judei, perchè dissero alli Saraceni che soto quella capella staeva le sepoltura de David propheta.

The heart of Duke Philip of Burgundy was never buried in Jerusalem. Owing to the Turkish occupation of Negroponte, the Bishop who was carrying the relic was obliged to pass by way of Rome, where the Pope on hearing of the matter dispensed the Bishop from his pilgrimage, took the 6000 ducats, and buried the heart in St Peter's.

Fra Suriano, in another codex of the same MS., trusts to the future when the ruined convent would be repaired—"li frati la refaranno, et non haveranno respecto a danari." But within a few years the Franciscans were entirely banished from the place.

In another place (Cap. LVIII.) he speaks of the church in its ruined state:

in tempo de Christiani la nostra chiesia era tanto grande che con-
teniva in lei tuti li altri mysterii; ma al presente tuta e scarcata, excepto una de le ale, dove era el Cenaculo e lo Spirito Sancto. Nel
quale loco al presente officiamo e persolvemo le divine laude.
Appresso al qual loco i lo monasterio de le Bizoche nostre per spatio
de cinquanta braza. (This last paragraph refers to the female convent
and hospice.)

The House of Caiaphas.—A special interest attaches to this
venerable sanctuary, because, however modern the present
Armenian buildings on the site may be, there seems little doubt
that here stood throughout the ages a succession of chapels
commemorating the existence of the first Christian Hospice of
Jerusalem. It was from the Domus Caiaphæ that the first known
Christian Pilgrim (*Itinerarium Burdigalense*) set out to explore
the Holy City of Ælia Capitolina, and there is no reason to

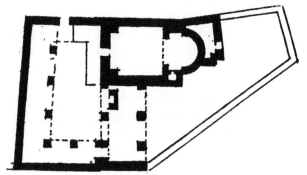

Fig. 47. House of Caiaphas, from the Palestine Survey of 1864.
Scale, $\frac{1}{500}$.

suppose that the exact position of the ancient hospice of nearly
sixteen centuries ago has ever been changed.[1]

The shrine dedicated to the memory of the Trial of Christ and
the affecting story of Peter's denial of His Master seems to have
occupied a less important place in the estimation of mediæval
pilgrims. It presumably passed into the exclusive ownership of
the Georgian Armenian Church at some period antecedent to
the Crusades, as there does not appear to be any record of it as
a Latin property.

[1] Inde eadem via ascenditur Sion et paret ubi fuit domus Caiaphæ
sacerdotis (*Itinerarium, c.* A.D. 350).

The existing convent, which has the appearance of having been rebuilt in a particularly plain and utilitarian style of the nineteenth century, consists of an upper story of chambers carried on an arched substructure round a very small courtyard, in one corner of which is a small and unarchitectural, and very dark, chapel—a mere square chamber with a semicircular apse. The convent stands surrounded by a great graveyard, one of the series of cemeteries which crown Mount Sion. It would seem to be especially associated with cemetery purposes, for within the arches of its courtyard are many large and elaborate tombs of Armenian ecclesiastical dignitaries of the last century or two.

The New German Church of the "Dormition."—Midway between the "Cœnaculum" and the "House of Caiaphas" is a large and imposing Benedictine monastery enclosing a singular circular domical church. This most important German monument in the Holy City is designed in a Rhenish Romanesque style with an immense dome supported on eight surrounding piers or buttresses with intervening semicircular chapels. The plan is, of course, reminiscent of Aix-la-Chapelle, but the construction is different. The superb mosaic decorations of the interior are advanced but a short way towards completion.

The Church of the Tomb of the Virgin.—From an archæological point of view, second only to the great church of the Holy Sepulchre, this singular little monument is perhaps the most untouched relic of a remote past to be found in or near Jerusalem. The drawing by De Vogüé made more than fifty years ago shows it in precisely the same condition as at present, and that condition seems to have been unchanged since the crusading epoch (?).

The tomb of the Blessed Virgin Mary is first mentioned historically by John Damascenus (A.D. 730), who states that the Empress Pulcheria (390–450) sent to Jerusalem for some relic of the Virgin which she desired to preserve in Constantinople. Bishop Arculf describes a circular church built over the tomb (seventh century), and Bernard Sapiens saw this circular church in ruins (ninth century).

During the crusading period a monastery of the Order of Cluny was established on the site, the first Abbot, Hugh, being appointed in 1117 (De Vogüé). Of this Abbey the only trace

Fig. 48. Tomb of the Virgin, Jerusalem.

surviving is the square chamber at the top of the remarkable flight of steps leading down to the rock-hewn tomb; the fine ramping vault and some portion of the staircase with the two tomb niches half-way down also form part of this same building.

An upper church, which is not very clearly recorded, may also have existed above the subterranean chapel, but no trace of it survives, nor does it seem easy to account for its position in relation to the front of the building as at present constituted.

When the Saracens occupied Jerusalem in the thirteenth century they pulled down the Cluniac monastery, to use the materials for rebuilding the city wall. At a subsequent period the Franciscans were permitted to occupy the subterranean church, but they were displaced in the eighteenth century by the Greeks and Armenians who now constitute its guardians.

As will be seen by reference to the accompanying photograph the square building which has constituted the upper church in recent times is evidently the untouched work of c. 1117. The moulded arches supported on nook shafts with "Corinthian" capitals are precisely similar in character to the oldest portion of the Gothic work of the Holy Sepulchre. These two buildings —the tomb-houses of the Virgin and of her Son—appear identical in date; they have evidently been carried out by the same masons and the same architect. The stilting of the inner arch reminds one of the same treatment in the doorways of the Holy Sepulchre, the mouldings—a hollow between two rolls— are also precisely similar, but the carved detail of capitals is perhaps more ordinary and less elaborate. Above the outer arch is a row of small brackets which once supported the beams of an outer flat-roofed loggia or porch, of which no other trace now remains, or they may have supported a cornice somewhat re-sembling the main string-course of the Holy Sepulchre front; the gable above has been rebuilt.

Within, the building, with its impressive gloom and mystery resulting from an almost entire obscurity, has also an appearance of singular preservation. The vulgar frippery of Eastern church ornamentation is fortunately invisible in the darkness, and it is evidently thought useless to waste the usual display of hideous icons and childish toys in a place where such evidences of taste would be lost to view. In recent centuries pilgrims have noted the presence of inscriptions and verses painted on the sloping vault of the staircase and on other parts, but at the present day nothing of the sort remains.

The entrance porch[1] has a blocked-up window on either side, apparently without mouldings. The vaulted crypt at the bottom of the stairs is without any architectural character, and the actual tomb of the Virgin is now reduced to a mere fragment of rock. Half-way down the staircase are two recesses containing tombs, one on either hand. That on the east side is coeval with the building of the church, it consists of a plain arch about 8 feet wide and 6 feet in depth, ornamented on the side towards the stairs with voussoirs of a regular size, panelled on the face. Within this recess is a plain altar tomb placed north and south with a small altar on the north side. These two structures are now known as the "tombs of Joachim and Anna," but in reality this little chantry contains the tomb of Queen Milicent, widow of Fulk of Anjou (*dec.* about 1155). Possibly the altar of the Queen's chantry may have been dedicated to the parents of the Blessed Virgin Mary, and hence the modern appellation. It would seem probable that the Queen's body may still rest undisturbed within this chantry, although the iron grille in front of it, mentioned by William of Tyre, has been removed, and both the tomb and the little side altar have been covered over to some extent with woodwork by the modern Armenians.

There would seem to have been another staircase descending to this crypt on the north side corresponding to the existing one on the south, but there is no record of its use, it merely shows on the plan of the building and is blocked.

The crypt of the Virgin's Tomb creates a singular impression on the visitor. It seems hardly possible that it can always have been so entirely devoid of daylight as at present. Its singular position at the bottom of a deep valley has occasioned the gradual accumulation of earth and rubbish around its walls, and such external windows as at one time existed have become blocked. A window, like a pavement light in a London street, exists over the ritual choir behind the tomb, and serves to some

---

[1] This, and the frontispiece of this book have been reproduced from photographs kindly lent for the purpose by the "American Colony," Jerusalem.

extent for light and air. The singular obscurity of the place is all
the more surprising when we consider that the walls of the

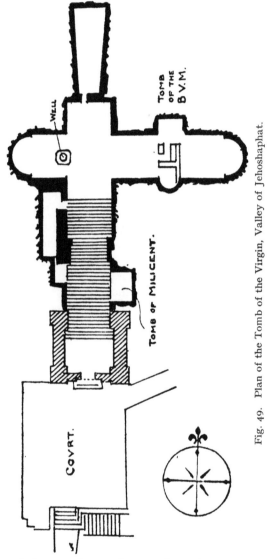

Fig. 49. Plan of the Tomb of the Virgin, Valley of Jehoshaphat.

interior, and the ramping vault over the stairs, were at one time
covered with paintings and legends in verse in the popular

metrical hymn style. Over the altar behind the tomb in the apse
was a fresco representing the B.V.M. seated amongst angels,
underneath which was the inscription preserved by John of
Wurzburg:

HIC JOSOPHAT VALLIS HINC EST AD SIDERA CALLIS
IN DOMINO FULTA FUIT MARIA SEPULTA
HINC EXALTATA CAELOS PETIT INVIOLATA
SPES CAPTIVORUM VIA LUX ET MATER EORUM

In the narthex or porch, a chamber about 8 m. square, were
tombs of early crusaders: Werner de Gray, cousin of king
Godfrey, and Arnulph d'Oudenarde were buried here about
1107. A passage way conducted from this porch to the adjacent
"Grotto of the Agony"; and the monastery of the Cluniacs
seems to have been built over these two Holy Sites. The Cluniac
monks must have entirely rebuilt whatever they found on this
site, for the present crypt does not agree with the description of
a circular church in two stories as seen by Bishop Arculf and
the early pilgrims.

Sandys the sixteenth-century English traveller describes the
Virgin's Tomb as "made thus by the mother of Constantine"
and that "In this place burneth 18 lamps continually; partly
maintained by the Christians, partly by the Mahometans, who
have this place in an especial veneration."

Fra Bernardino Amico describes the place with his curious
drawings, or "corpo trasparento" method of illustration. In
his time the Franciscans seem to have had the exclusive right to
celebrate mass upon the altar of the Tomb. The Armenians,
Greeks, Syrians, Copts, and Abyssinians each possessed a particular altar, and the Moslems claimed a mihrab or niche on
the south side of the tomb, and in fact almost the nearest point
to it. The tomb chantry of Queen Milicent on the staircase had
been appropriated by the Georgians, and the chantry on the
opposite side was in possession of the Abyssinians. These
arrangements have survived until the present day, and even
still the Moslem prays within the mihrab in its dark interior,
continuing the strange traditions of crusading times when many
of the eastern shrines were common both to Islam and to
Christianity.

The Churches on the Mount of Olives.—The principal ancient shrine of Olivet is the site of the Ascension. Here a church-enclosure, very similar to the circular shrine of the Anastasis in general idea, was constructed during the Constantinian epoch, and seems to have been called IMBOMON (*vide* St Sylvia). The late Herr Baurath Schick published a set of plans, with a lengthy account of his investigations on the site in 1895, in the *Palestine Exploration Fund Quarterly Statement*. His conclusions were apparently correct and agree with those of others who have studied the subject.

The ancient circular church-enclosure, over 100 feet diameter, seems to have completely resembled a circular *impluvium* of the Roman style of architecture; a colonnaded court with a series of chambers on the outside forming an outer ring of walls recalled the usual house construction of the period. Of this, of course, hardly a trace remains at the present day, but Herr Schick seems to have identified the general plan from evidences in the later buildings on the spot, and from the position of the "Grotto of St Pelagia," a partly rock-hewn chamber which may have formed a partial crypt at the west side of the buildings.

The Church of the Ascension has been exposed to all the destructive circumstances which have arisen from time to time in the history of Jerusalem, it is therefore not surprising that even fewer traces remain from a remote antiquity than in the other great primitive shrine of the Holy Sepulchre. Successive churches have been built upon the site until the coming of the Crusaders, who seem to have erected a sort of copy of its primitive form, but on a reduced scale. At the present day a few bases of piers with engaged columns are the only souvenirs of the circular church in its latest form; everything else has completely disappeared.

In the centre of the modern irregular enclosure (used as a mosque, and at the same time with occasional services held by different Christian sects within its walls) is the Kubbet enclosing the holy stone of the Ascension footprint. This Kubbet has a certain architectural interest. It has all the appearance of being the work of mediæval Christian masons, but of a period subsequent to the twelfth century. De Vogüé thought this to be Moslem work, with perhaps some details of the ancient crusading church used up in its construction. To the present writer it would seem more probably of the same period and workmanship as the "Upper Chamber" of the Cœnaculum, which is usually attributed to the period of Frederick II in Jerusalem, and is supposed to be by Cypriot masons. This little monument is remarkably well preserved, and forms an interesting example of the small class of religious shrines shared in by Moslems and Christians with apparent perfect harmony.

The earlier Church of the Ascension built by the Crusaders, of which so little now remains, is described by John of Wurzburg (1170):—

Hodie exstat magna ecclesia in cujus medio magno foramine quodam aperto designatur locus Ascensionis Domini.

Sæwulf (1102) apparently describes the site as it stood before the Crusaders' building, very much as it appears at present.

The primitive church-enclosure built in the fourth century and restored by Modestus is described by all the earlier pilgrims. It seems to have been illuminated with lamps on the great festival of the Ascension in a manner very impressive to the feelings of Arculf, Willibald, and others—an illumination of Olivet which is still practised by the modern Orthodox. At this earlier period the footprint of Christ was surrounded by a bronze screen the height of a man, instead of being covered with anything resembling the modern "Kubbet."

Eusebius, Bishop of Cæsarea, alludes in the course of his description of the place of the Ascension to a cave as the real spot where the Saviour initiated the Apostles into the mysteries of their religion, and from which He ascended. (Euseb. *Vita Const.* III. 41, and *Demonst. Evang.* VI. 18.) This cave is probably the ancient tomb or cistern cut in the rock, now known as the Chapel of the Creed. Above this cave was built at some doubtful period an early Christian church, with its narthex immediately over the crypt, and its three aisles to the east of it. Only rough traces of the walls of this church and some portions of mosaic flooring in the *diaconicon* remain; they have recently been unearthed, and possess some interest.

The learned Père Vincent of the Dominicans has written a very interesting article in the *Revue Biblique*, April 1911, on the remains discovered and fully explored on this site in 1910–11. It results from these investigations that a church of the familiar basilican plan with a triapsal east end, a raised choir above a *confessio*, and approached by a colonnaded narthex and atrium once occupied the site. The colonnaded narthex was above the present cave of the "Credo," and a large cistern was below the centre of the atrium.

This church was of the Bethlehem type—a type which seems to have been frequently copied at a period somewhat difficult to define. The exact date of the Bethlehem Basilica is not known, and one singular thing is that it resembles so much the style of the Roman churches of a period when there was but little European influence in the Holy Land. Numerous details of stone carving of an early Byzantine type were found on this site; details of a style which may have begun earlier in this district, as it certainly continued longer here than elsewhere.

The enthusiastic discoverers of these ruins were carried away with the idea that they belonged to Constantine's "Imbomon" on Olivet, but there is no mention of any basilica having been attached to that monumental enclosure, and these ornamental details are of too late a type for such a theory.

The crypt of the Creed was restored as a sanctuary in recent years; during the Middle Ages it was hardly so much as mentioned.

The Ancient Crypt of the "Creed," with its Byzantine church ruins, is now within the enclosure of the French Carmelite Convent of the "Lord's Prayer." This institution is built to the east of the ancient remains, and is of some architectural and historical interest amongst the modern ecclesiastical monuments of the Mount of Olives. It appears to have been founded about 1875 by the Duchesse de la Tour d'Auvergne, an eccentric lady who at one time resided on Olivet and had the intention of being buried within this little cloister which forms the approach to the small chapel of the convent. The sumptuous marble tomb, with a life-size effigy of the Duchesse, decorates one side of this cloister. The buildings of the convent were originally designed by M. Mauss, the French Government Colonial Architect, who did so much architectural work in Jerusalem during the 'sixties of the last century, but since his time many additions have been made to the premises. The cloistered court, which forms the principal architectural feature of the convent, is to some extent a copy of the cloister of Kulaat el Hozn, the crusading castle in the north of Syria. The work is a lifeless reproduction of the twelfth-century style, the carved details are executed in a mechanical manner by some inferior European mason, and the exceedingly small chapel to which the cloister forms an approach is a bare and characterless interior. The cloister, with its versions of the Lord's Prayer in panels of painted tile-work, is a curious monument to the memory of an eccentric lady, and an example of French Gothic architecture of the revival at the end of the last century which has an unique historical interest from being found in such a position.

The Mount of Olives was covered with churches and houses, forming almost a suburb of Jerusalem at a period immediately preceding the Arab conquest of the seventh century. Mosaic floors and ornamental details of all kinds are found all over the summit, wherever the modern monks and nuns dig foundations for their new residences, and these remains are invariably of the sixth- and seventh-century types.

Russian Church of the Ascension.—The high campanile attached to this church, which dominates Jerusalem in every view, and can be seen from the Jordan banks and the Dead Sea, was built about 1870. It is over 150 feet high to the metal spire which crowns its summit. Without any particular architectural character it serves its purpose as an inoffensive landmark—the purpose for which it was built—and owing to the large openings in its sides, which detract from its really large scale, it looks much smaller than it really is. Close to the foot of this immense tower is a pretty little Russian church of a very plain design, cruciform in plan and covered with a central dome and the usual semi-domes over the four arms of the cross.

Russian Church of Gethsemane.—This is quite one of the most remarkable modern monuments of the Jerusalem suburbs. It was built about 1880 and completed with various adornments and the marvellous gilding of its bulbous cupolas in 1895. It is a sheer importation of the peculiar Moscow style of church which is supposed to originate in the Tartar tent church of primitive times (*vide* Neale's *Russian Ecclesiology*). Its general design is a cruciform interior of great height and domical construction supported on four corner towers. Externally the upper part of the walls between the towers are carried inwards in tiers of small dormer windows arranged like the steps of an Indian temple. The centre part of the building finishes in a great onion-shaped dome, and the four surrounding towers are also crowned with similar but smaller domes. The five domes are entirely covered with heavy gilding, which seen at a distance is sufficiently conspicuous, and at the same time affords a strange contrast with the surrounding tombs and the grey walls of the city.

Like the Russian churches which are familiar to most tourists on the Continent, standing in strange contrast with their surroundings of a French or German city, this Church of Gethsemane has a strangely foreign look, although one might expect its Asiatic character to harmonise with a Syrian landscape and climate.

The Church of the Pool of Siloam. (See Mr Archibald Dickie's Paper read before the R.I.B.A. 6th March, 1899.)—This most interesting building, which was laid bare by the Palestine Exploration Fund explorers Bliss and Dickie in 1896, has unfortunately been completely covered up again by order of the Turkish Government, for fear that a desire to possess the Holy Site might lead to fresh contentions and troubles between the Christians. For some unexplained but probably similar motive the Turks have built a small minaret adjacent to the spot, giving as it were an additional Moslem ownership to the place. The ruins as described by Mr Dickie can, therefore, only be studied with the aid of the excellent drawings published in the *Journal* of the R.I.B.A.

The famous Siloam Tunnel, which forms a part of the ancient construction of the Siloam Pool, was placed in the hands of a very mysterious party of young Englishmen some years ago with a firman for exploring the site of the tunnel and the "Virgin's Spring." These gentlemen, according to all reports, were interested chiefly in finding some supposed treasures on the site, but in any case they found nothing of an unexpected character in the mysterious ramifications of the still unexplored "underground Jerusalem."

The Modern Buildings outside the Walls of Jerusalem.—The

enormous influx of pilgrims and tourists into Palestine since the middle of the nineteenth century has naturally produced a remarkable demand for religious buildings in the Holy City. The value of property, fluctuating according to circumstances of political and missionary developments, has arisen within the past fifty years from francs to napoleons—one might almost say from centimes into napoleons. Fifty years ago a piece of land without the walls which was recently sold for £3000 cost sixteen napoleons. In almost the same proportion the properties within a radius of perhaps a mile of the city have risen from a mere agricultural value into a fabulous estimation. Of course every square inch of land within the old walls is at the present day almost unsaleable owing to the competition of religious factions and the difficulties of transferring title. Many persons, Jew bankers and others who invested a few pounds in properties about the middle of the nineteenth century have long since retired with fortunes.

About the time of the Crimean War (1855) the Sublime Porte seems to have been induced to present a large area of ground, formerly used as the "Meidan" of the Jerusalem garrison, to the Russian Palestine Society, an institution supported by voluntary contributions in Russia for the regulation of the gigantic pilgrimages of Russian subjects to the Holy Land. This property was secured with a high wall and four great iron gates, and within the enclosure a large church was built.

Ever since the building of the great Russian hospice the different nations of Europe seem to have vied with each other in erecting immense blocks of buildings, very few of which can be considered satisfactory additions to the modern city springing up without the walls to the north. The French Hospice of Notre Dame de France is the most pretentious and most unsatisfactory of what may be called the native productions, i.e. built without any European architect. But in poverty of design and total absence of all keeping with its surroundings perhaps the great German Hospice of St Paul near the old Damascus Gate is even more successful. School buildings, Protestant chapels, hospitals, etc., all the constituent institutions of a large and remarkably mixed community are coming into existence daily, and they are all marked with a singularly commonplace utilitarianism, which is also conferred upon the religious buildings in suburban Jerusalem. In this northern district of the city the only group of buildings which can lay claim to any serious architectural character is the Anglican College of St George, built by the present writer (1895–1910).

The Dominican Church of St Stephen, near the Damascus Gate, is a poor meanly built modern church, of which the original design by M. Boutard, of Paris, made in 1885,[1] may have possessed some merit as a copy of one of the remarkable primitive churches in North Syria; but as carried out by the Dominican friars in Jerusalem the result is quite deplorable. The exterior is devoid of architecture, and the interior is a *mélange* of cheap Parisian religious art and poor construction. It is regrettable that this church replaces the interesting ruin of an early basilica of probably the fourth or fifth century, of which large traces remained so late as 1890.

One of the most imposing of the modern churches in the new suburbs of the city is certainly that of the Abyssinians. It was built about 1890 from the designs of a French architect. The Abyssinians or Ethiopian Christians are described by Ludolph von Sudheim as distinguished in his day (1350) by having a cross "in fronte ferro ignito impressam," possibly a mediæval version of the tattooing which is still customary with many sects of pilgrims at the present day. The Abyssinians have not left any trace of their presence on the monumental history of the Holy City, until the present day.

[1] Published in *S. Étienne et son sanctuaire*, by Père Lagrange, Paris, 1894. A curious divergence from the design of M. Boutard was made by introducing flying buttresses on the outside, which reminds one that the constructors were Frenchmen, and were not at home in the primitive Syrian style selected by the original designer.

PART IV

THE HOLY SEPULCHRE IN JERU-SALEM REPRODUCED AS A PILGRIM SHRINE IN EUROPE

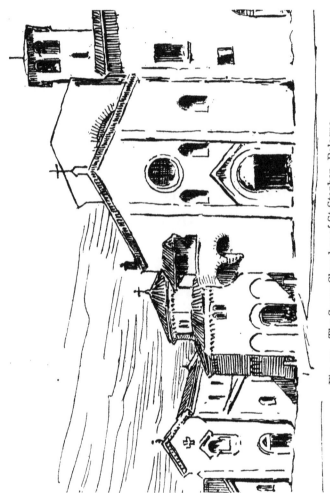

Fig. 50. The Seven Churches of St Stephen, Bologna.

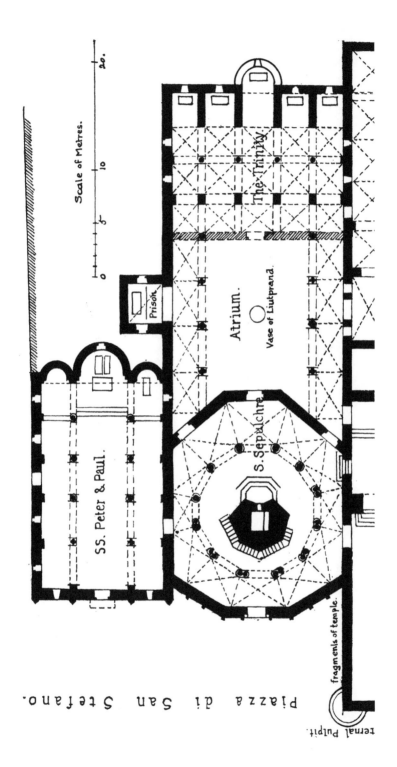

Scale of Metres.

20.

10

5

0

The Trinity.

Prison.

Atrium.

Vase of Liutprand.

S. Sepulchre.

SS. Peter & Paul.

fragments of temple.

ternal Pulpit.

Piazza di San Stefano.

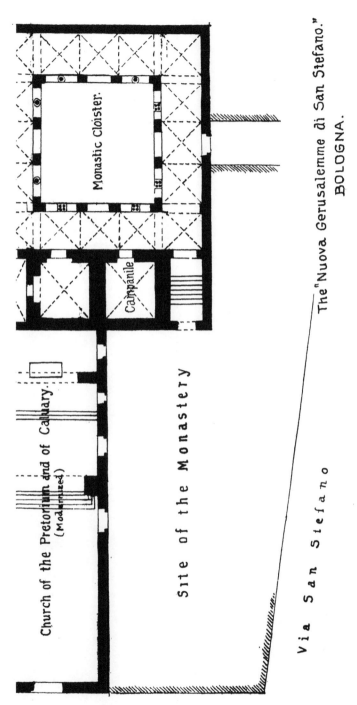

Plan of the "Nuova Gerusalemme," San Stefano

CHAPTER I

THE CHURCH OF SAN STEFANO, BOLOGNA

THE Crusading Kingdom of Jerusalem was a brief interval in the history of the Holy Land, during which pilgrimage to the greatest shrine of mediæval Christianity was comparatively easy. Before and after that period the difficulties of the way, the tediousness of the journey, and the hostility to be met with, were the causes which led to a very general desire in Christendom to transport all movable relics as far as possible away from the power of the infidels, and to represent by copies the immovable, but most precious of all—the Holy Sepulchre. Even the removal of this most valued record of the great Christian epic seems to have been seriously contemplated in the seventeenth century (*vide* p. 35).

At the time of the loss of Acre and the termination of the Latin Kingdom, the "Holy House" of Loretto is supposed to have been transported bodily across the sea to the shores of the Adriatic—a comparatively simple thing for the Venetian traders to undertake with their experience in transporting the immense quantities of building materials from ruined temples and sites in the Ægean which have gone towards the building of mediæval Venice.

Many of the relics preserved in St Peter's and elsewhere in Rome are supposed to have come from the Holy Sites around the Holy Sepulchre, the dates of their "invention" are perhaps uncertain, but as a rule they were probably added to the collection in Europe at different periods of religious enthusiasm connected with the barbarian inroads of the "Dark Ages."

Many remarkable monuments in Europe are to be attributed to this desire to possess, if not the original, at least a full size copy of the Tomb of Christ. In some few cases the names of famous artists are associated with these erections, although their history is often obscured by subsequent alteration or diversion to other uses. The majority of such monuments are necessarily subsequent in date of construction if not of foundation to the crusading epoch; but several especially interesting examples of an earlier period belong to the centuries when Palestine groaned beneath the tyranny of Byzantine and Moslem fanatics—the tyranny which occasioned the mission of Peter the Hermit, and those crusading ambitions of the Middle Ages which, however discounted by mere commercial or colonising enterprises, seem sufficiently superior to the usual selfish ideals of mankind.

As has already been shown the circular rock-cut enclosure around the tomb in Jerusalem would very much resemble in arrangement the circular tomb monument common enough all over Europe, from Stonehenge and the Druidical circles of the north to the Etruscan and Roman circular monuments of historical times. A circular tomb-temple would be very natural and quite in harmony with its surroundings in those early ages, anywhere in the West, as much as in the East.

At an early date the circular tomb develops into the Christian church, as in the circular churches of the Roman villas or of St George, Thessalonica, or the Tomb of St Luke, Ephesus.

The most ancient replica, or copy, in Europe of the Memorial of Christ in Jerusalem is the group of churches and other buildings known as the "Nuova Gerusalemme" in Bologna.

In spite of various rebuildings and "restorations" since its legendary foundation in the fifth century, it still possesses a singular air of the most profound antiquity. The fragments of an ancient temple of Isis, once occupying the spot and now inserted in the wall of one of the churches, serve to impress the visitor with this idea.

The group of buildings consists of a number of churches and chapels communicating with each other but of the most varied plans, and different dates. The general scheme and arrangement of the different parts has however been clearly maintained throughout the ages.

The general appearance and character of the "Nuova Gerusalemme" at the present day suggest the probability that in its primitive condition—the fifth century according to the legend—it may have represented the Constantinian buildings of Jerusalem: as these were modified in subsequent ages, so the European copy may have been somewhat altered in harmony with the statements of returning pilgrims from Palestine. Whether or not the primitive design at Jerusalem may have been copied, there is no doubt that the condition of the Holy Sepulchre and its adjuncts in the period between the seventh and eleventh centuries has been carefully reproduced and still survives in a most remarkable manner.

In attempting to give a description of this curious monument it is necessary to begin with a résumé of its known history. This is perhaps most easily obtained from a twelfth-century Codex preserved in the University Library, Bologna, assisted by references to Sigonio's *History of the Bishops of Bologna*,[1] and also to two small books published in the eighteenth century: *Nuova Gerusalemme* by Don Antonio Casale, and the *Abbaziale Basilica di San Stefano* by Don Celestino Petracchi.[2]

The Codex of the University Library referred to is numbered 1473, and commences: "Vitæ Sanctorum et Sancti Petronii. Anno ab Incarnatione Domini MCLXXX. Dominus Landulfi Abbate, etc." The portion referring to the building of San Stefano, or the New Jerusalem, may be translated as follows:—

The venerable father having taken possession of his pontifical throne, devoted his attention first of all to the repair of churches, which were in a ruined condition. He built a monastery outside the city towards the east in honour of St Stephen the Protomartyr; a spacious building with lofty walls, and constructed with many columns of porphyry and precious marbles, having capitals carved with the figures of men, animals, and birds. He devoted the greatest attention to this building, and with special care in the reproduction of the Lord's Sepulchre set out the work himself with a measuring reed, for he had passed many days in Judea collecting all the vestiges of Christian antiquity. He decorated the copy of the Sepulchre, both inside and out, with polished marble slabs.

The Bishop built another edifice in that place with many columns, consisting of an atrium surrounded with two galleries one above the other; in the upper gallery were columns of precious marble. In

---

[1] 1580.   [2] 1747.

this way the buildings extended to the place which represented Golgotha, or Calvary, where the cross of Christ stood; this place also was decorated with various coloured pictures. The pavement consisted of the most beautiful coloured stones and marbles. Thus did he endeavour with the most ardent desire to render the place beautiful.

In the place called Golgotha he placed the wooden cross, which in length and width corresponded with the cross of Jesus Christ.

A "Vestibulum," paved with stone of a milk-white colour, and with walls ornamented with beautiful pictures, is described as in front of the "atrium," and steps led up from it on to the higher level of Golgotha. This "Vestibulum" is evidently represented at the present day by the twelfth-century cloister on the south side of the monastery—in other words the monastic cloister proper, round which the different monastic buildings are ranged.

The Codex contains an account of the destruction of Bologna and the monastery of San Stefano by the Huns in A.D. 903, and the above description must have a special reference to the condition of the buildings after that event. They are however described as if they were still in their primitive form as planned by St Petronius, and reference is made to certain adjuncts of the group, which have either disappeared or been much altered since their enclosure within the city walls of the tenth and eleventh centuries. An artificial mound at a short distance to the south-east of San Stefano, on which was a church of St John Evangelist, seems to have formed a part of the group; possibly representing the "Cœnaculum" of Mount Sion. This church is still standing on its mound in the form of a fine Gothic edifice rebuilt in 1221, and known as "San Giovanni del Monte." The Pool of Siloam (represented by a cistern), the Valley of Jehoshaphat, and other Holy Places, were more or less adequately reproduced, but such things have of course entirely disappeared in the development of the city of Bologna as one of the chief communities of mediæval Italy.

According to the Codex the destruction of San Stefano by the Huns seems to have been very complete; the place was burnt to the ground, but as was not unusual in those days the relic most venerated by pious pilgrims—the Cross of St Petronius—

was miraculously preserved, both from the conflagration and from the hands of the robber Huns.

According to the legends of the founding of the Christian Church in Bologna, the ancient *Felsina*, the first Bishop St Petronius was a scion of the Imperial family, and born in Constantinople about the middle of the fourth century. He appears to have passed his youth in Palestine, probably as a hermit or priest, and in those early days of a Byzantine influence in Italy, was selected for the important bishopric of Bologna, and the province of Emilia.

At this time the city of Bologna was comprised within a very limited enceinte, and the new Bishop does not seem to have proposed setting up his *cathedra* within it, but selected a spot in the suburbs towards the east, already occupied by two churches, one of which had been a temple of Isis. He united these two churches by building a third in the form of the Holy Sepulchre at Jerusalem, which was also to constitute his own eventual tomb, and in one of the churches he set the pontifical throne and the seats of the presbytery in accordance with the fashion of the period. To these three churches he added four chapels to represent certain Holy Sites in Jerusalem.

The new foundation was in the form of a monastery, of which the Bishop acted as the Abbot: "Petronius Monasterium fecit, quod Hierusalem appellavit, et ibi inter Monachos habitavit... more a Sancto Eusebio Episcopo Vercellensi instituto" (Sigonio, *Hist. Vesc. Bon.*). This monastery continued to exist as originally constituted with Egyptian (Syrian) monks, until the year 543, when becoming deserted it was handed over to the recently founded Benedictine Order, and colonised by a number of monks from Monte Cassino, who remained in possession until 1447. In the middle of the fifteenth century the *commendatore* of the property was a certain Don Coppiero, who disposed of it to a community of priests, but they, not finding the revenues sufficient for their support, passed it on to the Celestines, an Order of hermits, founded in the thirteenth century but now extinct.

The episcopal throne of Bologna was removed from San Stefano to the church, afterwards rebuilt in its present form and known as San Pietro in the centre of the city, some time during the tenth century. This was due to the reconstitution of the enceinte of the city at that period of barbarian invasion, and a natural desire on the part of the clergy to take refuge within the new fortifications.

In 903 the province of Emilia was ravaged by the Huns, and the "New Jerusalem" in the suburbs of Bologna was completely destroyed by fire and pillage. The mosaic façade of the church representing the "Cross-finding" chapel at Jerusalem is referred to amongst the monumental decorations which disappeared.

Although no precise account of the restoration of the monument after these disasters survives, there is little doubt that such a restoration was quickly set in hand, and many of the buildings as we now see them must date from the tenth century. Such a restoration would synchronise with that period during which the pilgrimage to the Holy Land was a matter of the greatest difficulty, and when the savage treatment of the western pilgrims by the Moslem rulers of Palestine was becoming intolerable and arousing the warlike spirit of the first crusade all over Europe.

San Stefano attracted considerable interest as a pilgrimage shrine in the twelfth century. In 1141 a great "invention" of relics took place, and a safe conduct was issued to all pilgrims to Bologna on that occasion. Shortly after the Abbot caused the church which represented "Mount Calvary" to be pulled down and rebuilt in a more substantial manner. During this operation the bodies of the "Forty Martyrs" (evidently an allusion to similar relics in Jerusalem) were discovered or "invented" and at the same time a "Volto Santo" was introduced amongst the attractions of the place. This "Volto Santo" is described as of "pietra paragona" or mosaic work, and survived into the seventeenth century.

During the twelfth century an historical figure of interest to Englishmen—Pope Adrian IV, the only Englishman who ever filled the throne of St Peter—was an inmate of this monastery.

The last event of historical importance connected with San Stefano is the occupancy of the property "in commendam" by the famous Cardinal Giuliano della Rovere (afterwards Pope Julius II), who amongst the many stormy scenes of his career was the object of a popular demonstration by the people of Bologna, in which the "New Jerusalem" was attacked, and the monastic kitchen and some other parts of the premises were burnt to the ground. Cardinal Giuliano appears to have restored the buildings after this event, and to have reopened the church of SS. Peter and Paul, which had been shut up for more than sixty years.

The general plan of the seven churches at Bologna, and their relative position with regard to each other, is of the greatest importance in studying them as illustrating the history of the original monument in Jerusalem.

According to the earliest legends, the site in Bologna was already occupied in the fourth century by two churches (one of them an ancient temple of Isis), and therefore the arrangement of the group by St Petronius may have been somewhat influenced by this circumstance; but at the same time it is remarkable how closely the grouping of the churches follows the model in the Holy City.

By examining the plans of the original and its copy it will be found that although dimensions are entirely different, the Sepulchre occupies its correct position relatively to the atrium of pre-crusading days, with the "Cross-finding" chapel beneath on its east side; the adjuncts of this atrium can also clearly be traced. The church of Calvary is in its proper position on the south-east of the Sepulchre, and by a strange circumstance the "Pretorium" is still identified with it (or attached to it) much in the way in which it is supposed to have existed according to the theory demonstrated in the modern Russian church in Jerusalem (*vide* p. 49).

. Before proceeding to describe the different churches in detail it must be mentioned that in modern times the name of the "Cross-finding" chapel, or the Basilica, has been changed into the "Trinity," and that several of the dedications of side chapels are also evidently of recent times.

The church of the "Trinity" evidently reproduces the shrine or shrines which stood on the site of the Basilica in Jerusalem, with the cave beneath wherein the miraculous finding of the three crosses was supposed to have taken place. This is the Basilica or "Martyrion" of the early description and plan by

Bp Arculf, but the change in its designation at Bologna is not easily accounted for. The confusion in the dedication of this particular shrine may be due to the presence of a convent of the "Trinity" at Jerusalem (*vide* plan of the buildings in Jerusalem) of an indeterminate age—probably a Byzantine foundation of the tenth century.

During the earlier and Middle Ages the "Trinity," or more properly speaking "Cross-finding," chapel, contained three large crosses of wood: one of them was covered with copper, the others with iron, to protect them from the teeth of the faithful who were in the habit of kissing them and gnawing at them at the same time. A precisely similar savagery is referred to by St Silvia of Aquitaine as practised by the earliest visitors to the shrines in Jerusalem in the fourth century. One of the crosses here referred to now stands on the top of the Tomb in the Holy Sepulchre Church at Bologna; it was placed in this position in the year 1712.

It would seem as if the church of the "Trinity" was originally little more than the eastern side or cloister of the "Atrium" with a row of chapels forming its eastern wall. This may very well represent the appearance of the original atrium in Jerusalem after the rebuildings by Modestus in A.D. 628. The church has been enlarged, and the atrium proportionately curtailed, by a wall built across its eastern part to enclose the chapels, at a subsequent period, probably after the destruction by the Huns in 903, or when a certain Bishop Bernard was buried within its precincts in 1104.

The general appearance, arrangement, and dimensions of the interior of the dodecagonal church at Bologna remain very much as they were in the Middle Ages, although it must be remembered that much "restoration" has taken place at subsequent periods, notably after 1860. This domed building is in the regular style of early Lombardic architecture, with its characteristic yellow and red brickwork, and the usual admixture of marble and stone details from ancient ruins.

The arches supporting the central cupola, and the quadripartite vaulting of the ambulatory, spring in an odd manner from coupled columns on the west side, and from single columns on the east side. Where these columns are coupled one is of marble, the other of brick. This strange and defective construction points to some rebuilding of the upper portion at some later period, and perhaps accounts for a certain irregularity in the shape of the twelve-sided plan.

The representation of the Tomb in the centre of the church is of more archæological importance than any other part of the

Fig. 51.   Interior of the Holy Sepulchre Church, St Stephen's, Bologna.

Bolognese replica. The original in Jerusalem has suffered more changes in its structure and arrangement than perhaps its immediate surroundings ; it is therefore most interesting to find in Bologna sufficient records of the appearance of the Holy

Sepulchre previous to the first crusade of 1099, and corresponding most accurately with the pilgrims' accounts of the period.

The altar on the top of the Tomb, as it exists at Bologna, and as it is described by the Abbot Daniel and the Englishman Sæwulf, had two staircases for approach. These staircases must have been removed from the original previously to 1555, as they are not shown on any of the ancient copperplates of that period. A similar suggestion of a double staircase is also to be found in the Segovia replica. The balustrade of these staircases continues round the sides of the Tomb forming an enclosure to the altar.

About 1250–1300 there would seem to have been a "restoration" of the Bolognese replica, or at least the veneering of a new face upon its construction. On the east side the large recess, within which is the entrance to the Tomb, was treated as a trefoiled archway with elegant nook-shafts, and three panels of the refined sculpture of the thirteenth century representing the "Resurrection"; in the centre panel sits an angel, the three Maries in a panel on one side are balanced by three sleeping soldiers on the other. The staircases already mentioned are decorated with a balustrade of small columns with carved capitals of the same period of embellishment.

Against the south side of the Tomb replica is a square pulpit or ambo of early Lombardic character, decorated with rudely carved lions; the origin or significance of this feature in the interior is difficult to explain: in all probability it has been placed in this position without any particular meaning, and it certainly represents nothing in Jerusalem.

A detail which may perhaps favour the traditional early origin of the Bolognese copy is the fact that instead of the floor of the Tomb being as at Jerusalem a little above the level of the surrounding church, it is approached by a descent or sloping floor. This is of course easily accounted for by the universal raising of ground levels on ancient sites.

The church, or station, known as the "Atrium" is of a particular interest, both as a characteristic specimen of early Lombardic art as well as a representation of the famous atrium of the early church in Jerusalem. It consists of an open space

surrounded on north and south sides by vaulted arcades of the
usual brick round arched type of N. Italy. On the west side is
the octagonal church of St Sepulchre, whilst on the east is the
entrance front of the church built to represent the restored
Basilica. with the crypt of the "Cross-finding" below.

Fig. 52. Interior of the Holy Sepulchre Church, St Stephen's, Bologna.

In the centre of the atrium stands a singular object: at first
sight it appears to be either a holy water stoup or a font, but in
reality, it is an alms-dish of stone. It occupies much the same

position with regard to surrounding buildings as the vase-shaped monument in the "Chorus Dominorum" at Jerusalem, known as the "Centre of the World."

In the Bolognese example an interesting inscription runs round the edge of the bowl, somewhat difficult to read owing to contractions and misspelling of words; as generally translated it reads:—

RECEIVE O LORD THE HUMBLE GIFTS OF LIUPRANTE. BARBATUS BEING THE BISHOP. THIS VASE BEING FILLED IN THE SERVICE OF THE LORD'S SUPPER. IF ANY SHALL DIMINISH IT THE LORD SHALL JUDGE HIM.

This rather unusual form of offertory bowl is decorated on the underside with a fluted surface in addition to the above inscription.

The date and donor of the bowl are not easy to identify. A certain Liutprand, a famous Lombard author, was Bishop of Cremona between 922–972. Another famous Liutprand was the Lombard king who endeavoured to unite all Italy under his sceptre, and who flourished between 712–744. In any case it is evidently very ancient, and recalls a custom which still survives in Jerusalem for the pilgrims to place their offerings in bowls or trays standing on the Holy Sites.

The bowl at Bologna stood at one time on the ground or pavement of the atrium, but since the restoration of the buildings by Pope Julius II it has been raised on a pedestal, decorated with the papal arms, and has all the appearance of a holy water stoup.

On the north side of the atrium is a representation of the "Prison" in its correct position as at Jerusalem. It is a small square chapel, in which is an altar, formerly decorated with a picture by Francia, removed in 1747. It is still known as the "Carcere," but also passes for the "Casa di Caipha."

Around the atrium various Holy Sites are commemorated by white marble crosses let into the walls. These Holy Sites are difficult to identify since the destruction of the original atrium in Jerusalem by the building of the Crusaders' Chorus Dominorum, and in any case they may be fanciful additions of a later period.

At Bologna the reproduction of "Mount Calvary" on an artificial mound with a church on its summit has been some-what obscured by subsequent alterations.

It is evident that in the fourteenth century a church of the period took the place of the original building (whatever that may have been) regarded as the ancient temple of Isis, con-

Fig. 53. View in the Atrium with the Vase of Liutprand in the centre. St Sepulchre, Bologna.

verted into a replica of Golgotha. (Perhaps the ruins of the temple and its podium may have formed a mound which suggested the idea to the first planners of the "New Jerusalem.") The brick walls of this square Gothic church still stand untouched externally with a curious little outside pulpit built in brickwork on stone corbels at its north-west corner, very reminiscent of the famous "relic-exhibition" pulpit by

Donatello at Prato,[1] and the inscribed lintel of the Isis temple is inserted in the north wall near by. This Gothic church is apparently dated 1330, according to a record of its dedication by a certain Francesco Lombrano, preserved in the University Library.

In 1637 this Gothic church was altered into a pseudo-classic edifice as far as its interior is concerned; and its name was changed into "la chiesa del Crocifisso."

In its original plan the Calvary church was divided into two parts (perhaps by the screen), one being called "Casa di Pilato," the other forming the chapel of SS. John and Mary Magdalene.

The "Casa di Pilato" is of a particular interest for comparison with the topography of the "Holy Sites" immediately around the "Sepulchre" in Jerusalem. The placing of the "Judgment-seat" or "Pretorium" close against Calvary seems to be in harmony with the theory advanced of recent years that the true Pretorium at Jerusalem was discovered within the Russian hospice in 1887. If this be so it is evident that the "New Jerusalem" of Bologna must be considered a monument of the earlier Christian antiquity, as the "Pretorium" of crusading traditions has always been where it is at present—at the start of the "Via Dolorosa" in the Holy City.

In the "Casa di Pilato" a round marble disc was let into the floor to represent the "Station of Jesus"; at one side was a window called the "Ecce Homo." The communicating door between this church and that of the "Sepulchre" was known as the "Scala Santa," much frequented by gravid women.

A staircase leads down from the Calvary church into the very interesting cloister on the south-east of the group of buildings constituting the monastery of many different occupations. The architecture of this cloister is characteristic of the twelfth century, its round arches in two stories rest on capitals of the elaborate Lombardic carving of human and animal forms. Around this cloister were originally grouped the usual buildings

[1] It appears that in the Middle Ages there was amongst the numerous relics preserved at the "New Jerusalem" a "Girdle of the B.V.M."; this would account for the presence of the little outside pulpit so much like the Prato example, which was used for the exhibition of such a relic to the pilgrim crowd in the piazza beneath.

of a monastery: Benedictine, Celestine, or perhaps the original cathedral chapter of primitive times. These buildings have since been secularised and the cloister alone remains as their record.

On the north side of the Holy Sepulchre stands the venerable basilica of SS. Peter and Paul, occupying the site of one of the two churches said to have been found by St Petronius in the place where he established his cathedral. The original church was used by the first Bishops of Bologna—SS. Petronius, Faustinianus, and others—as their cathedral, but the present church is a rebuilding of probably the twelfth century. It is an interesting design in the Lombardic round-arched style, and the interior consisting of three aisles covered by quadripartite vaulting, supported on arcades of alternate single and clustered columns, is exceedingly effective. At the east end are three apses, containing altars and ancient sarcophagi supposed to enshrine the relics of St Isidor (Syrian Martyr) and three of the Holy Innocents. The steps up to these shrines are much worn by the feet of innumerable pilgrims.

This church of SS. Peter and Paul has no reference to the group of the seven churches of the New Jerusalem, its presence is in a sense accidental. It appears to have lain in an abandoned condition for very many years in the fifteenth century, and to have been restored by Pope Julius II.

Considering the circumstances of that remote age when it seems presumable that the copy of the Holy Sepulchre was initiated, or of equally rude periods when modifications may have been attempted in the original design, and the difficulties in either case of conveying the impression of the monument in Jerusalem to the average builder or mason of those early centuries, it is not surprising if the copy should somewhat fail; the fact that there is so much resemblance is a very great cause of astonishment.

The materials for the early history of Lombardic architecture are very scanty. There appears to have been a very remarkable period of its development in the days of the Gothic kingdom of Ravenna, and the stupendous monument of Theodoric (c. 525) justifies the theory of those archæologists who imagine a development of the fine arts under the Lombards, the traces of which have mostly disappeared in consequence of the social and even racial changes of later times.

The earliest identified examples of true Lombard style are: S. Salvatore, Brescia; S. Vincenzo, Milan; S. Maria delle Carcere, Pavia; all these are of basilican plan. Later examples are: S. Michaele, Pavia; the cathedrals of Parma and Modena; the church of Borgo San Donnino; all suggesting a cruciform vaulted construction. In S. Ambrogio, Milan, the triple apse, the crypt and the campanile alone remain from the ninth century. Many ancient baptisteries survive from the most remote period of Lombardic art: Gravedona, Albengo, Biella, Asti, etc.

In the true Lombard style, although the materials employed in construction are generally second-hand and the decorations merely clumsy copies of Roman work, there is a genuine originality of design which confers a very great sense of appropriateness on many a time worn detail intended originally for some entirely different purpose. In this style the roofs were invariably of wood, and their eaves were also invariably decorated with the arched gallery on short columns so characteristic of the Rhine and North Italy.

The chief reason for supposing the period of the Lombard kingdom one of great artistic activity and importance, is the traditional history of the *Magistri Comacini*, or Freemasons of Como, who are credited with having recovered the architectural art after the ruin of the Roman Empire and the incursions of the Germanic barbarians in the sixth and eighth centuries. This confraternity is said to date in its foundation from an edict published by Liutprand, the Lombard king (712–744), regulating the standard measure for artificers work, and in other words establishing the basis for estimating the cost of buildings by measurement. The "Piede Liutprando" or "Liprando" is perhaps in reality only the more ancient Roman foot standardised by the *Magistri* for use in their church buildings, but the mode of calculating the cost of such edifices by a standard of measurement may have been an invention of the period, as the ancient Roman buildings are not usually associated with any estimates of this kind.

The above remarks on the style are suggested by the fact that San Stefano is a characteristic and early example of the true

Lombard period (eighth century), and possibly a restoration, as we see it now, of the original building of 400 years before. The name of Liuprante, or Liutprand, mentioned on the offertory bowl, would in that case doubtless mean that the restorer of the buildings was the Lombard king famous for his patronage of architects and builders. Such a theory is in harmony with all the arrangements and appearances existing on the site, in spite of several "restorations" in subsequent ages.

A striking divergence in the plan of the Sepulchre itself from the original in Jerusalem must be noted: at Jerusalem the loculus, where the sacred body is supposed to have lain, is on the north side of the chamber, at Bologna it occupies the opposite side. This is explained by the legend that when St Petronius was planning the monument, partly as his own tomb, he was induced out of a greater reverence for the original to reverse the order, and avoid too close a copy.

The "Sepulchre" church at Bologna was at one time full of tombs belonging to various Bolognese families; these were removed in the course of different restorations.

The "New Jerusalem" was undergoing restoration between 1860 and 1880, and closed to the public.

CHAPTER II

LESSER COPIES OF THE HOLY SEPULCHRE IN DIFFERENT PARTS OF EUROPE

DURING the Middle Ages a very considerable number of these replicas existed in almost every country of Christendom, and at a later period the "Way of the Cross" or "Sacro Monte" of Italy appears to be a development of the same idea. Next in order of date to the remarkable "New Jerusalem" of Bologna come some French examples, of which unfortunately no vestiges of importance remain beyond mere documentary record.

At Neuvy-St-Sépulcre in the Department of the Indre, France, is a very large circular church, supposed to date from the eleventh century, with a later square church added on one side. This interesting building was almost completely destroyed by alterations in the eighteenth century, and the simulacrum of the Holy Sepulchre has entirely disappeared (*vide* V.-le-Duc, *Dictionnaire, sub voce*).

Of minor examples the most important is the "Vera Cruz" church at Segovia, Spain. Standing at a distance from the city of Segovia it suggests the idea of a pilgrimage shrine of the type of that of Bologna, but without the adjacent chapels—possibly the intention may have been to make a similar "New Jerusalem," but the scheme miscarried.

Street in his *Gothic Architecture in Spain* describes the building as of the thirteenth century, founding his opinion on the following date inscribed on a wall:—

DEDICATIS ECCLESIA BEATI SEPULCHRI XTI IDUS APRILIS ERA MCCXLVI

but it would seem probable that this inscription refers to some restoration of the edifice, as its plan would certainly not agree with the actual church of the Holy Sepulchre in Jerusalem of that period.

The church consists of an octagonal central building in two stories, surrounded by a wide encircling aisle of the same height, and covered with pointed ribbed vaulting of the thirteenth century or later. Street describes the interior as follows :—

This central chamber is of two stories in height, the lower entered by archways in the cardinal sides, and the upper by a double flight of steps leading to a door in its western side. The upper room is vaulted with a domical roof which has below it four ribs, two parallel north and south, and two parallel east and west, and it retains the original altar. ....The upper chapel is lighted by seven little windows

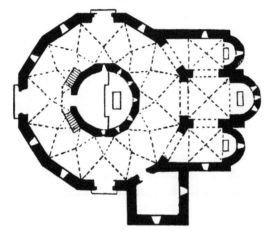

Fig. 54.   Plan of La Vera Cruz, Segovia, Spain. (Not to scale.)

opening into the aisle around it. The room below the chapel has also a dome, with ribs on its underside.

On the east side of this church is an apsidal chancel, of no great length, with a chapel on either side. These chapels, the three entrance doorways, and the lower walls are in the early Romanesque style of Spain, whilst the vaulting of the building seems a later addition.

The principal interest attaching to this copy of the Holy Sepulchre lies in its apparently reproducing the arrangements of the original in the eleventh century. The plan of the three eastern chapels is certainly the same as existed in Jerusalem at the time of Sæwulf's pilgrimage, or that of the Abbot Daniel, just after the crusaders had taken the city; the chapel on top of the Tomb is exactly what these pilgrims refer to. The double staircase up to it corresponds exactly with the Bologna example.

In an old church in Florence (probably of the thirteenth or early fourteenth century) called S. Pancrazio, now desecrated, and in the days of the Grand Dukes used as the law-courts, stands a very interesting work of art designed by the famous Leone Battista Alberti, one of the "Admirable Crichtons" of the early Renaissance. This little known masterpiece of classical detail and marble inlay represents the Holy Sepulchre in Jerusalem; but although an object of great beauty in itself it has of course little to do with the present subject beyond serving as an example of the later attempts to reproduce the appearance of the original in the Holy City.

As Leone Battista Alberti died in 1472 his version of the original would be founded on its mediæval form before the alterations by Fra Bonifazio, and accordingly we find it without the modern "Angel Chapel" and with a very small cupola on the roof.

This version in S. Pancrazio was commissioned by the Rucellai family of Florence, the great patrons of Alberti for whom he designed the family palace in the neighbouring Via Vigna Nuova, the alterations to S. Maria Novella and other things in the city of flowers.

Florence has always been a remarkable place for customs and memorials associated with the Holy Land, many of which seem to have an early origin. A representation of the Holy Fire ceremony in Jerusalem on the Saturday before Easter is still observed with great pomp and ceremony. The small church of S. Biagio, where the paraphernalia of this annual custom is preserved, is said to be built with stones brought from Palestine by the Pazzi family at the time of the Crusades, and the tradition survives that a particular member of this family brought a portion of the fire in a carefully tended lantern all the way from Jerusalem to be kept perpetually alight in Florence. At the present day this bequest of the mediæval Pazzi family takes the form of an annual display of fireworks in the Duomo at the High Mass on the Saturday in Holy Week when a great crowd of the contadini of the district assemble, and an idea seems to prevail that the successful ignition of crackers and catherine-wheels outside the cathedral by means of a rocket discharged

Fig. 55. Reproduction of the Holy Sepulchre by Leone Battista Alberti (c. 1450) in the Church of S. Pancrazio, Florence, Italy.

down a wire from the high altar is an augury for the coming wheat harvest.

The very remarkable ambition of the Medicean Grand Dukes to possess the actual Holy Sepulchre of Jerusalem, and the preparations they made for its reception within their magnificent tomb-house in the centre of Florence, have already been referred to on a previous page. It is interesting to remark that this idea of removing the actual monument synchronises with the restoration by the Guardian of Mount Sion, Fra Bonifazio, in 1550. Carrying on the tradition of these copies of the Holy Sepulchre in Western Europe is a small example which stands in the Uniat-Armenian church in Rome. It is of small size and of no historical importance beyond recording the survival of such efforts to reproduce the original in Jerusalem in the seventeenth or early eighteenth century. It is hardly an attempt to copy the original—a mere commercial advertisement by some speculative Armenian monk of the period. The church itself, in which this copy is located, is much more interesting, being an ancient Roman temple.

The *Sacro Monte* of North Italy is a feature in the development of mediæval Christianity. It is invariably intended to be a more or less approximate representation of the Holy Sites of Jerusalem, for the purpose of making a pilgrimage or procession similar to that made by the pilgrims in Jerusalem itself, along the so-called Via Dolorosa on Fridays. Very few of these Sacri Monti have any other signification—that of the Lake of Orta with its life of St Francis of Assisi being an exception. None of them are older than the early Renaissance period of art, which is often represented by works of great masters in their decoration.

The most famous Sacri Monti are Varallo in the Val de Sezia, which forms almost a town with its numerous buildings, inns, etc.; that of Crea near Casale Monferrato, with eighteen chapels; and the smaller example of S. Vivaldo near Volterra in Tuscany, with about a dozen shrines. In these the scenes of the Passion are pictured in more or less of a regular series to be visited by the pilgrim as if he were performing the round of the actual "Stations" in the Holy City. In the case of the celebrated Sacro Monte of Varese the groups of life-size statues embrace the whole Gospel story.

In quite modern days the familiar Stations of the Cross which decorate almost every modern Catholic church seem to be the descendants of the Sacro Monte.

It seems probable that the Via Dolorosa procession in Jerusa-

lem may be an unconscious survival of the primitive custom of
the early Church as described by St Sylvia of Aquitaine, when
the pilgrims visited the "Imbomon" on the Mount of Olives at
night-time, and returned to Jerusalem to attend mass in the
Holy Sepulchre "at the hour of the morning when one man can

Fig. 56. Chapel of the Holy Sepulchre, Sacro Monte of
S. Vivaldo, Tuscany.

distinguish another"; but at that period the various Holy Sites
were collected together around the hill of Calvary, and the Via
Dolorosa had no existence as we know it now.

The subject of pilgrimage—a characteristic of all civilised humanity in all ages—demands some mention in the architectural history of the Holy Sepulchre and its imitations. These imitations began to appear in Europe soon after the erection of the memorials on the Holy Sites attributed to Constantine and Helena. Innumerable pilgrims are however said to have visited Palestine in the course of the first three centuries of the Christian era, but their objects in view seem to have been confined within the walls of the Cœnaculum on Mount Sion, according to the contemporary writer Epiphanius. Christian pilgrimages to the tombs of Saints and Apostles were customary amongst the western nations at the same time that the longer journey to Jerusalem and the Holy Land was becoming popular, and the sentiment was naturally encouraged by the discovery of the greatest of Christian memorials—the Tomb of Christ.

One curious architectural detail which belongs to the subject of mediæval pilgrimage is to be found in many old churches in Europe; it is the maze or labyrinth made of coloured marbles, sometimes forming part of the church floor, sometimes introduced into the carved or mural decorations; it is supposed to have afforded a means of making an imaginary pilgrimage with the finger or on the knees.

The "Easter Sepulchre" of the mediæval churches in England has a certain relationship to the present subject, and the custom of erecting such monuments in the fourteenth and fifteenth centuries afforded an opportunity for the display of much charming architectural design. The "Easter Sepulchre" was often a private tomb honoured by being used for the ceremonies of Passion Week—a sentiment resembling the ambition of St Petronius in the erection of his own tomb-house at Bologna. But in England—with the exception of the chapel of the Sepulchre in Winchester Cathedral—very few examples seem to have taken the form of separate buildings or chapels, and but a few parish churches were dedicated in honour of Saint Sepulchre. In the cathedral of Constance (Germany) is a beautiful thirteenth century shrine representing the "Easter Sepulchre," but hardly in any way resembling the Holy Sepulchre, Jerusalem; it occupies the centre of a chapel used by some knightly Order, whose coats of arms decorate its walls.

In conclusion it must be observed that the above attempt to illustrate the archæology and history of the Holy Sepulchre in Jerusalem has been compiled chiefly with the desire to assist in the study of the most important of all Christian relics, by presenting the matter viewed from an architectural standpoint, and unbiased by any foregone conclusions.

It is true that we have at present no very clear historical evidence of the condition of the Holy Sites before c. 333 A.D., but to most minds this fact is reasonably accounted for by the known circumstances of the first three centuries of the Christian Era. The Gospel history is not out of harmony with this state of oblivion, or at least absence of records, succeeding the Apostolic age, and such records may even still survive for future explorers to unearth in Egypt or elsewhere.

The matter presents itself as a monumental evidence of a series of events which has occupied the attention of a great proportion of mankind for more than nineteen centuries, and the humble ambition of the author has been to be permitted to assist in elucidating the exceedingly interesting mass of information which has accumulated around this most important of monuments.

CHRONOLOGICAL TABLES

ECCLESIASTICAL CHRONOLOGY OF JERUSALEM
AFTER A.D. 333

THE BISHOPS. (From Le Quien, *Oriens Christianus*, tom. 3.)

39. Macarius (Quiriacus) I
    (*c*. 330).
40. Maximus II.
41. Cyrillus.
42. Joannes II.
43. Praylius.
44. Juvenalis.
45. Anastasius.
46. Martyrius.
47. Salustius.
48. Elias I.
49 Joannes III.
50. Petrus.
51. Eustochius.
52. Macarius II.
53. Joannes IV.
54. Amos.
55. Isacius.
56. Zacharias.
57. Modestus.
58. Sophronius I, *ob*. 644. Sedes
    Hierosolymitana multos
    annos vacat.
59. Joannes V, 705.
60. Theodorus I.
61. Eusebius.
62. Elias II.
63. Georgius (*c*. 800).
64. Thomas I.
65. Basilius.
66. Sergius I.
67. Salomon.
68. Theodosius.
69. Elias III.
70. Sergius II.

71. Leontius.
72. Anastasius (Nicolaus)
73. Christophorus I.
74. Agatho.
75. Joannes VI.
76. Christophorus II.
77. Thomas II.
78. Joseph II.
79. Alexander.
80. Agapius.
81. Hieremias (Orestes).
82. Theophilus I.
83. Arsenius I.
84. Jordanus.
85. Nicephorus I.
86. Sophronius II.
87. Euthymius.
88. Simon (Simeon II).
89: Sabbas I.
90. Jacobus II.
91. Arsenius II.
92. Joannes VII.
93. Nicephorus II.
94. Athanasius II.
95. Leontius.
96. Dositheus I (1193).
97. Marcus II.
98. Theophanes I.
99. Gregorius II.
100. Athanasius III.
101. Thaddeus.
102. Sophronius III.
103. Athanasius IV.
104. Gabriel Brula.
105. Lazarus.

106. Sophronius IV.
107. Dorotheus I.
108. Theophilus II.
109. Theophanes II.
110. Joachim.
111. Theophanes III.
112. Abraham.
113. Jacobus III.
114. Marcus III.
115. Gregorius III.

116. Dorotheus II.
117. Germanus.
118. Sophronius V.
119. Theophanes IV.
120. Paisius.
121. Nectarius.
122. Dositheus II (c. 1672).
123. Chrysanthus.
124. Milatheus (1733).

Until the year 451, Jerusalem was the see-town of an ordinary Bishopric of the Early Church, under the authority of the Metropolitan of Cæsarea. The Council of Chalcedon constituted it a Patriarchate with jurisdiction over the province of Palestine, and at the present day the Patriarch rules over five archbishops and five bishops.

CHRONOLOGY OF THE CIVIL GOVERNMENT OF JERUSALEM FROM A.D. 333 TO THE TURKISH OCCUPATION IN A.D. 1517

THE ROMAN EMPIRE.

333. Constantine I.
337. Constantine II.
351. Constantius.

361. Julian.
363. Jovian.
364. Valentinian I.

367. Gratian.
368. Valens.
379. Theodosius I.

THE BYZANTINE EMPIRE.

395. Arcadius.
406. Theodosius II.
450. Marcian.
457. Leo I.
474. Zeno.

491. Anastasius I.
518. Justin I.
527. Justinian I.
565. Justin II.

578. Tiberius II.
582. Maurice.
602. Phocas.
610. Heraclius.

OMAYYAD CALIPHATE, BAGDAD.

637. Omar I.
644. Othman.
656. Moawiya I.
680. Yazid I.
683. Moawiya II.

684. Merwan I.
685. Abdelmelek.
705. Walid I.
715. Sulieman.
717. Omar II.

720. Yazid II.
724. Hisham.
743. Walid II.
744. Yazid III.
744. Merwan II.

ABBASIDE CALIPHATE, BAGDAD.

748. Abulabbas.	833. Motazim.	892. Moktafi.
754. Mansur.	842. Vathiq.	908. Moqtadir.
775. Mahdi.	847. Motawakkel.	932. Qadhir.
785. Hadi.	861. Montasir.	934. Radi.
786. Haroun er	862. Mostani.	941. Motaqi.
Raschid.	866. Motazz.	944. Mostaqfi.
810. Amin.	868. Mothadi.	946. Moti.
813. Mamun.	870. Motamid.	

FATIMITE CALIPHATE, EGYPT.

969. Moizz.	996. Hakim.	1035. Mostanzir.
975. Aziz.	1020. Zahir.	1094. Mostali.

LATIN KINGDOM.

1099. Godfrey de Bouillon (Advocate of the Holy Sepulchre).

1100. Baldwin I.	1146. Baldwin III.	1183. Baldwin V.
1118. Baldwin II.	1162. Amalric I.	1186. Guy de Lusi-
1131. Fulk (Foulques).	1174. Baldwin IV.	gnan.

AYYUBITE RULERS OF EGYPT.

1187. Saladin.	1198. Mansur.	1218. Kamel.
1193. Aziz.	1199. Adil.	

LATIN KINGDOM RESTORED.

1229. Frederick II crowns himself in the Holy Sepulchre.
1239. Richard, Earl of Cornwall, and William, Earl of Salisbury,
maintain the Christian Government in its last years.

AYYUBITE RULERS OF EGYPT RESTORED.

1244. Salih Najm.	1249. Turanshah.	1250. Ashraf.

BAHRI MAMLUKES, EGYPT.

1250. Shajar, Moizz'	1293. Nasir.	1345. Shaban I.
Izz.	1294. Kitboga.	1346. Hajji.
1257. Mansur I.	1296. Lajin.	1347. Hasan.
1259. Mozaffer.	1308. Bibars II.	1351. Salih.
1260. Bibars I.	1341. Abu Bakr,	1361. Mansur II.
1277. Said Nasir.	Kuchuk.	1363. Shaban II.
1279. Adil.	1342. Ahmad, Salih	1377. Ali.
1290. Khalil.	Imad.	1381. Salih Hajji.

BURJI MAMLUKES, EGYPT.

1382. Barquq.	1438. Aziz.	1495. Nasir Moham-
1398. Faraj.	1453. Mansur,	med.
1405. Abdelaziz.	Ashraf.	1498. Kansu.
1412. Mostain,	1461. Muayyad II,	1499. Jan Bulat.
Muayyad I.	Koshkadam.	1501. Tumanbai,
1421. Mozaffer, Zahir,	1467. Bilbai,	Kansuh Ghuri.
Mohammed.	Timurboga.	1516. Ashraf.
1422. Barsbai.	1468. Kaitbai.	

CHRONOLOGY OF EVENTS AND BIBLIOGRAPHICAL NOTES

	A.D.
The Crucifixion. According to the ordinary computation .	33
The Gospel of St Luke [Smith's *Dict. of Bible*, p. 712] .	64
Persecution of the Christians and Martyrdom of St James [Smith, p. 1010]	64
Siege of Jerusalem by Titus	70

Jerusalem disappears from history.

Colonia Aelia Capitolina, founded by Hadrian . . .	136
Coins with a representation of a temple of Astarte and the inscription C. A. C.	136
Aristeas and Hecatæus of Abdera [P.P.T.S., uncertain date]	?
Origen refers to "Golgotha" [Migne, *Pat. Gr.* xiii. col. 1777]	185–253
Chronicon Paschale [P.P.T.S.]	270
Eusebii et Hieronymi Onomasticon Urbium et Locorum SS. [var. editions]	330–400

The New Jerusalem built by Constantine.

The Martyrion consecrated in the presence of Eusebius, Bishop of Cæsarea	335
Catechetical Lectures of St Cyril [var. edit.] . . .	350
Itinerarium Burdigalense [Bordeaux Pilgrim, P.P.T.S.] .	?
Itinerarium Antonini Augusti [Reland, p. 416] . .	?
Pilgrimage of Paula described by St Jerome [P.P.T.S.] .	382
Letter of Paula and Eustochium to Marcella [P.P.T.S.] .	382
Peregrinatio ad Loca Sancta S. Silviæ Aquitanæ. Discovered by Sig. G. Gamurrini at Arezzo, 1883. Edited in 1887, and published by the Palestine Societies of England, Russia, and Germany . .	385
S. Eucherii Epitome de Locis Sanctis aliquibus [P.P.T.S.]	440
Jerusalem made an independent patriarchate . . .	453

The building of the Holy Sepulchre Church as we see it
at the present day.

During the Middle Ages, and since the final Moslem occupation of Jerusalem, innumerable accounts of travels, pilgrimages, etc., have been written, of which the most important are the following:—

The following early printed books on Jerusalem also contain valuable information on the Church of the Holy Sepulchre, in the form of more or less accurate drawings and plans:—

A.D.

Bernardo Amico. "Trattato delle piante e immagine de' sacri edifizi di Terra Santa." Roma. Valuable drawings of the period 1609

George Sandys' "Travailes, containing a History of the Turkish Empire, etc., with fifty graven Maps and Figures." London 1615

Christopher Fuerer. "Itinerarium." Nurnb. . . . 1621

F. Quaresmius. "Historica, theologica, et moralis Terræ Sanctæ elucidatio." Antwerp 1639

J. Doubdan. "Voyage de la Terre Sainte." Paris . . 1661

Cornelius de Bruyn (le Brun). "Reyzen door der Levant, etc." Delft. Interesting illustrations 1672

Numerous books of travels were published during the eighteenth century but of little individual interest, and when illustrations are attempted they are of a deplorable character. In 1741, Jonas Korte, a German bookseller, visited Jerusalem and started a theory as to the genuineness of the "Tomb of Christ" which has induced a certain feeling of partisanship amongst Christians ever since.

Burning of the Holy Sepulchre Church 1808

Holy Land occupied by Mohammed Ali Pasha of Egypt . 1832

Holy Land becomes a vilayet of the Turkish Empire . 1840

During the nineteenth century a continual publication of accounts of tours and pilgrimages, explorations, identifications, etc., in the Holy Land in all languages, and with the most varied objects in view, renders any attempt at a comprehensive bibliography almost impossible. Setting aside works of a Missionary character, and those written in support of some new and remarkable identifications of Holy Sites, the more serious and important modern contributions to the history of the Holy Sepulchre are the following:—

E. D. Clarke. "Travels in the Holy Land," Cambridge . 1823

F. de Chateaubriand. "Itinéraire," Paris 1837

Edward Robinson, D.D. "Biblical Researches," New York 1838

Rev. George Williams. "The Holy City." London . . 1845

Prof. R. Willis, F.R.S., republishes the above with additions of an architectural character. Plan of the Holy Sepulchre by Scoles 1849

Salzmann, a German photographer, visits Jerusalem and publishes a collection of views of the Holy Sepulchre

A.D.

[amongst the first productions of the new art ever
published]. Paris. Large folio 1854
M. de Vogüé, "Les Églises de la Terre Sainte," Paris . 1860
Ordnance Survey conducted by Sir Henry James and Col.
Chas. Wilson at the expense of Lady Burdett-Coutts 1864
P.E.F. founded 1864
Col. Warren's Excavations in Jerusalem [published by
P.E.F. 1884][1] 1867
Palestine Exploration Fund Quarterly Statement first
published 1869
Publications of *L'Orient Latin* [mediæval history] . . 1870
Building of the great iron dome over the Holy Sepulchre . 1870
American Palestine Exploration Society instituted . . 1871
Clearing of portion of the Muristan by German Govern-
ment 1872
Publications of the German Palestine Society commence . 1878
The large 4to Survey of Palestine, with supplements, com-
menced 1881
This is intended to contain serious results of investiga-
tions by the Society extracted from the Quarterly State-
ments.

Discovery of the remains of Constantine's Basilica by the
Russians on their property to the east of the Holy
Sepulchre 1887
Hayter Lewis, F.S.A. "Holy places of Jerusalem" . . 1888
Röhricht. "Regesta Regni Hierosol." 1890
Guy Le Strange. "Palestine under the Moslems" . . 1890
Revue Biblique de l'école S. Étienne, Jerusalem, com-
menced 1892
Bulletin of the Russian Palestine Society commences . 1894
G. Jeffery. "The Buildings of the Holy Sepulchre,"
Florence [privately printed]. This contains the first
reference to the mosaic in St Pudenziana, Rome, as a
probable representation 1894
Discovery of the Madeba mosaic 1897
Rev. A. Headlam. Review of the above in "Quarterly."
July 1899
Arch. C. Dickie. "Some Early Christian Churches in
Palestine." R.I.B.A. Journal 1899
G. Jeffery. "Drawings of the Basilica of Constantine" in
Publ. of Russian Palestine Society 1900
C. Mauss. "Église du S. Sépulcre," Paris 1900
Colonel Warren examined the remains of the Basilica, *see* Plate
XX, Ordnance Survey.

English Palestine Exploration Society appears to accept the
idea that the mosaic of St Pudenziana represents the
fourth-century buildings on the Holy Sites. See Sir
Chas. Wilson in P.E.F.Q.S., p. 149.   .   .   .   1902
Arch. C. Dickie. "Masonry Remains around the Church of
the Holy Sepulchre." P.E.F.Q.S., p. 298 .   .   .   1908

In 1865 the Palestine Exploration Society of London
commissioned Col. Chas. Wilson to make a plan of the Holy
Sepulchre Church. This plan agrees in a general way with
the older plaȟ made by Scoles for Williams' "Holy City."
It is more accurate and detailed than the older work, and
with the plans made by Herr Schick at about the same
period forms the basis of most modern investigations of the
Holy Site.

The best handbook of an archæological kind on
Jerusalem is that which was published by Fr. Barnabas
Meistermann, O.F.M. in 1907. It contains excellent plans
of the various monuments drawn to a small scale.   Fr.
Barnabas suggests one or two identifications of his own
which are worthy of attention.

INDEX

CAMBRIDGE : PRINTED BY
J. B. PEACE, M.A.,
AT THE UNIVERSITY PRESS

For EU product safety concerns, contact us at Calle de José Abascal, 56–1°, 28003 Madrid, Spain or eugpsr@cambridge.org.

www.ingramcontent.com/pod-product-compliance
Ingram Content Group UK Ltd.
Pitfield, Milton Keynes, MK11 3LW, UK
UKHW010341140625
459647UK00010B/750